Best of the Best from the
Midwest
Cookbook

Selected Recipes from the
Favorite Cookbooks of
Iowa, Illinois, Indiana, and Ohio

Most of the corn grown in the United States is produced in the Corn Belt, which primarily includes Iowa, Illinois, Indiana, and Ohio. Approximately 50% of all corn grown in the United States is from these four states. Corn is the most widely grown crop in America.

Best of the Best from the
Midwest
Cookbook

Selected Recipes from the
Favorite Cookbooks of
Iowa, Illinois, Indiana, and Ohio

EDITED BY

Gwen McKee

AND

Barbara Moseley

Illustrated by Tupper England

QUAIL RIDGE PRESS
Preserving America's Food Heritage

Recipe Collection ©2009 Quail Ridge Press, Inc.

Library of Congress Cataloging-in-Publication Data

Best of the best from the Midwest cookbook : selected recipes from the favorite cookbooks of Iowa, Illinois, Indiana, and Ohio / edited by Gwen McKee
and Barbara Moseley ; illustrated by Tupper England. — 1st ed.
  p. cm.. — (Best of the best state cookbook series)
  ISBN-13: 978-1-934193-27-3
  ISBN-10: 1-934193-27-5
    1. Cookery, American--Midwestern style. 2. Cookery--Middle West.
I. McKee, Gwen. II. Moseley, Barbara.
TX715.2.M53B47 2009
  641.5977--dc22   2008054253

ISBN-13: 978-1-934193-27-3 • ISBN-10: 1-934193-27-5

Book design by Cynthia Clark • Cover photo by Greg Campbell
Printed in Canada

First edition, July 2009

On the cover: Iowa Chops, page 153

QUAIL RIDGE PRESS
P. O. Box 123 • Brandon, MS 39043
info©quailridge.com• www.quailridge.com

CONTENTS

This is a replica of the blacksmith shop in Grand Detour, Illinois, where John Deere set up shop in 1837. It was here that Deere developed the self-polishing steel plow, making it possible for farmers to cultivate the sticky Midwestern soil, and thus opened the prairie to agriculture.

Quest for the Best
Regional Cooking

It seems that everywhere Barbara and I travel, we find that people love to talk about food. Invariably they mention specific dishes that have been an important part of their family's heritage and tradition, and do so with exuberance and pride.

"My mother always serves her fabulous cornbread dressing with our Thanksgiving turkey, and it is simply 'the best.'"

"Aunt Susan's famous pecan pie is always the first to go."

"No family occasion would be complete without Uncle Joe's chicken salad sandwiches."

Well, we heard, we researched, and we captured these bragged-about recipes so that people all over the country —and the world—could enjoy them.

My co-editor Barbara Moseley and I have been searching for the country's best recipes for three decades, and home cooks everywhere have learned to trust and rely on our cookbooks to bring them fabulous meals their friends and family will love! We always choose recipes based first and foremost on taste. In addition, the ingredients have to be readily available, and the recipes simple, with easy-to-follow instructions and never-fail results.

While touring the country and tasting the local fare, we delight in finding the little secrets that make the big difference. We have eaten buffalo in Wyoming, halibut in Alaska, lobster in Maine, gumbo in Louisiana, each prepared in a variety of creative ways. Finding out about conch in Florida and boysenberries in Oregon and poi in Hawaii. . . . No matter where we venture, this part of our job is always fun, often surprising, and definitely inspiring!

You would probably think first of pork chops and corn coming from the Midwest . . . and you would be right. But there are so many good comfort foods that inevitably go along with them. From the states of Ohio, Illinois, Indiana, and Iowa come delicious recipes that simply

taste like home. Treat yourself to time-tested recipes like
Hoosier Biscuits, Buckeyes, Iowa Corn Pancakes . . . and
famous recipes like Chicago-Style Pizza, Cincinnati Chili,
and Harry Caray's Chicken Vesuvio. . . . There's always a
whole lot of good cookin' going on in the Midwest. Put
on your appetite and come on in!

Gwen McKee

Gwen McKee and Barbara Moseley, editors
of Best of the Best State Cookbook Series

Beverages and Appetizers

Fulton County, Indiana, is considered the Round Barn Capital of the World, although only eight remain standing of its original seventeen. The circular design is not compatible with mechanized farming, and so they were eventually abandoned. The Fulton County Historical Society has established a National Round Barn Center of Information to help find ways to save them.

Friendship Tea

A hot drink especially for holidays.

FOR 30-CUP PERCOLATOR:

9 cups unsweetened pineapple
  juice
9 cups cranberry juice cocktail
4½ cups water

1 cup brown sugar
4½ teaspoons whole cloves
4 broken cinnamon sticks
¼ teaspoon salt

FOR 10-CUP PERCOLATOR:

3 cups unsweetened pineapple
  juice
3 cups cranberry juice cocktail
1½ cups water

⅓ cup brown sugar
1½ teaspoons whole cloves
1 broken cinnamon stick
⅛ teaspoon salt

Combine pineapple juice, cranberry juice, and water in automatic percolator. Combine remaining ingredients in basket. Allow to go through perk cycle. Remove basket and stem from coffee maker. Serve piping hot.

Taste & See (Indiana)

Orange Smoothie

Like a Creamsicle in a glass.

1 cup nonfat vanilla frozen
  yogurt
¾ cup low-fat (1%) milk

¼ cup frozen orange juice
  concentrate

Combine ingredients in a blender; blend until smooth. Serves 1.

Cooking with Hope Ridge Families (Ohio)

Cheesecake Kahlúa Milkshake

2 scoops vanilla ice cream
1 slice cheesecake
1 cup milk

2 shots Kahlúa
Whipped cream
1 maraschino cherry

Combine ice cream, cheesecake, milk, and Kahlúa in blender or food processor. Process until smooth. Pour into chilled stemmed glasses and garnish with whipped cream and a maraschino cherry. Serves 2.

Note: I keep a frozen cheesecake in the freezer just for this purpose. You'll be glad you did, too! People will kill for this recipe.

50 Years and Still Cookin'! (Ohio)

Bailey's Nog

6 eggs, beaten until foamy
½ cup sugar
3 cups milk
1½ cups Bailey's Irish Cream

½ teaspoon ground nutmeg
½ cup whipping cream, whipped
Ground nutmeg

Gradually add sugar to beaten eggs. Beat 5 minutes, until thick and lemony. Reduce speed on mixer to low; gradually add milk, Bailey's, and nutmeg. Beat until combined. Chill thoroughly.

Stir whipped cream into chilled mixture until thoroughly combined. Sprinkle with nutmeg. Yields 2 quarts.

Champions: Favorite Foods of Indy Car Racing (Indiana)

Yellow Birds

Perfect for a summer afternoon with friends.

1 (6-ounce) can frozen orange juice
12 ounces canned pineapple juice

12 ounces white rum
6 ounces crème de banana
18 ounces water

Mix together in a large glass pitcher. Add a generous amount of ice and serve in your most summery glasses. Serves 8.

Recipes from Iowa with Love (Iowa)

Bloody Mary Deluxe

1 (46-ounce) can tomato juice
½ cup beef broth
6 tablespoons fresh lime juice
¼ cup Worcestershire
2 teaspoons sea salt or coarse
 salt
1 teaspoon ground pepper

1 teaspoon celery salt
1 teaspoon dill
½–1 teaspoon hot pepper
 sauce
1 teaspoon prepared horseradish
1–2 cups vodka

Put all ingredients except vodka in pitcher; mix well. Fill 12-ounce glasses with ice. Add 1–2 ounces vodka to each glass. Add tomato mixture. Garnish with celery sticks, cucumber sticks or slices, and lime. Makes 8–10 servings.

SoupÇon II (Illinois)

Cincinnati Red

This famous beer recipe from the Hudepohl Brewing Company is suggested as a "pick up" for breakfast or brunch. Some residents claim it is a good hangover cure.

12 ounces Hudepohl beer,
 chilled
12 ounces tomato juice, chilled

Dash of cayenne
Dash of Worcestershire

Combine ingredients in large pitcher. Stir well and serve chilled or over ice. Makes 6 servings.

Cincinnati Recipe Treasury (Ohio)

The Cincinnati Red Stockings, so-named for the color of their game hosiery, were the first professional baseball team in U.S. history. The Red Stockings began playing in 1869. Long stockings were then a novelty in team uniforms. The team, now simply called the Reds, dominated the National League from 1970 to 1976, winning five National League Western Division titles, four National League pennants, and two back-to-back World Series titles. Dubbed the "Big Red Machine," the team consisted of manager Sparky Anderson, Pete Rose, Johnny Bench, Joe Morgan, and Tony Pérez, and was supported by César Gerónimo, Ken Griffey, Sr., and Dave Concepción. The team's most recent World Series championship came in 1990 when Lou Piniella led the team to a four-game sweep of the heavily-favored Oakland Athletics.

Hot Spiced Cider

2 quarts cider
½ cup packed brown sugar
1 teaspoon whole cloves
1 teaspoon allspice
1 teaspoon ground cinnamon
3 (3-inch) sticks cinnamon
⅛ teaspoon nutmeg

Place cider in a 2-quart capacity electric percolator. Place all remaining ingredients in percolator basket. Perk for 7 minutes. Serve hot in mugs . . . with doughnuts of course! Yields 2 quarts.

Discover Dayton (Ohio)

Blackberry Wine

4 quarts blackberries
10 quarts water
10 pounds sugar
Juice of 3 lemons
Juice of 4 oranges
1 yeast cake
3 pounds ground raisins
10 quarts water

Boil blackberries in 10 quarts water for 15 minutes. Add sugar while mixture is hot. Cool and add juice from lemons and oranges, then stir in yeast and mix well. Put in a large crock. Stir twice a day for 7 days. Add ground raisins and 10 quarts water. Stir twice a day for 10 days until wine stops working. Strain and bottle with loose caps.

Wildlife Harvest Game Cookbook (Iowa)

Tequila-Champagne Punch

Perfect for brunch parties or luncheons.

2 quarts white wine, chilled
2 (6-ounce) cans frozen
  concentrated pineapple juice,
  reconstituted with water
1 (fifth) bottle tequila
2 (fifth) bottles champagne,
  chilled
2 quarts soda water, chilled
Strawberry halves or orange
  slices

In punch bowl, combine wine, pineapple juice, and tequila (or mix in the proportions you punch bowl will hold). Just before serving, add champagne and soda water. Float fruits in punch. Or freeze strawberries or other fruits with water in ring mold; unmold and float in punch. Makes about 2 gallons.

SoupÇon I (Illinois)

Triconas
(Hot Cheese Pastries)

FILLING:

2 (8-ounce) packages cream
  cheese, softened
½ pound Greek cheese (feta),
  crumbled

1 egg
3 tablespoons butter or
  margarine, melted

Cream cheeses, egg, and butter in small bowl of electric mixer and beat at medium speed until well blended and smooth.

PASTRY:

1 package prepared phyllo-
  pastry or strudel-pastry
  leaves

1 cup butter or margarine,
  melted

Preheat oven to 350°. Place 2 leaves of phyllo-pastry on board; brush with melted butter. Cut lengthwise into strips about 2 inches wide. Place 1 teaspoon Filling at end of a strip. Fold over one corner to opposite side, to make a triangle.

Continue folding, keeping triangle shape, to other end of strip. Arrange the filled triangle on an ungreased cookie sheet. Repeat with remaining strips. Repeat with other pastry leaves. Bake 20 minutes or until deep golden-brown. Serve hot. Yields 7 dozen.

Note: If desired, make and bake ahead. Cool; then refrigerate, covered, overnight. To serve: Arrange on cookie sheet; bake in 350° oven about 10 minutes, or until heated.

C-U in the Kitchen (Illinois)

Italian Cheese Twists

¼ cup butter or margarine, melted
¼ teaspoon each, crushed: basil, oregano, and marjoram
¼ teaspoon garlic powder
1 (16-ounce) loaf frozen bread dough, thawed
¾ cup shredded mozzarella cheese
1 egg, slightly beaten
1 tablespoon water
2 tablespoons sesame seeds

In a small bowl, combine butter, basil, oregano, marjoram, and garlic powder; set aside. On a lightly floured surface, roll bread dough into a 12-inch square.

Spread butter mixture evenly over dough and sprinkle with cheese. Fold dough into thirds. With a sharp knife, cut dough crosswise into 20 (4½-inch) strips. Twist each strip twice and pinch ends to seal. Place about 2 inches apart on a greased baking sheet. Cover, let rise in a warm place until almost double, about 30 minutes.

Combine egg and water. Brush each twist and sprinkle with sesame seeds. Bake at 375° for 10–12 minutes or until golden. Yields 24 twists.

Favorite Herbal Recipes Vol. III (Illinois)

Boursin

This is the real thing. A purist will tell you one can't make boursin with dried herbs—only fresh ones. Well, maybe he's right.

1 (8-ounce) package cream cheese, softened
1 tablespoon fresh lemon juice
1 minced clove garlic
½ teaspoon Worcestershire
½ teaspoon dry mustard
1 tablespoon finely chopped fresh parsley
1 tablespoon finely chopped fresh chives
4 tablespoons minced fresh herbs*

Combine all ingredients, but don't beat—just mix gently and thoroughly. Cover tightly and refrigerate. When ready to serve, bring to room temperature. Makes about 1 cup.

*Use at least 4 of the following herbs—the more, the better! Rosemary, thyme, dill, Greek oregano, marjoram, summer savory, basil, sage.

It's About Thyme (Indiana)

Fried Mozzarella

Nothing more is needed with this filling appetizer than a glass of chilled white wine.

8 ounces mozzarella cheese
¼ cup Wondra flour
2 extra large eggs
1 teaspoon salt
½ teaspoon freshly milled black
  pepper
1½ cups fine dry bread crumbs
1½ cups corn oil

Cut mozzarella into ½-inch slices and then into ½-inch strips. Place flour in a shallow bowl. In another shallow bowl, beat eggs, salt, and pepper thoroughly with a fork. Place bread crumbs in the bowl.

Dip mozzarella strips in flour, then in beaten eggs. Dredge thoroughly in bread crumbs, making sure cheese is thoroughly coated with crumbs so that it does not ooze in frying.

Arrange strips in a single layer on a large platter lined with wax paper. Chill at least 1 hour (chilling will prevent bread crumb coating from falling off when frying).

In a 12-inch skillet, heat oil over medium-high heat until haze forms. Fry mozzarella in 2 batches, turning once, until lightly golden on both sides. Drain on paper towels. To serve, arrange on platter and serve immediately. Serves 6–8.

Herrin's Favorite Italian Recipes Cookbook (Illinois)

In 1969, Sears, Roebuck & Co. was the largest retailer in the world. Sears executives decided to consolidate the thousands of employees in offices distributed throughout the Chicago area into one building in downtown Chicago, Illinois. The Sears Tower, completed in 1973, is one of the tallest and most recognizable landmarks in the Chicago skyline and in the world. Including its antennas, the total height of Sears Tower is 1,725 feet. The Sears Tower has gone through several owners over the years, but Sears has retained the naming rights for the building. However, in March 2009, London-based insurance broker Willis Group Holdings, Ltd. leased a large portion of the building and obtained its naming rights. The building is now called Willis Tower.

Pizza Crackers

HiHo or Ritz Crackers
1 small jar pizza sauce

Mozzarella cheese
Pepperoni

Spread 4 crackers at a time with pizza sauce. Top with cheese and pepperoni. Place on a paper plate and microwave at 50% for 30–60 seconds or until cheese melts. Rotate after 30 seconds. The more you place in the microwave, the longer it takes to cook.

Share with Love (Ohio)

Mimi Party Pizzas

½ pound sausage or
 hamburger meat
1 teaspoon oregano
1 clove garlic, minced

1 tube refrigerator biscuits
1 (6-ounce) can tomato paste
1 cup shredded Cheddar cheese
¼ cup grated Parmesan cheese

Brown and drain meat. Add oregano and garlic. On greased baking sheet, flatten 10 refrigerator biscuits to 4-inch circles with a rim. Fill with tomato paste and meat. Sprinkle with cheese. Bake at 450° for 10 minutes.

New Beginnings (Iowa)

Hot Dog Rolls

These are remarkable tasty, and worthy of being elevated on your hors d'oeuvre table.

1 pound hot dogs (wieners)
1 pound bacon slices

1 pound brown sugar

Cut hot dogs in thirds. Cut bacon slices in half. Wrap each hot dog third with bacon slice. Arrange in 9x13-inch baking dish. Sprinkle with brown sugar. Bake at 350° for 1 hour. Arrange on footed cake plate and spear with toothpicks.

The Lucy Miele 6-5-4- Cookbook (Illinois)

Artichoke Puffs

1 (10-count) can buttermilk
  biscuits
1 (18-ounce) can artichoke
  hearts in water

½ cup mayonnaise
½ cup freshly grated Parmesan
  cheese

Remove biscuits from can; pinch each one in half and re-from into 2 smaller biscuits to yield 20. Bake according to instructions on can. When done, remove from oven and cool. Slice each in half horizontally to make 40 pieces. Place ¼ artichoke hearts on top of each biscuit piece. Mix mayonnaise and cheese together until smooth. Use this mixture to "ice" the top of each artichoke. When ready to serve, broil for 1–1½ minutes, until lightly browned. (Watch closely; they brown quickly!)

I Love You (Iowa)

Artichoke Bread

A hearty appetizer.

1 or 2 loaves frozen bread
  (1, if large)
½ cup butter
2 tablespoons sesame seeds
2 cloves garlic, crushed
1½ cups sour cream
2 cups cubed Monterey Jack
  cheese

½ cup grated Parmesan cheese
2 tablespoons parsley flakes
1 (14-ounce) can artichoke
  hearts, drained, chopped
1 cup shredded Cheddar cheese

Slice through bread horizontally. Scoop center from bread. Sauté bread pieces in butter with sesame seeds and garlic. Remove from stove. Stir in sour cream, Jack cheese, Parmesan cheese, parsley, and artichokes.

Put filling into scooped bread shells. Top with Cheddar cheese. Bake at 350° for 30 minutes, uncovered. Slice bread with bread knife on angle.

Favorite Recipes from Poland Women's Club (Ohio)

Tortilla Temptations

1 (8-ounce) package cream
  cheese, softened
1 (2¼-ounce) can ripe olives,
  drained, sliced or chopped

4 green onions, including tops,
  chopped
4 small flour tortillas
Picante or salsa sauce

Combine cream cheese, olives, and green onions with an electric mixer until mixed well. Evenly spread thin layer of filling on tortillas, jellyroll fashion. Cover and refrigerate at least 2 hours until cream cheese mixture sets. Cut each tortilla into 1-inch slices. Serve with picante or salsa sauce for dipping. Makes 24 pieces.

Honest to Goodness (Illinois)

Seafood Appetizers

1 package Hidden Valley Ranch
  Italian dry mix
6 ounces fat-free Swiss cheese
  slices, chopped
8 ounces nonfat sour cream

¾ cup nonfat mayonnaise
8 ounces imitation crabmeat,
  finely chopped
1 (1-pound) loaf cocktail rye
  bread

Preheat oven to 350°. Combine all ingredients in a medium bowl. Spread mixture evenly on individual rye slices. Place on ungreased baking sheet. Bake 10–15 minutes, or until lightly browned. Makes 40 servings.

The Heart of Cooking II (Indiana)

Hot Crabmeat Puffs

MINIATURE CREAM PUFFS:

1 cup water
½ cup margarine or butter
1 cup all-purpose flour

Salt to taste
4 eggs

Preheat oven to 400°. Bring water and margarine to a boil. Add flour and salt. Stir vigorously over low heat until mixture forms a ball. Add eggs, one at a time, beating until smooth. Drop teaspoonfuls of batter onto ungreased baking sheet. Bake for 30–35 minutes and remove from baking sheet.

CRABMEAT FILLING:

1 (8-ounce) package cream
  cheese, softened
1 tablespoon milk
½ teaspoon horseradish sauce
Pepper to taste
1 (6½-ounce) can crabmeat,
  drained

½ cup slivered almonds,
  toasted
2 tablespoons finely chopped
  onion

Lower oven temperature to 375°. Combine cream cheese, milk, horseradish sauce, and pepper; mix until well blended. Stir in crabmeat, almonds, and onion.

To assemble cream puffs, cut tops from cream puffs and fill with crab mixture. Replace tops. Bake 10 minutes and serve. Yields 36 appetizers.

Note: Easier than it looks. Be sure to make cream puffs small.

Five Star Sensations (Ohio)

Crab Puffs

1 cup water
½ cup butter
1 cup all-purpose flour
4 whole eggs
1 egg, separated
2 (8-ounce) packages cream
   cheese, softened
½ teaspoon milk

2 packages frozen crabmeat,
   thawed, drained (or 2 cans,
   drained)
1 teaspoon pepper
Greens of 6 green onions,
   chopped
2½ teaspoons dill weeds

Preheat oven to 400°. Combine water and butter in medium sauce-pan; bring to a boil and add flour all at once. Stir vigorously with wooden spoon until dough leaves sides of pan and forms smooth ball. Remove from heat and beat in 4 whole eggs, one at a time, until thick dough is formed. Place level teaspoons of dough 1 inch apart on foil-lined cookie sheet. Mix separated egg yolk and milk, and brush dough with this mixture.

Bake 10 minutes at 400°, then reduce heat to 300° and continue cooking for 25–30 minutes until puffs are high, but not all the way through, to prepare for filling.

Combine all remaining ingredients and stuff puffs with mixture. Yields 50–60 puffs.

Note: Puffs may be frozen and reheated on cookie sheet for 10 minutes at 375°.

An Apple for the Teacher (Illinois)

Won Ton Quiche

1–3 packages won ton wrappers
1 dozen eggs
1 quart heavy whipping cream
2 cups milk
Salt to taste

White pepper to taste (optional)
4 ounces or more smoked ham,
   chopped
4–6 cups grated Swiss cheese

Spray muffin tins with nonstick cooking spray. Place 2 won ton wrappers over each muffin tin at opposing angles. Push down into tin to form crust for quiche.

Whisk together eggs, heavy cream, milk, salt, and pepper. Pour mixture into each crust until they are about ¾ full. Add ham and cheese to taste. Bake at 350° for 20 minutes, or until crusts are browned and center is set. Makes about 5 dozen.

Cooking Up a Cure (Ohio)

Lumpies

1 pound ground beef
½ cup chopped onions
   (optional)
Salt and pepper to taste

Won ton skins (found in produce
   department)
Taco sauce

Mix beef, onions, salt and pepper in a bowl. Lay a square of dough down (if you use "large" squares cut into 4 squares) and place small amount of meat mixture in center. Roll up like a cigarette. Roll all Lumpies before cooking. You may have to wet side of dough to keep together. Drop each roll into hot oil. Cook for 2–3 minutes or until golden brown. Serve hot. Dip in taco sauce.

Franklin County Homemakers Extension Cookbook (Illinois)

Sausage Stars

Won ton wrappers
1 pound sausage, cooked,
   drained
1½ cups shredded Monterey
   Jack cheese
1½ cups shredded sharp
   Cheddar cheese

1 cup Hidden Valley Original
   Ranch Dressing Mix
   (prepared)
½ cup sliced ripe olives
½ cup chopped red pepper

Form wrappers into lightly greased muffin tins, brush lightly with oil. Bake in 350° oven 5–7 minutes, or until golden. Take out of tins, put onto a cookie sheet; fill with mixture of remaining ingredients. Bake at 350° about 7–10 minutes until hot and bubbly. Makes 3–4 dozen.

Note: You can find won ton wrappers in the produce section of your grocery store.

Tried and True by Mothers of 2's (Ohio)

Eggrolls

Easy and delicious.

2 tablespoons vegetable oil
2 cloves garlic, minced
1 medium onion, thinly sliced
½ pound lean ground pork
Soy sauce to taste

2 packages cole slaw blend
 (prepackaged)
Salt and pepper to taste
15 eggroll wrappers

Heat vegetable oil in skillet and sauté garlic and onion until tender. Add pork and soy sauce and sauté until browned. Remove and drain in strainer. Stir in cole slaw mix and salt and pepper; let cool 10–15 minutes.

Carefully separate eggroll wrappers. Lay one wrapper on clean surface with corner of roll pointing toward you. Place about 2 table-spoons of filling near corner facing you, and roll edge toward middle. Fold in both sides and continue rolling. Moisten opposite edge with water to seal. Repeat with other wrappers.

Fill basket of small fryer with 3–4 rolls at a time; fry in 375° oil until golden brown, about 3 minutes on each side. Drain on paper towels.

Note: May use ground turkey, chicken, or shrimp for the pork. Easy to freeze for future use.

Asthma Walk Cook Book (Ohio)

On February 20, 1962, Ohio native John Glenn was the first American to orbit the Earth, aboard *Friendship 7*. He was also the oldest living person to have flown in space when, at the age of 77 in 1998, he flew aboard the Space Shuttle *Discovery* mission STS-95. Glenn served as a United States Senator (D-Ohio, 1974–1999), and received the Congressional Space Medal of Honor.

Sauerkraut Balls

1 pound bulk sausage
¼ pound ground beef
½ cup chopped onion
3 tablespoons snipped fresh
  parsley
1 teaspoon each: garlic powder,
  salt, and sugar
½ teaspoon dry mustard
⅛ teaspoon pepper
1–2 pounds drained sauerkraut,
  chopped
½ cup bread crumbs
3 eggs, beaten, divided
¼ cup milk
Seasoned bread crumbs

Brown sausage and ground beef with onion, parsley, garlic powder, salt, sugar, dry mustard, and pepper in a skillet, stirring until sausage and ground beef are crumbly; drain. Stir in sauerkraut. Add ½ cup bread crumbs and 1 egg and mix well. Chill, covered, in refrigerator.

Shape sausage mixture into 1-inch balls. Dip balls in a mixture of milk and remaining 2 eggs. Coat with seasoned bread crumbs. Arrange balls on a broiler pan. Broil in a preheated oven until golden brown; drain. May freeze sauerkraut balls before broiling for future use.

Note: May be served with hot sweet mustard sauce.

Beginnings (Ohio)

Sauerkraut Balls

A favorite at New Year's Eve parties in our German settlement.

2½ cups sauerkraut, drained
1 medium onion
1 pound ground chuck,
  browned
4½ tablespoons flour
2 eggs, beaten
1 cup instant potatoes
¼ teaspoon each: salt, pepper,
  and garlic salt
1 beef bouillon cube dissolved in
  ¼ cup hot water
Cracker crumbs

Drain sauerkraut well. In food processor place sauerkraut and onion and pulsate until onion and sauerkraut are chopped fine. Place mixture in a bowl and add browned meat, flour, eggs, instant potatoes, seasonings, and beef bouillon mixture.

Bend well and roll into 1-inch balls, then roll in cracker crumbs. Deep fry until brown. Drain on paper towels. Serve hot or cold.

Touches of the Hands & Heart (Ohio)

Spinach Balls

1 (12-ounce) twin pack
  chicken flavor stuffing mix
  (mix according to directions)
2 sticks margarine, melted
6 eggs, slightly beaten

2 (10-ounce) packages frozen
  chopped spinach, thawed
  and squeezed dry
1 cup grated Parmesan cheese

In a large bowl, stir together all ingredients. Form into bite-size balls and freeze uncovered on cookie sheets. When frozen remove spinach balls and store in freezer in freezer bags. When ready to serve, remove the number needed and bake while still frozen in preheated 350° oven 20 minutes. Makes 120 balls.

Family Celebrations Cookbook (Illinois)

Spinach Appetizers

4 eggs, slightly beaten
2 (10-ounce) boxes frozen
  chopped spinach
1 (16-ounce) box Pepperidge
  Farm Herb Stuffing Mix
1 cup grated Cheddar cheese

¾ cup grated Parmesan cheese
½ teaspoon garlic salt
½ teaspoon thyme
1 cup finely chopped onion
¾ cup butter, melted

Mix everything together with hands. Let stand for awhile. Roll into balls. Chill for 30 minutes or longer. Bake at 350° for 15–20 minutes. Can be frozen after baked.

Sharing Our Best —Ashland Church of God (Ohio)

Meredith Willson was inspired by his boyhood in Mason City, Iowa, in writing and composing his first musical, *The Music Man*. The hit Broadway musical won the Tony Award for Best Musical in 1958. The cast recording of *The Music Man* won the first Grammy Award given for best cast album, and its 1962 film adaptation was a success.

Laura's Marinated Vegetables

Everyone will ask for the recipe!

MARINADE:

1⅓ cups vinegar
⅔ cup vegetable oil
3 tablespoons lemon juice
½ cup sugar

2 teaspoons oregano
1 teaspoon salt
½ teaspoon pepper
Dash of Tabasco

In a large bowl, combine ingredients. Stir to dissolve sugar.

VEGETABLES:

2 medium red onions, thinly
  sliced
1 pound fresh mushroom caps,
  cleaned
1 large head broccoli, cut into
  flowerets

1 head cauliflower, cut into
  flowerets
1 (6-ounce) can large, pitted
  black olives, drained

Add Vegetables to Marinade and stir gently to coat well. Refrigerate for several hours, or overnight, stirring occasionally. At serving time, drain and arrange on a plate with the broccoli forming a "wreath" around the other vegetables. Serve with toothpicks.

Variation: You may substitute or add 1 pound fresh or frozen shrimp and cherry tomatoes. Add tomatoes at serving time. Serve as a luncheon salad. Serves 8–10.

Nutbread and Nostalgia (Indiana)

True to its motto, "Cross Roads of America," Indiana has more miles of Interstate Highway per square mile than any other state. The Indiana state motto can be traced back to the early 1800s. In the early years river traffic, especially along the Ohio, was a major means of transportation. The National Road, a major westward route, and the north-south Michigan Road crossed in Indianapolis. Today more major highways intersect in Indiana than in any other state.

Vegetable Frittata

2 tablespoons extra virgin
olive oil
1 onion, chopped
2 small zucchini, sliced
1 large red pepper, cut into
strips
3 new potatoes, peeled,
cooked, sliced

8 pitted black olives, sliced
8 eggs
⅓ cup milk
½ teaspoon salt
¼ teaspoon white pepper
½ cup freshly grated Parmesan
cheese

In a large skillet heat olive oil and sauté onion 5 minutes. Add zucchini and red pepper and sauté 5 minutes or until soft. Stir in potatoes and olives. Cool. Preheat oven to 350°. In a bowl, beat eggs with remaining ingredients.

Line a 9-inch square baking pan with foil. Heavily butter bottom and sides of foil. Spoon in vegetables, spreading them in an even layer. Pour egg mixture evenly over vegetables. Bake 35–40 minutes, or until puffed and golden brown. Remove from heat and cool 10 minutes.

To serve warm, use foil to lift frittata from pan. Turn down sides of foil and cut into 2-inch squares. To serve cold, chill frittata in pan, then remove and cut. Garnish top of each square as desired. Yields 16 (2-inch) squares.

SUGGESTED GARNISHES:

Asparagus tips and pimento strips; mushroom slices, white onion rings, and parsley; small stuffed olives and parsley; pickle fan and black olive slices; cherry tomato slices topped with pumpkin seeds.

One Magnificent Cookbook (Illinois)

Gazpacho Salsa with Creole Spiced Tortilla Chips

2½–3 pounds tomatoes, chopped
1 hothouse or English cucumber, chopped
1 medium red onion, chopped
1 yellow bell pepper, chopped
½ bunch cilantro
2 jalapeño peppers

2 garlic cloves
2–3 tablespoons olive oil
1–2 tablespoons red wine vinegar
½–1 teaspoon sugar
Salt and freshly ground pepper to taste

Combine tomatoes, cucumber, red onion, and yellow pepper in a bowl and toss to mix well. Remove leaves from cilantro and discard stems. Process cilantro leaves, jalapeños, garlic, olive oil, red wine vinegar, sugar, salt and pepper in a blender until smooth. Add vegetable mixture and mix well. Chill, tightly covered, in refrigerator. Drain slightly before serving. Serve with Creole Spiced Tortilla Chips. Yields 3½–4 cups.

CREOLE SPICED TORTILLA CHIPS:

2 (10-count) packages 7-inch tortillas

1–2 tablespoons Creole seasoning or chili powder

Cut each package of tortillas into halves. Cut each half into 4 wedges. Arrange in single layers on baking sheets. Spray wedges lightly with nonstick cooking spray. Sprinkle with seasoning. Bake at 350° for 5 minutes. Cool and store in an airtight container.

America Celebrates Columbus (Ohio)

Watermelon Fire and Ice Salsa

3 cups watermelon, seeded,
  chopped
½ cup chopped green pepper
2 tablespoons lime juice
1 tablespoon chopped cilantro
1 tablespoon chopped green
  onions

1–2 tablespoons minced
  jalapeño pepper
½ teaspoon garlic salt
1 cup sour cream
Tortilla chips

Combine first 7 ingredients. Cover and refrigerate one hour. Serve over sour cream with tortilla chips.

Cook, Line & Sinker (Ohio)

Easy Party Dip

Sure to be one of your favorite dips. You will be surprised.

1 cup Hellmann's mayonnaise
1 cup chopped onion
8 ounces Swiss cheese,
  shredded

2 artificial lobster tails, or 3 sea
  legs, or 12 cooked shrimp
1 box Ritz Crackers

Simply mix first 3 ingredients in a small casserole dish. For color and added taste, shred one or a combination of seafood mentioned above. Mix well. Cover casserole dish. Bake at 350° until cheese is melted, approximately 15–20 minutes. Serve warm on Ritz Crackers.

Indiana's Finest Recipes (Indiana)

Baked Reuben Dip

1 cup grated Swiss cheese
1 cup sauerkraut, drained
½ cup sour cream
2 teaspoons spicy brown
  mustard
1 tablespoon ketchup
2 teaspoons minced onion
1 (8-ounce) package cream
  cheese, cubed
8 ounces corned beef, cut into
  small pieces

Combine all ingredients. Place in glass baking dish. Cover and bake 30 minutes at 350°. Uncover and bake an additional 5–10 minutes until golden. Serve with crackers. Serves 4–6.

Sharing Traditions from People You Know (Iowa)

Mustard Dip

8 ounces sour cream
8 ounces mayonnaise
8 ounces yellow mustard
¼ cup chopped onion
1 package Original Hidden
  Valley Ranch Dressing
½ cup sugar
3 teaspoons horseradish

Mix all together. Serve with pretzels.

Sharing Our Best (Iowa)

Nutty Cereal Snack

1 (12-ounce) package square
  bite-size rice cereal
1 (12-ounce) package M&M's
2 (2-ounce) packages slivered
  almonds
1 (3¼-ounce) package shelled
  sunflower seeds

1 cup plus 2 tablespoons
  margarine or butter
1½ cups sugar
1½ cups light corn syrup
1½ teaspoons vanilla

In a very large container combine cereal, M&M's, almonds, and sun-flower seeds; set aside. In a large saucepan melt margarine. Add sugar and syrup to saucepan and stir to combine. Bring mixture to a boil over medium heat. Boil gently for 3 minutes, stirring frequently. Remove pan from heat and stir in vanilla. Pour syrup over cereal mixture, while stirring, until pieces are coated. Turn out onto wax paper and let stand, covered with wax paper for several hours.

Iowa Granges: Celebrating 125 Years of Cooking (Iowa)

Hidden Valley Ranch
Oyster Crackers

1 (1-ounce) package Hidden
  Valley Ranch Salad Dressing
  Mix
½ teaspoon dill weed

¾ cup oil
¼ teaspoon lemon pepper
¼ teaspoon garlic powder
5 cups plain oyster crackers

Preheat oven to 250°. Combine salad dressing mix with dill weed and oil. Pour over crackers; stir to coat. Sprinkle with lemon pepper and garlic powder; toss to coat. Place in oven for 15–20 minutes. Stir gently halfway through baking.

Carroll County Humane Society Members & Friends Cookbook
Volume II (Ohio)

Hunker Down Popcorn

Light the fire, find a book, and hunker down with a bowl of this dynamite popcorn. It almost makes winter worthwhile.

18 cups popped corn
1 tablespoon butter or light
margarine
⅔ cup light corn syrup
1½–2 teaspoons vanilla

1 (3-ounce) package butter
pecan, butterscotch, or vanilla
instant pudding mix
½ teaspoon salt

Preheat oven to 300°. Pam spray a big roasting pan. Pop corn in air popper (enough kernels to make 18 cups popped corn). Put popped corn in pan and keep warm in 300° oven. In glass measuring cup, microwave butter until melted (or melt in saucepan on stove). Stir in corn syrup, vanilla, and pudding mix with a fork. Pour syrup over popcorn and toss with wooden spoon. Sprinkle salt over corn. Toss; taste; sprinkle. Do it again until it says, "Hello!" Return to 300° oven for 8 minutes. Toss. Return to 300° oven for 8 minutes. Toss again. Determine if it needs another few minutes to make it glossy. Toss. Taste. (My oven dictates another 8 minutes, but all ovens are different. Use your infallible good taste.) Turn out on large pieces of foil to cool. Break into bits. Store leftovers (if any) in covered tin box.

The Lucy Miele Too Good to Be Low-Fat Cookbook (Illinois)

Bread and Breakfast

The Longaberger Company in Newark, Ohio, is a maker of handcrafted maple wood baskets. The company's corporate headquarters on State Route 16 is a local landmark and takes the shape of their biggest seller, the Medium Market Basket.

Swiss Cheese Bread

Hearty and delicious—people love it!

1 loaf French or Italian bread
1 pound Swiss cheese, thinly
  sliced
1 cup butter, melted
2 tablespoons minced onion
1 tablespoon poppy seeds

1 teaspoon seasoned salt
1 (4-ounce) can mushrooms,
  drained
1 tablespoon dry mustard
1 tablespoon lemon juice

Slice bread loaf partly through, diagonally in both directions, making little diamonds. Stuff slices of cheese in openings. Place loaf of bread on foil on cookie sheet. Mix remaining ingredients and pour mixture over bread. Seal foil tightly around loaf.

Bake at 350° for 45-60 minutes. Check several times to be sure bottom is not browning too quickly. Serves 6-8.

Brunch Basket (Illinois)

American Gothic Cheese Loaf

Mrs. Nan Wood Graham, sister of Grant Wood and model for the woman in American Gothic, submitted this recipe as a convenient, tasty favorite.

1 long loaf unsliced French or
  sourdough bread
1 pound or 2½ cups shredded
  Cheddar cheese
⅓ cup (or more) mayonnaise
2 tablespoons chopped or dry
  parsley

2 tablespoons prepared mustard
2 teaspoons finely chopped onion
2 tablespoons lemon juice
⅓ teaspoon salt

Slice the long loaf into thick slices (about 14) on the bias, cutting through just to bottom crust. Mix together all filling ingredients; mix well. Spread thickly between bread slices. Wrap loaf in aluminum foil and place in prepared (400°) oven for 25 minutes, or until piping hot and crusty.

The American Gothic Cookbook (Iowa)

Garlic Bubble Bread

Frozen white bread loaf
¼ cup margarine, melted
1 egg, beaten
1 tablespoon dried parsley
   flakes

1 teaspoon garlic powder
¼ teaspoon salt

Thaw frozen bread loaf according to package. Cut bread into walnut-size shapes and dip into mixture of margarine, egg, parsley flakes, garlic powder, and salt. Place into greased loaf pan, cover, and let rise. Bake at 350° until brown.

Madison County Cookbook (Iowa)

Italian Style Garlic Butter

Ideal for spaghetti dinner!

½ cup butter or margarine,
   softened
¼ cup lite mayonnaise or salad
   dressing
2 tablespoons grated Parmesan
   cheese

1 teaspoon crushed dried basil
½ teaspoon crushed dried
   oregano
1 clove garlic, minced

Beat together all ingredients with an electric mixer. Store in a covered container in refrigerator up to one month. To serve, spread evenly on slices of French bread or split bagels; place on an ungreased baking sheet. Broil 4 inches from heat 2–3 minutes or until golden. Makes ¾ cup.

kinderFun Kuisine (Ohio)

Ham & Swiss Cheese Biscuits

2 cups all-purpose flour
2 teaspoons baking powder
½ teaspoon baking soda
½ cup butter or margarine,
  chilled, cut into pieces
½ cup shredded Swiss cheese
¼ cup minced ham
About ⅔ cup buttermilk

Preheat oven to 450°. Grease baking sheet. Sift flour, baking powder, and baking soda into medium bowl. Using pastry blender or 2 knives, cut in butter until mixture resembles coarse crumbs. Stir in cheese, ham, and enough buttermilk to make a soft dough. Turn out dough onto lightly floured surface; knead lightly. Roll out dough ½ inch thick. Cut biscuit rounds with 2-inch cutter. Place on greased baking sheet. Bake about 10 minutes or until browned. Makes 18 biscuits.

Dawn to Dusk (Ohio)

Sister Lettie's Buttermilk Biscuits

2 cups all-purpose flour
½ teaspoon salt
1 tablespoon baking powder
½ teaspoon baking soda
3 tablespoons chilled butter
¾ cup buttermilk, chilled
3 tablespoons butter, melted

Sift flour, salt, baking powder, and soda together 3 times. Cut in chilled butter with pastry blender or 2 knives, scissors fashion, until mixture resembles coarse meal. Chill mixture in the refrigerator about 1 hour or longer.

Add buttermilk and knead lightly, 10–15 times. Roll to ¾-inch thickness and cut with a 1½-inch round biscuit cutter, and place on lightly greased cookie sheet; or press dough quickly into a shallow greased and floured 9 x 10-inch pan, and cut dough into diamond or square-shaped biscuits.

Brush with melted butter and bake 12 minutes at 450° for round biscuits, or at 400° for 18 minutes for pan biscuits. Makes 10 (2-inch) or 15 (1½-inch) round biscuits. The pan biscuits will have tender, soft sides and must be separated. These biscuits are extremely light and delicious. There never seem to be enough!.

The Shaker Cookbook (Ohio)

Cheese Garlic Biscuits

2 cups Bisquick
²⁄₃ cup milk
½ cup shredded Cheddar
  cheese

½ stick butter or margarine,
  melted
¼ teaspoon garlic powder

Preheat oven to 450°. Mix Bisquick, milk, and cheese until soft dough forms; beat vigorously for 30 seconds. Drop dough by spoonfuls onto ungreased cookie sheet. Bake 8–10 minutes or until golden brown. Mix margarine and garlic powder; brush over warm biscuits before removing from cookie sheet. Serve warm. Makes about 10–12 biscuits.

Gardener's Delight (Ohio)

Hoosier Biscuits

1 teaspoon salt
1 pint milk
3–4 cups all-purpose flour
2 tablespoons yeast

1 teaspoon cream of tartar
2 tablespoons hot water
2–3 eggs

Add a teaspoon of salt to a pint of new milk, warm from the cow. Stir in flour until it becomes a stiff batter; add great spoonfuls of lively brewer's yeast; put in a warm place and let it rise as much as it will. When well raised, stir in a teaspoon of saleratus (cream of tartar), stir with batter, and add flour until it becomes a tolerable stiff dough. Knead it thoroughly, set it by the fire until it begins to rise, and then roll out, cut to biscuit form, put it in pans, cover it over with a thick clothe, set by the fire until it rises again, then bake in a quick (400°) oven for about 30 minutes, or until golden brown.

The Conner Prairie Cookbook (Indiana)

Residents of Indiana are known as Hoosiers. Although many stories are told, the origin of the term is unknown, but it has been in use since at least 1826. The state of Indiana adopted the nickname "Hoosier State" more than 150 years ago. Today, "Hoosiers" is also the mascot for the Indiana University athletic teams, and the title of an award-winning 1986 movie *Hoosiers* starring Gene Hackman, based on the story of the Milan High School basketball team and its road to winning the state championship.

Corn Festival Biscuits

¾ stick butter or margarine
1 (8½-ounce) can cream-style
  corn

1½ cups Bisquick

Melt butter or margarine in cookie sheet with sides. Stir corn and biscuit mix together. Drop by teaspoons into melted butter, turn to coat the other side. Bake at 400° for 20 minutes or until nicely browned. Makes 8–10.

The French-Icarian Persimmon Tree Cookbook (Illinois)

Corn Fritters

1 egg
¼ cup milk
1 cup pancake mix
1 (12-ounce) can whole-kernel
  corn, drained

Vegetable oil
Maple syrup

Blend egg with milk. Stir in pancake mix until smooth. Fold in corn. Drop by teaspoonfuls into hot vegetable oil. Cook 4 minutes or until golden brown. Serve with maple syrup.

T. W. and Anna Elliott Family Recipes (Iowa)

The Best Cornbread

1 cup sour cream
1 cup cream-style corn
1 cup cornmeal
½ cup vegetable oil

2 eggs
3 teaspoons baking powder
Pinch of salt

Preheat oven to 350°. In medium bowl combine all ingredients; mix well. Pour into a 9-inch square greased pan or 9-inch cast-iron skillet. Bake 25–30 minutes or until golden brown. Yields 8 servings.

Cooking on the Wild Side (Ohio)

1990s Melt in Your Mouth Dinner Rolls

You had better double this one, as they disappear quickly.

1 package dry yeast
½ cup warm water
1 tablespoon sugar plus ⅓ cup
   sugar, divided
1 teaspoon baking powder
1 cup milk

⅓ cup margarine
Dash of salt
2 eggs, beaten
4½–5½ cups all-purpose
   flour

Add yeast to warm water. Add 1 tablespoon sugar and baking powder. Let stand 20 minutes. Meanwhile, scald 1 cup milk. Add margarine, remaining ⅓ cup sugar, and a dash of salt. Cool. Then add eggs. Add flour and mix. Refrigerate overnight.

   Roll out half the dough as you would for pie and brush with melted margarine. Cut 12 pie-shaped pieces. Roll each from wide end to pointed end. Place on cookie sheet which has been sprayed and let rise. Do the same with remaining dough. Bake at 400° for 10 minutes. Makes 24 rolls.

Touches of the Hands & Heart (Ohio)

Butter Crust Rolls

1 package yeast
¼ cup warm water
½ cup shortening
¾ cup milk

½ cup sugar
3 eggs, slightly beaten
1 teaspoon salt
4½ cups all-purpose flour

Dissolve yeast in warm water. Melt shortening in milk over low heat. Combine all ingredients and mix well. Let dough rise until double in bulk. Divide dough into thirds. Roll each third out on floured board into a circle. Spread melted butter or margarine on each circle and then cut into 12 pie-shaped pieces. Starting at the big end, roll each piece. Place in greased pan and let rise for 1 hour. Bake at 375° for about 15 minutes. Makes 3 dozen rolls.

Home Cooking (Indiana)

Refrigerator Rolls

¾ cup hot water
½ cup sugar
1 tablespoon salt
3 tablespoons margarine
2 packages dry yeast

1 cup warm water
1 egg, beaten
5¼ cups all-purpose flour,
   divided

Mix hot water, sugar, salt, and margarine; cool to lukewarm. Dissolve yeast in warm water. Stir egg and 3 cups flour in lukewarm mixture. Beat until smooth. Add rest of flour, mixing well. Place dough in greased bowl; brush top with soft margarine. Cover tightly with wax paper or foil. (I like bowls with lids that fit tightly.) Refrigerate until double or until needed (up to 4 days).

To use, cut off amount of dough required and form into favorite shapes. Cover. Let rise in warm draft-free place until doubled, about 1 hour. Brush with melted margarine. Bake in 400° oven about 10–15 minutes.

The Great Iowa Home Cooking Expedition (Iowa)

Norma's Surprise Breakfast Rolls

¼ cup sugar
1 teaspoon cinnamon
2 (8-count) cans crescent rolls

16 large marshmallows
¼ cup butter, melted
¼ cup chopped nuts

GLAZE:

½ teaspoon vanilla
½ cup powdered sugar

2–3 teaspoons milk

Combine sugar and cinnamon. Separate crescent rolls into 16 triangles. Dip marshmallows in melted butter and dip in sugar and cinnamon mixture. Wrap triangle around marshmallows and seal tightly. Dip in remaining melted butter. Place buttered-side-down in deep muffin cup. Place on foil or on cookie sheet. Bake at 375° for 10–15 minutes. Remove immediately from pan and drizzle Glaze over top.

Cooking with Daisy's Descendants (Illinois)

Christmas Morning Rolls

1 (24-count) bag frozen dinner
   rolls
1 (3¾-ounce) package
   butterscotch pudding (not
   instant)

½ cup butter
¾ cup brown sugar
½ cup chopped nuts

Arrange rolls in greased tube pan. Sprinkle dry pudding mix over rolls. Cook butter and remaining ingredients over low heat until sugar is dissolved and mixture is bubbly. Pour over rolls. Cover tightly with foil and let stand on counter top overnight.

The next morning, bake at 350° for 30 minutes. Let stand 5 minutes, then invert carefully on serving dish.

Treasured Recipes (Ohio)

Overnight Cinnamon Rolls

1 package yeast
¼ cup warm water
2 eggs, beaten
⅓ cup white sugar
½ teaspoon salt

1 cup milk, scalded
½ cup margarine
3½ cups all-purpose flour
Butter, cinnamon, and brown
   sugar

Dissolve yeast in warm water. Add rest of ingredients and refrigerate overnight.

Roll out cold dough. Sprinkle with butter, cinnamon, and a little brown sugar. Roll up and cut in slices. Put Pecan Topping in bottom of a greased pan, then put rolls on top of that. Let rise, then bake. When rolls are done baking (about 25 minutes), flip out on plate.

PECAN TOPPING:
⅓ cup butter, softened
½ cup brown sugar

½ cup pecan pieces
1 tablespoon corn syrup or water

Combine ingredients and pour into bottom of greased pan.

Favorite Recipes from the Heart of Amish Country (Ohio)

Shenkli

(A Swiss Donut)

¾ cup butter, softened
3 cups sugar
8 eggs, beaten
2 lemons, grated, rind only
1 teaspoon lemon flavor

9–9½ cups all-purpose flour
  divided
½ teaspoon salt
1 teaspoon baking soda
2 teaspoons cream of tartar

Cream butter and sugar. Add eggs, grated lemon rind, and flavoring. Mix 4 cups flour, salt, soda, and cream of tartar. Sift. Add remaining flour, 1 cup at a time and mix well. Dough will be very stiff. Roll out by hand in long 1-inch thick rolls. Cut 1-inch long and shape into the size of a fat finger. Cool 3–4 hours or overnight in refrigerator.

Fry in oil until brown. Drain on paper towels. Can be frozen. Makes 115–125.

Recipes from "The Little Switzerland of Ohio" (Ohio)

Scottish Oat Scones

1½ cups all-purpose flour
1 cup quick or old-fashioned
  oats, uncooked
¼ cup sugar
1 tablespoon baking powder
¼ teaspoon salt
1 stick butter, chilled, cut in
  pieces

½ cup craisins
⅓ cup milk
1 egg, lightly beaten
1 tablespoon sugar
⅛ teaspoon cinnamon

Heat oven to 400°. Spray cookie sheet with nonstick spray. In large bowl, combine flour, oats, sugar, baking powder, and salt. Mix well. Cut in butter with pastry blender until like coarse crumbs. Stir in craisins.

In small bowl, mix milk and egg. Add to dry mix all at once. Stir with fork just until all ingredients are moistened. Do not overmix. Turn dough out onto lightly floured surface. Knead gently 8–10 times. Roll or pat dough into 8-inch circle, about ½ inch thick. Combine sugar and cinnamon and sprinkle over dough. Cut into 10 wedges. Bake on cookie sheet 12–15 minutes until light golden brown. Serve with honey, jam, apple butter, or favorite spread.

Rose Hill Recipes (Ohio)

Sticky Bagels

8 ounces fat-free Ultra Promise
   Margarine
½ teaspoon vanilla

1 cup brown sugar
2 teaspoons cinnamon
1 dozen bagels, cut in half

Beat margarine, vanilla, brown sugar, and cinnamon for 1 minute on medium speed with blender. Take bagel and dip top with spread just prepared. If needed, spread with knife. Broil at 450° for 4–5 minutes, until bubbly and brown. Serve warm. Yields 24 servings.

Down Home Cookin' without the Down Home Fat (Ohio)

Mrs. Rockne's Swedish Coffee Cake

For over half a century, Knute Rockne was one of the most dominant figures in college football. During his 13 years as head coach, Rockne transformed the University of Notre Dame from an unheralded Midwestern school into a national institution.

½ pound butter
2 cups sugar
3 eggs
3 teaspoons baking powder

3 cups all-purpose flour
1 (12-ounce) can evaporated
   milk

TOPPING:

¾ cup brown sugar
¾ cup coconut

4 tablespoons flour
4 tablespoons butter, melted

Cream butter with sugar; add eggs and beat well. Combine baking powder with flour; sift. Add milk alternately with the sifted flour mixture. Pour batter into 2 greased pans—1 (9x13-inch) pan and 1 (9x9-inch) pan. (Or use an 8x8-inch pan for the small cake; it makes it a little higher.) Mix Topping and sprinkle over batter. Bake 30–35 minutes at 350°. This coffee cake freezes well.

Aspic and Old Lace (Indiana)

Peach Pudding Coffee Cake

This is a great Sunday morning brunch treat, served warm.

2 cups sliced peaches	1 cup all-purpose flour
Lemon juice	½ teaspoon salt
Cinnamon	4 tablespoons butter
¾ cup sugar	½ cup milk
1 teaspoon baking powder	

In an 8-inch square pan, slice peaches. Sprinkle with lemon juice and cinnamon. Combine sugar, baking powder, flour, and salt in mixing bowl. Blend in butter and add milk. Spread this batter on top of peaches. Sprinkle batter with Topping.

TOPPING:

¾ cup sugar	1 cup boiling water
1 tablespoon cornstarch	

Sprinkle sugar and cornstarch over batter. Add 1 cup boiling water over top. Do not stir. Bake at 350° for 45 minutes.

Blue Willow's "Sweet Treasures" (Iowa)

Coffee Cake

1 (18¼-ounce) box yellow cake mix (without pudding)	½ cup oil
	4 eggs
1 (3-ounce) package French vanilla instant pudding	½ cup sugar
	1 cup chopped nuts
1⅓ cups milk	1 teaspoon cinnamon

Mix cake mix, pudding, milk, oil, and eggs. Set aside. Combine sugar, chopped nuts, and cinnamon. Alternate cake batter with filling mixture in well-greased tube pan. Alternate layers beginning and ending with batter. Bake in 350° oven for 60 minutes.

A Sprinkling of Favorite Recipes (Ohio)

Rhubarb Nut Bread

1½ cups brown sugar
⅔ cup oil
1 egg
1 cup sour milk or buttermilk
2½ cups all-purpose flour

½ cup chopped nuts
1 teaspoon baking soda
¼ teaspoon salt
1 teaspoon vanilla
1½ cups diced rhubarb

TOPPING:

1 tablespoon butter, melted   ½ cup sugar

In a bowl, combine sugar, oil, egg, and rest of ingredients. Beat until well mixed. Sprinkle with Topping mixture. Bake in greased 9x5-inch loaf pan or 9x13-inch baking pan at 325° for 1 hour. Cool on rack.

The French-Icarian Persimmon Tree Cookbook (Illinois)

Strawberry Bread

3 cups all-purpose flour, sifted
1 teaspoon baking soda
1 teaspoon salt
2 teaspoons cinnamon
2 cups sugar

4 eggs, beaten
1½ cups vegetable oil
1 cup chopped pecans
1½ pints fresh strawberries,
  sliced

Preheat oven to 350°. In a bowl combine flour, soda, salt, cinnamon, and sugar, and mix well.

Mix eggs and oil and add to dry ingredients. Stir in pecans. Fold in strawberries until moistened.

Pour into 2 greased 9x5-inch loaf pans and bake 50–60 minutes or until toothpick inserted in center comes out clean. Yields 2 loaves.

One Magnificent Cookbook (Illinois)

Nabisco's plant in Chicago, Illinois, is one of the largest bakeries in the world, employing more than 2,000 workers and turning out some 320 million pounds of snack foods annually. Originally known as the National Biscuit Company, Nabisco opened corporate offices in the world's first skyscraper, the Home Insurance Building, in the Chicago Loop in 1898. (The building was demolished in 1931.)

Strawberry Nut Bread with Strawberry Butter

3 cups all-purpose flour
2 cups sugar
1 teaspoon baking soda
1 teaspoon salt
1 teaspoon cinnamon
4 eggs, beaten
¼ cup vegetable oil
2 (10-ounce) packages frozen
  strawberries, thawed, juice
  reserved
1 cup chopped nuts of choice
½ cup butter, softened
¾ cup powdered sugar

In large mixing bowl, combine flour, sugar, baking soda, salt, and cinnamon. Make a well in center of dry ingredients. Pour eggs, oil, and strawberries into well. Mix thoroughly. Stir in nuts. Butter 2 (9x5x3-inch) loaf pans or 5 miniature loaf pans.

Bake at 350° for 50–60 minutes for large loaves, or 20–25 minutes for small loaves. Cool in pans for 10 minutes, then remove and cool on wire rack.

Combine ½ cup strawberry juice, butter, and powdered sugar. Mix by hand on in food processor until smooth. Offer with sliced bread, or pour over loaves.

I'll Cook When Pigs Fly (Ohio)

Strawberry Banana Bread

½ cup butter or margarine
¾ cup sugar
1 egg
3 tablespoons milk
1 (3-ounce) package strawberry
  gelatin
½ teaspoon baking soda
1 cup mashed bananas
1 teaspoon baking powder
2 cups all-purpose flour

Cream butter and sugar; add beaten egg. In separate bowl, mix milk, gelatin, and soda. Use high bowl (as this mixture will fizz). Add bananas. Mix together with butter mixture. Sift together dry ingredients and add to mixture. Pour into greased loaf pan. Bake at 350° for 40 minutes or until done.

Country Lady Nibbling and Scribbling (Iowa)

Best Ever Banana Bread

You'll never use another banana bread recipe after tasting this one.

1 cup butter or margarine, softened	4 teaspoons baking soda
3 cups sugar	2 teaspoons vanilla
6 eggs	4–5 bananas, mashed
3 cups sour cream	1 teaspoon salt
	5 cups all-purpose flour

Cream together butter, sugar, and eggs. Mix sour cream and soda together in separate bowl, and let stand until foamy. Add rest of ingredients to above mixtures; mix well. Place into 4 greased and floured 9x5-inch bread pans and bake 50 minutes at 350° or until toothpick inserted comes out clean.

Marcus, Iowa, Quasquicentennial Cookbook (Iowa)

Canned Holiday Bread

Gather 6 wide-mouth pint canning jars, lids, and rings. Grease jars with shortening. Place lids in pan; pour boiling water over them. Don't boil, but leave in water until ready to use. (Do this when bread is about ready to come out of oven.)

⅔ cup shortening	1½ teaspoons salt
2⅔ cups sugar	½ teaspoon baking powder
4 eggs	2 teaspoons baking soda
2 cups shredded apples	1 teaspoon cinnamon
⅔ cup water	1 teaspoon ground cloves
3⅓ cups all-purpose flour	⅔ cup chopped nuts

Cream shortening and sugar. Beat in eggs, apples, and water. Sift together flour, baking powder, baking soda, salt, and spices. Add to apple mixture, and stir in nuts. Pour batter into jars, filling about ½ full. Bake at 325° for 45–53 minutes. When done, remove one jar at a time from oven. Cut off excess, wipe edges of jar clean, put on scalded lid, and screw band tight. After cooling, you can tighten band.

Variations: (1) Two cups canned pumpkin, (2) 2 cups applesauce, (3) or 1¾ cups applesauce and ¼ cup crushed pineapple.

Seasoned with Love (Illinois)

Maple Bread

2 packages yeast
¼ cup warm water
1 cup rolled oats
¾ cup boiling water
1 cup hot coffee
⅓ cup butter-flavored Crisco

½ cup maple syrup or molasses
½ cup sugar
2 teaspoons salt
2 eggs, beaten
5 cups all-purpose flour

Dissolve yeast in warm water. Mix oats, boiling water, and coffee together; let stand until lukewarm. Mix in Crisco, syrup, sugar, salt, and eggs. Add dissolved yeast. Add flour and knead on floured surface. Let rise until double in size. Punch down and shape into loaves or rolls. Let rise. Bake at 350° for about 30 minutes.

Our Collection of Heavenly Recipes (Ohio)

Corn Muffins

Requested in our favorite restaurant dish survey. By Chef Ed Kromko, French Loaf Restaurant.

¾ cup and 2 tablespoons sugar
1½ teaspoons salt
¾ cup shortening
1½ tablespoons corn syrup
4 eggs
1½ cups milk
2 teaspoons vanilla

3¾ cups and 2 tablespoons cake
  flour
5¼ teaspoons baking powder
¾ cup and 1 tablespoon yellow
  cornmeal
½ cup water

Cream sugar, salt, shortening, and corn syrup until soft and smooth. Add eggs one at a time, mixing thoroughly after each addition. Gradually stir in milk and vanilla. Set aside. Sift together cake flour and baking powder. Add cornmeal. Add flour-cornmeal mixture to first mixture and stir until flour is absorbed. Add water and mix to a smooth batter (do not overmix or muffins will become tough). Drop batter into well-greased muffin tins, filling them about half full. Bake at 400° for 15–20 minutes, or until muffin springs back when center is pressed with a finger. Makes about 36 muffins.

A Taste of Columbus Vol. III (Ohio)

Cranberry Hazelnut Muffins

Hazelnuts, golden raisins, cranberries, cinnamon, cloves, and brandy provide a rich blend of flavors in this spicy muffin recipe.

1½ cups all-purpose flour
1 teaspoon ground cinnamon
½ teaspoon baking powder
¼ teaspoon baking soda
¼ teaspoon ground cloves
1 cup fresh cranberries
⅓ cup golden raisins

⅓ cup chopped hazelnuts
2 eggs
¾ cup packed light brown
  sugar
½ cup orange juice
⅓ cup corn oil
1 teaspoon brandy

Heat oven to 350°. In a large bowl, sift together flour, cinnamon, baking powder, baking soda, and cloves. In a food processor, finely chop cranberries, raisins, and hazelnuts.

In a medium bowl, beat eggs. Stir in brown sugar, orange juice, corn oil, and brandy. Mix in brown sugar, orange juice, corn oil, and brandy. Mix in chopped cranberries, raisins, and hazelnuts, then pour egg mixture into flour mixture. Stir well. Fill greased muffin tins. Bake 20 minutes. Makes 12 muffins.

Muffins—104 Recipes from A to Z (Illinois)

Refrigerator Bran Muffins

1 (15-ounce) box raisin bran
  cereal
5 cups all-purpose flour
3 cups sugar
5 teaspoons baking soda
2 teaspoons salt

1 tablespoon pumpkin pie spice
  (optional)
4 eggs, beaten
1 cup vegetable oil (or melted
  shortening)
4 cups buttermilk

Mix dry ingredients together in a large bowl. Add eggs, shortening, and buttermilk; mix until dry ingredients are moistened. Store in covered container in refrigerator. For muffins, fill greased muffin pans ⅔ full and bake at 400° for 15–20 minutes. Batter keeps for 6 weeks.

More Hoosier Cooking (Indiana)

Pumpkin Crème Muffins

BATTER:

2 eggs
1 cup sugar
½ cup chopped nuts
1¼ cups all-purpose flour
2 teaspoons cinnamon

¾ cup oil
1 cup canned pumpkin
1 teaspoon baking soda
½ teaspoon salt

FILLING:

1 (8-ounce) package cream
   cheese, softened

1 egg
⅓ cup sugar

STREUSEL TOPPING:

¼ cup sugar
¼ teaspoon cinnamon

3 tablespoons all-purpose flour
2 tablespoons butter

Mix Batter ingredients together; set aside. Blend Filling ingredients until smooth; set aside. Combine Streusel ingredients; set aside. Pour pumpkin batter into greased or lined muffin tins. Fill ⅔ full. spoon heaping teaspoon crème mixture in center. Sprinkle with 1 teaspoon Streusel Topping. Bake at 350° for 15–18 minutes. Makes 18 muffins.

Carol's Kitchen (Illinois)

Ohio Bran 'n' Raisin Muffins

Best muffins ever!

2 cups bran
1 cup raisins
¾ cup milk
⅔ cup molasses
2 eggs, beaten

½ cup vegetable oil
1 cup all-purpose flour
2 teaspoons baking powder
1 teaspoon baking soda
½ teaspoon salt

Heat oven to 400°. Grease 16 (2–2½-inch) muffin cups. Stir bran, raisins, milk, and molasses in medium-size bowl. Stir well. Allow to stand 15 minutes. Stir in eggs and vegetable oil. Mix flour, baking powder, baking soda, and salt in large bowl. Stir bran mixture into flour mixture until blended. Spoon batter into prepared muffin cups. Bake 15–18 minutes until lightly browned and sharp knife inserted in muffins comes out clean. Makes 16 muffins.

Seasoned with Love (Ohio)

Apple-Pumpkin Streusel Muffins

This is a favorite especially in the fall when the flavors of pumpkins and apples come to mind.

BATTER:

2½ cups all-purpose flour
3 cups sugar
1 teaspoon ground cinnamon
1 teaspoon baking soda
½ teaspoon ground ginger
½ teaspoon salt
¼ teaspoon ground nutmeg

2 eggs, slightly beaten
1 cup canned pumpkin*
½ cup vegetable oil
2 cups peeled, cored, grated
    all-purpose apples
½ cup finely chopped nuts

Preheat oven to 375°. In large bowl, combine flour, sugar, cinnamon, baking soda, ginger, salt, and nutmeg. In medium bowl, combine eggs, pumpkin, and oil; add to dry ingredients, stir until just moistened. Add apples and nuts. Fill paper-lined or greased muffin cups ¾ full.

TOPPING:

2 tablespoons flour
1 tablespoon butter or
    margarine, softened

¼ cup sugar
½ teaspoon cinnamon

Combine ingredients; sprinkle evenly over muffins. Bake 20–25 minutes, or until golden brown. Cool 5 minutes; remove from pans. Makes 18–24 muffins.

*Since pumpkin usually comes packed in 16-ounce cans, use half the can and freeze the remainder for another batch of muffins at a later date. You'll need it, and not much later, either.

Bountiful Ohio (Ohio)

Iowa Corn Pancakes

Try them. You will like them!

1½ cups sifted enriched flour
2 tablespoons sugar
1 teaspoon baking soda
1 teaspoon salt
1 teaspoon baking powder
  (optional)

½ cup yellow cornmeal
2 eggs, slightly beaten
2 cups buttermilk,
  approximately
2 tablespoons butter, melted, or
  bacon fat

Mix all dry ingredients together well. Beat eggs lightly with a fork and then mix well with 1 cup buttermilk. Mix dry mixture with egg/buttermilk mixture. Mix well with a hand beater, not a machine mixer. Add melted butter to mixture and mix. Add buttermilk to mixture until it is the proper thickness for cooking.

Fry in a nonstick skillet heated between medium-high and high. The skillet is ready for frying when drops of water bounce around and quickly evaporate.

Spanning the Bridge of Time (Iowa)

Pancake Mix

This mixture makes light and fluffy pancakes, easy to prepare. It keeps well for months on your kitchen shelf—it doesn't have to refrigerated.

12 cups all-purpose flour
4 cups dry instant powdered
  milk

¾ cup baking powder
¾ cup sugar
2 tablespoons salt

Combine flour, powdered milk, baking powder, sugar, and salt. Sift several times. Be sure it is mixed well.

TO MAKE PANCAKES:
1½ cups mix
1 cup water

1 egg
2 tablespoons oil

Beat until smooth and fry cakes on hot griddle.

Sharing Our Best (Indiana)

High Rise Apple Pancake

1 medium apple	½ cup plus 2 tablespoons milk
1 teaspoon lemon juice	3 eggs or one carton egg
2 tablespoons sugar	substitute
1 teaspoon cinnamon	5 tablespoons butter
½ cup plus 2 tablespoons all-purpose flour	Powdered sugar

Preheat oven to 425°. Peel and slice apple into ¼-inch slices and place in a small mixing bowl. Toss with lemon juice, sugar, and cinnamon. In large mixing bowl, combine flour and milk, and mix until just incorporated. Add eggs and mix. Batter should be slightly lumpy.

In skillet, heat butter until foamy. Remove from heat and quickly add batter. Arrange apples in pinwheel design and place in oven. Bake 25 minutes, or until pancake is puffed up and golden brown. Sprinkle with powdered sugar and serve with warm apple sauce, syrup, or jam. Yields 2 generous servings.

Holy Cow, Chicago's Cooking! (Illinois)

German Apple Pancake

PANCAKE:

3 large eggs	½ teaspoon salt
¾ cup milk	½ teaspoon vanilla
¾ cup all-purpose flour	1½ tablespoons butter

Preheat oven to 450°. Beat eggs, milk, flour, salt, and vanilla until smooth. In a heavy 12-inch skillet, melt butter; pour batter into skillet. Bake 15 minutes; lower temperature to 350°; bake 10 minutes more.

FILLING:

1 pound tart apples (and/or peaches and pears), peeled, cored, sliced	¼ cup butter, melted
	¼ cup brown sugar
	Ground cinnamon and nutmeg

Sauté apples in butter and sugar; season to taste with cinnamon and nutmeg. Place pancake on serving dish, then with slotted spoon, add apples to half of pancake; fold over. Pour remaining apple syrup in pan over folded pancake. Serve with additional maple syrup if desired, although not necessary.

Dawn to Dusk (Ohio)

Blueberry Cream Cheese-Stuffed Baked French Toast

1½ loaves French bread or
   sourdough bread, presliced
   (no crust), divided
1 (12-ounce) bag frozen
   blueberries, rinsed
1 (8-ounce) package cream
   cheese
½ cup sugar

½ cup sour cream
1 teaspoon vanilla
8 eggs
½ cup milk
1 pint half-and-half
1 teaspoon cinnamon
1 teaspoon nutmeg
½ cup powdered sugar

Cut 1 loaf bread into cubes and place into bottom of a greased 9x13-inch baking dish. Dish should be ¾ full. Sprinkle blueberries evenly over bread. Microwave cream cheese in bowl for 2 minutes. Stir carefully and add sugar, sour cream, and vanilla. Spread over blueberries. Place remaining 6–8 large slices of bread over cream cheese. (Judge by how many guests you are serving.) Beat eggs, milk, half-and-half, cinnamon, and nutmeg, and pour over bread. Make holes with knife so liquid goes throughout. Cover and refrigerate overnight.

Bake at 350°, covered, 1 hour, then uncovered, 25–30 minutes, until top is golden brown. Let sit 10 minutes before slicing. Sift powdered sugar over before serving.

Don't Forget the INNgredients! (Ohio)

Seven U.S. presidents were born in Ohio, second only to Virginia's eight. Ulysses S. Grant (1869–1877); Rutherford B. Hayes (1877–1881); James A. Garfield (1881); Benjamin Harrison (1889–1893); William McKinley (1897–1901); William Howard Taft (1909–1913); Warren G. Harding (1921–1923).

Grant   *Hayes*   *Garfield*   *Harrison*   *McKinley*   *Taft*   *Harding*

Peach French Toast

1 cup brown sugar
½ cup butter or margarine
2 tablespoons water
1 (29-ounce) can sliced peaches,
   drained

12–14 (1-inch-thick) slices French
   bread
5 large eggs
1½ cups milk
3 teaspoons vanilla

Over medium-low heat, stir brown sugar and butter until butter melts. Add water and cook until sauce is thick and foamy. Pour into 9x13-inch baking dish. Let cool 10 minutes. Place peaches on top of sauce. Cover with bread, trimming to fit in one layer. Whisk together eggs, milk, and vanilla. Pour over bread. Cover and refrigerate overnight. Bake at 350°, uncovered, 40 minutes or until set and golden. Cover with foil if browning too quickly. Serve with warmed reserved peach syrup, if desired. This is rich and yummy!

The Fifth Generation Cookbook (Ohio)

Crispy Yeast Waffles

2⅔ cups all-purpose flour
1 package active dry yeast
2 tablespoons sugar
1 teaspoon salt

1¾ cups milk
¼ cup water
¼ cup margarine or butter
3 eggs

In large mixer bowl, combine flour, yeast, sugar, and salt; mix well. In saucepan, heat milk, water, and butter until very warm (120°–130°); butter does not need to melt. Add to flour mixture. Add eggs. Blend at low speed until moistened; beat 1 minute at medium speed. Cover bowl with plastic wrap and foil; refrigerate several hours or overnight.

Stir down batter. Bake on waffle iron on medium heat. Serve hot with butter and toppings.

Home Cookin' Is a Family Affair (Illinois)

Cheese and Onion Bake

Good side dish with roasts. Also good for breakfast buffet.

2 tablespoons butter
2 large onions, sliced
1 (10¾-ounce) can cream of
  chicken soup
1 soup can milk

½–¾ cup grated Swiss
  cheese
Salt and pepper
6 slices French bread, buttered
  (preferably sourdough)

Slowly cook onions in butter until limp and golden, about 20 minutes. Place in a 2-quart casserole. Combine soup, milk, cheese, salt, and pepper. Heat. Pour ½ the mixture over onions. Place 6 slices of bread on top (if bread is too fresh, toast slightly). Pour remaining soup mixture over bread. May be made a day ahead. Bake at 350° for 1½ hours. Makes 8 servings.

SoupÇon I (Illinois)

Sausage-Wrapped Eggs

4 hard-boiled eggs, shelled   1 pound bulk pork sausage

Preheat oven to 400°. Wrap each egg, using wet hands, in ¼ pound of the sausage to form a ball. Place in shallow baking dish. Bake at 400° for 30–40 minutes, or until browned. Drain. Serve with Cream Curry Sauce. Makes 4 servings.

CREAM CURRY SAUCE:
2 teaspoons Sun Brand Madras   2 cups medium white sauce
  Curry Powder, or to taste

Combine curry powder with white sauce in small saucepan. Cook over low heat until warm. Serve warm. Makes 2 cups sauce.

The Elsah Landing Restaurant Cookbook (Illinois)

Cheese Blintz Casserole

This is a wonderful brunch dish, especially for entertaining, as it can be prepared the day before needed.

FILLING:

2 cups small-curd cottage
  cheese
2 egg yolks

1 tablespoon sugar
1 (8-ounce) package cream
  cheese, softened

Grease a 9x13-inch casserole dish. Beat together all Filling ingredients; set aside.

BATTER:

1½ cups sour cream
½ cup orange juice
6 eggs
¼ cup butter, softened

1 cup all-purpose flour
⅓ cup sugar
2 tablespoons baking powder
1 teaspoon cinnamon

Combine all ingredients in bowl or food processor. Beat or blend until smooth. Pour half the batter into the casserole dish. Drop Filling by teaspoonfuls over Batter; spread evenly (the Filling will mix slightly with the Batter). Pour remaining Batter over Filling. Cover and refrigerate 2 hours or overnight. Bake, uncovered, at 350° for 50–60 minutes, until light golden brown. Serve with additional sour cream and preserves. Serves 12.

Plain & Fancy Favorites (Ohio)

The legend of the Chicago Fire: After months without rain, Chicago was as dry as a tinder box. On the night of October 8, 1871, Mrs. O'Leary, a boarding housekeeper, went to the barn to milk her cow. She left her lighted lantern in the barn and the cow kicked it over, igniting straw in the stall. The fire took 2 days to control, killing 250 people and destroying much of the North Side of Chicago. Though the fire was one of the largest U.S. disasters of the 19th century, the rebuilding that began almost immediately spurred Chicago's development into one of the most populous and economically important American cities. Ironically, the Chicago Fire Academy was built on the fire's point of origin in 1956. A 33-foot bronze sculpture of stylized flames entitled "Pillar of Fire" was erected on the site in 1961.

Zesty Cheese Egg Bake

1 loaf French bread
1 (8-ounce) package cream
  cheese
1 (4-ounce) can green chiles,
  drained
2 cups grated Monterey Jack
  cheese

2 cups grated Cheddar cheese
8 eggs
1½ cups milk
1½ cups half-and-half
1½ teaspoons dried mustard
Paprika or red cayenne pepper

Grease a 9x13-inch baking dish. Cut enough bread into 1-inch cubes to fill baking dish half full. Set aside 8 whole slices to use for topping. Cut cream cheese into small cubes and place evenly over cubes. Combine grated cheeses and sprinkle over bread. Cover with remaining 8 slices of bread evenly over top.

In medium bowl, beat eggs well, then add milk, half-and-half, and dry mustard; blend well. Slowly pour egg mixture evenly over top giving it time to soak in. Spray tin foil with Pam and cover dish with it; let sit overnight.

Preheat oven to 350°. Leave foil on dish and place in oven. Bake for 45–50 minutes; remove foil (hopefully it did not stick to top of bread since you sprayed it with Pam) and bake another 15 minutes. Check often to make sure top does not get too brown. Knife inserted should come out clean. Let stand 10–15 minutes before serving. Sprinkle with paprika before serving. Serves 8.

Variation: One pound sausage, cooked and drained, may be added before covering with cheeses and bread slices.

Don't Forget the INNgredients!

Eggs Benedict Casserole

2½ cups cut-up cooked ham
10 eggs, poached
¼ teaspoon black pepper

1 cup crushed cornflakes or
    fine bread crumbs
¼ cup margarine, melted

Put ham in a 9x13-inch baking pan; place poached eggs on ham. Sprinkle with pepper. Prepare Mornay Sauce and pour over eggs. Toss butter and cornflakes, sprinkle over sauce in rectangle around each egg. Refrigerate no longer than 24 hours. Heat in 350° oven until sauce is bubbly.

MORNAY SAUCE:

¼ cup butter
¼ cup flour
½ teaspoon salt
⅛ teaspoon nutmeg

2½ cups milk
1½ cups shredded Gruyère
    or Swiss cheese
½ cup grated Parmesan

Heat butter over low heat till melted. Stir in flour, salt, and nutmeg. Cook, stirring constantly, till bubbly. Remove from heat, then stir in milk. Heat to boiling, stirring constantly. Boil 1 minute. Add cheese and stir till smooth.

Dawn to Dusk (Ohio)

©2002 STEVEN J. DUNLOP

Influenced by grain storage pits of the "old world" and corn cellars of Native Americans, the first known upright wooden silo was constructed in 1873 by Fred Hatch of McHenry County, Illinois. By storing silage (green fodder) in an air-tight container (silo), it stopped fermentation, thus preserving the feed until it was needed. The use of silos spread by word of mouth and through farming magazines. By 1924 there were more than 100,000 across the nation. During World War I farmers were asked to raise more food for the war effort. Building a silo was equated with patriotism. Silos have been built of wood, fieldstone, tile, brick, concrete and steel, and have ranged in height from 35 to 60 feet.

Winter Morning Peaches

2 (16-ounce) cans sliced peaches
2 tablespoons margarine or
   butter
⅓ cup brown sugar

½ teaspoon cinnamon
2 tablespoons cornstarch
¼ cup cold water

In saucepan over medium heat, heat peaches, margarine, brown sugar, and cinnamon. Stir cornstarch into cold water and add to peaches. Cook and stir until thickened. Cool slightly and spoon into individual dishes. Serve warm. Makes 6–8 servings.

Inn-describably Delicious (Illinois)

Fried Apples

4 tablespoons butter
4–6 Jonathan apples, unpeeled,
   sliced
Dash of salt

2 tablespoons sugar
2 tablespoons brown sugar

Melt butter in heavy skillet; stir in sliced apples sprinkled with sugars and salt. Cook over medium heat about 10 minutes, stirring and turning from time to time. Serve warm.

Dawdy Family Cookbook (Illinois)

Soups, Chilis, and Stews

Madison County, Iowa, is famous for its covered bridges, which were featured in a best-selling novel and film, The Bridges of Madison County. *Originally the county had nineteen covered bridges, but only six remain, all listed on the National Register of Historic Places. Hogback Covered Bridge, built in 1884, is still in its original location in a valley north of Winterset.*

White Bean Vegetable Soup

1 pound Great Northern beans
10 cups water
4 cups chicken stock or canned
  broth
2 pounds smoked ham hocks
1 onion, chopped

2 cups peeled potatoes, diced
2 carrots, peeled, diced
1 small head green cabbage,
  shredded
1 cup frozen lima beans, thawed

Soak beans overnight and drain. In large pot, put beans, water, chicken stock, and ham hocks. Cook until beans are tender, about 1½ hours. Add onion, potatoes, carrots, cabbage, and lima beans. Simmer 30 minutes longer, or until potatoes are done. Remove ham hocks and cut off meat; return meat to soup and eat.

College Avenue Presbyterian Church Cookbook (Illinois)

Bean Soup

Dried beans were used a lot by the Zoar people. This is my recipe and my husband's favorite soup.

1 (2-pound) bag Great Northern
  beans
2 cups diced ham
1 (46-ounce) can beef broth

1 large onion, chopped
2 cups diced celery
Salt and pepper to taste

Soak beans in water overnight; drain and rinse beans. In large kettle, combine soaked beans, ham, beef broth, onion, celery, and enough water to cover mixture. Salt and pepper to taste. Bring to a boil, then simmer 3 hours, adding a little more water if needed.

Heirloom Recipes and By Gone Days (Ohio)

Midwest Minestrone Soup

Soup is even better the second day!

1 pound Italian sweet sausage
1 tablespoon olive or vegetable
  oil
1 cup diced onion
1 clove garlic, finely minced
1 cup sliced carrots
1 teaspoon crumbled basil
2 small zucchini, sliced
1 (16-ounce) can Italian pear
  tomatoes, undrained, chopped

2 (10¾-ounce) cans beef
  bouillon
2 cups finely-shredded cabbage
1 teaspoon salt
¼ teaspoon pepper
1 (16-ounce) can Great Northern
  beans, undrained
Chopped fresh parsley

Slice sausage crosswise about ½-inch thick; brown in oil in a deep saucepan or Dutch oven. Add onion, garlic, carrots, and basil; cook 5 minutes. Add zucchini, tomatoes with liquid, bouillon, cabbage, salt, and pepper. Bring soup to a boil; reduce heat and simmer, covered, for 1 hour. Add beans with liquid; cook another 20 minutes. Garnish with parsley. Makes 8 servings.

Specialties of Indianapolis II (Indiana)

Hearty Italian Soup

1 pound mild link sausage
1 pound hot link sausage
4 carrots, peeled, diced
1½ pounds zucchini, diced
2 green peppers, diced
1 cup finely chopped onions
2 cloves garlic, minced
1 cup white cooking wine

10 cups chicken broth
2 large cans peeled whole
  tomatoes
2 teaspoons dried basil
1 teaspoon dried oregano
Black pepper to taste
1 cup uncooked orzo
1¼ cups Parmesan cheese

Remove casings from sausage, dice. Brown in soup pot; drain fat. Add diced vegetables, onions, and garlic to pot, stirring until soft. Add remaining ingredients except orzo and cheese, and bring to a boil. When boiling, add orzo and cook 20 minutes. Serve and sprinkle with Parmesan cheese. Serves 12.

The Kettle Cookbook (Ohio)

French Vegetable Beef Soup

A real "knife and fork" soup. Almost like a stew.

2 pounds beef stew meat, cut
    in ½-inch cubes
¼ cup oil
1 (10¾-ounce) can condensed
    onion soup
6 cans water
1 (6-ounce) can tomato paste
1½ teaspoons salt
¼ teaspoon pepper

1 tablespoon basil
1 (16-ounce) can wax beans,
    drained
1 (16-ounce) can kidney beans,
    drained
8 carrots, sliced
2 cups sliced celery
½ cup Parmesan cheese

Brown meat in oil. Reduce heat and stir in soup and water. Add tomato paste, salt, pepper, and basil. Simmer covered, 1½ hours.

Add all vegetables. Reheat to boiling, then simmer covered 30 minutes, or until meat and vegetables are tender. Stir in cheese. Yields 8 servings.

For Crying Out Loud . . . Let's Eat! (Indiana)

Corn Soup

A South African dish.

1 cup chopped yellow onion
2 ounces margarine
1 cup fresh tomatoes, coarsely
    diced
2 cups canned whole corn

2 cups canned cream-style corn
1 (12-ounce) can evaporated milk
3 chicken bouillon cubes
3 cups water
Salt and pepper to taste

In a 4-quart heavy pan, sauté onions in margarine until soft but not brown. Add tomatoes and simmer 3 minutes. Add corn, milk, and bouillon cubes dissolved in water. Add salt and pepper to taste. Simmer gently, covered, 15 minutes.

Country Cupboard Cookbook (Iowa)

The state of Iowa is named for the Ioway people, a Siouan tribe of Native Americans that formerly lived there. It is officially known as the "Hawkeye State" and unofficially known as the "Tall Corn State."

Beside The Point's Split Pea Soup

A "typically Ohio" recipe. Strictly Midwestern in origin.

8 cups water
1 (1-pound) bag split peas,
  rinsed, drained
1 ham bone with meat or 1 large
  ham hock
2 large onions, chopped
2–4 leeks, white part only,
  chopped

2 ribs celery, chopped (include
  some leaves)
1 large carrot, peeled, chopped
1 cup dry white wine
1 clove garlic, finely chopped
½ teaspoon marjoram leaves
¼ teaspoon thyme leaves
Salt and pepper to taste

In large kettle, combine all ingredients except salt and pepper; bring to a boil. Reduce heat, cover and simmer 2–2½ hours or until peas are soft. Remove ham bone; cool slightly. Remove meat from bone; return to kettle. Add salt and pepper to taste. Makes about 2 quarts.

Bountiful Ohio (Ohio)

Depression Potato Soup

This is an updated version of a soup my grandmother served at her boarding house during the Great Depression. It's as inexpensive, filling, and good now as it was then.

3 cups diced raw potatoes
1 cup diced onion
1 cup diced celery
Scant ½ cup uncooked fine
  noodles

2 cups water
1 (12-ounce) can evaporated skim
  milk
1 teaspoon dried parsley flakes
⅛ teaspoon black pepper

In a large saucepan, combine potatoes, onion, celery, noodles, and water. Cook over medium heat, stirring occasionally, until vegetables are tender, about 15 minutes. Drain, but reserve liquid. Return 1 cup of reserved liquid and drained vegetables back to pan. Stir in milk, parsley flakes, and black pepper. Lower heat. Simmer 10–15 minutes, stirring occasionally. Serves 4 (1½-cup) servings.

The Diabetic's Healthy Exchanges Cookbook (Iowa)

Duchess Potato Soup

6 cups fresh chicken stock, or
  1¼ tablespoons chicken
  stock base in 6 cups water
2 medium potatoes, peeled,
  cut in large chunks
2 medium carrots, peeled, cut
  in large chunks
1 small onion, cut in large
  chunks

1 teaspoon salt
⅜ teaspoon chervil
⅜ teaspoon pepper
¼ teaspoon onion salt
1 cup evaporated milk
¼ cup Cheddar cheese spread
Fresh parsley sprigs

Combine potatoes, carrots, and onion with chicken stock in large pot. Cover and cook over medium heat for 30 minutes, or until vegetables are tender. Add more water if soup becomes too thick. Blend in small batches in blender.

    Add salt, chervil, pepper, and onion salt. Taste and add more seasonings, if desired. Add milk and cheese. Add more milk, if needed, to get desired consistency. Heat, but do not boil. Garnish each serving with a parsley sprig. Makes 8 servings.

The Elsah Landing Restaurant Cookbook (Illinois)

Potato Soup

5 medium potatoes, peeled,
  cut in cubes
1 medium onion, diced
3 tablespoons butter
2 cups water

1 teaspoon salt
Pepper to taste
⅛–¼ teaspoon dill weed
1 chicken bouillon cube
2 cups milk

Cook potatoes and onion in hot butter until golden, about 10 minutes. Add water, salt, pepper, dill, and bouillon cube; heat over high heat till boiling. Reduce heat and simmer 15 minutes or until potatoes are tender. Remove from heat. Mash potatoes with potato masher. Add milk; heat through.

The PTA Pantry (Ohio)

Potato Cheese Soup

6–8 potatoes, peeled, diced
2–3 carrots, sliced
1–2 celery stalks, sliced
1 onion, chopped
1 (8-ounce) package cream
   cheese

¼ cup butter or margarine
1 (10¾-ounce) can cream of
   chicken soup, undiluted
2 cups milk
Salt and pepper to taste
4 bacon strips, fried, crumbled

Place potatoes, carrots, celery, and onion in a large kettle; cover with water. Cook until tender. Meanwhile, in a mixing bowl, combine cream cheese, butter, and soup; stir well. Add milk, seasoning, and bacon; add to vegetables and heat through. Yields 10–12 servings.

175th Anniversary Quilt Cookbook (Ohio)

Quick Broccoli Soup

1 (10-ounce) package broccoli,
   chopped
1 (10¾-ounce) can cream of
   mushroom soup (undiluted)
1½ cups milk

2 tablespoons butter or
   margarine
⅛ teaspoon pepper
4 ounces shredded Cheddar
   cheese

Cook broccoli in large saucepan, omitting salt; drain well. Stir in remaining ingredients. Cook over medium heat, stirring constantly until thoroughly heated.

Our Favorite Recipes (Illinois)

The Chicago Bears are one of three charter members of the NFL (National Football League) still in existence. The Arizona Cardinals, originally the Chicago Cardinals, along with the Green Bay Packers are the other two. The Bears have the most members (twenty-six) elected into the Pro Football Hall of Fame. The Bears have also recorded more regular season and overall victories than any other NFL franchise. The franchise recorded their 700th win on December 7, 2008.

Elegant Mushroom Soup

This soup is elegant enough to serve to dinner guests. Top servings with a dollop of Crème Fraîche or sour cream and chopped parsley or green onion tops.

1 pound mushrooms, coarsely
  chopped
4 green onions with tops,
  coarsely chopped
½ cup butter
⅓ cup all-purpose flour
¼ teaspoon dry mustard

2 teaspoons salt
Cayenne pepper to taste
¼ teaspoon black pepper
2 cups each chicken broth and
  whipping cream or
  half-and-half
⅓ cup sherry (optional)

Sauté mushrooms and green onions in butter in a saucepan for 5 minutes. Stir in flour, dry mustard, salt, cayenne pepper, and black pepper. Stir in chicken broth and cream gradually. Simmer until thickened and smooth, stirring constantly. Add sherry. Serves 4.

Generations (Illinois)

Sweet and Sour Cabbage Soup

6 cups shredded and diced
  cabbage
1 onion, coarsely chopped
5 cups beef broth
5 cups chicken broth
2–3 cups cooked chopped meat
  (sausage, ham, beef, pork
  roast, pot roast)
1 teaspoon minced garlic
¼ teaspoon dried thyme

¼ teaspoon ground allspice
½ teaspoon ground cayenne,
  or to taste
Salt and pepper to taste
2 cups chopped tomatoes
¼ cup tomato paste
¼ cup brown sugar
¼ cup cider vinegar
⅛ cup lemon juice

Simmer cabbage and onion in broth until tender, about ½ hour. Add meat, spices, tomatoes, and tomato paste, and simmer until reduced slightly and the flavors are blended. Add brown sugar, vinegar, and lemon juice, and reheat.

    This soup improves with 24 hours chilling and reheating. Makes a lot of hearty soup, but it freezes well. Serves 10.

More to Love . . . from The Mansion of Golconda (Illinois)

Asparagus Soup

One of the simplest, best soups you'll ever make.

2 tablespoons butter
1 (15-ounce) can drained
   asparagus tips;
   or 1 pound fresh asparagus
   tips; or 1 (10-ounce)
   package frozen asparagus
   pieces, thawed and drained,
   reserve juice

1 tablespoon butter
1 teaspoon curry powder
1 (10¾-ounce) can cream of
   asparagus soup
1 cup milk
Reserved asparagus juice
2 tablespoons cheap cocktail
   sherry

In saucepan, melt 2 tablespoons butter. Sauté asparagus in butter; remove and set aside. In same pan, melt butter; add curry powder. Stir and bubble 3–4 minutes. Add cream of asparagus soup, milk, reserved asparagus juice, and sherry; stir. Add sautéed asparagus. Correct seasoning—it may need a little salt. Heat gently through. Serve with dusting of paprika on top.

The Lucy Miele 6-5-4- Cookbook (Illinois)

Red Pepper Soup

This soup is absolutely gorgeous!!! It is not a 'hot' soup since it has sweet peppers.

4 red bell peppers, chopped
1 large onion, chopped
2 tablespoons margarine
¼ teaspoon ground cumin

¼ teaspoon cayenne pepper
3 cups chicken broth
½ teaspoon lemon juice

Sauté peppers and onions in margarine until they are soft. Add cumin and cayenne with chicken broth and simmer until vegetables are very soft.

Purée solids and then run them through a strainer to eliminate pepper skins. Return it all to soup pot and add lemon juice. Yields 6 cups.

Angiporto, Inc. (Illinois)

Shaker Tomato Soup

1 small onion, chopped
½ cup finely chopped celery
2 tablespoons butter
1 (10¾-ounce) can tomato soup
1 soup can water
1 teaspoon finely chopped
  parsley

1 tablespoon lemon juice
1 teaspoon sugar
Salt and pepper to taste
Whipped cream, unsweetened,
  for garnish
Parsley

Sauté onion and celery in butter until onion looks transparent. Add tomato soup, water, parsley, lemon juice, sugar, salt and pepper. Simmer 5 minutes. Celery will remain crisp. Top with unsweetened whipped cream and chopped parsley. Yields 6 servings.

Cincinnati Recipe Treasury (Ohio)

Chicken Curry Soup

1 chicken, cut up
6 peppercorns
2 ribs celery
1 medium onion, peeled
4 cups water
1 medium onion, finely diced
1 cup finely diced carrots
¼ cup butter

2 teaspoons curry powder
2 tablespoons cornstarch
¼ cup water
2 teaspoons salt
¼ teaspoon sugar
1 cup light cream (half-and-half)
Apple slices

Combine chicken, peppercorns, celery, and whole onion with water in a large saucepan. Cover and simmer 1 hour, or until chicken and vegetables are tender. Cool. Remove chicken from skin and bones, cut into bite-size pieces, and set aside. Discard skin and bones. Remove and strain liquid for stock.

Sauté diced onion and carrots in butter in medium saucepan over low heat for 5 minutes, or until onion is golden but not brown. Add curry powder and sauté for an additional 10 minutes. Add reserved stock, bring to a simmer and cook over medium heat for 5 minutes.

Mix cornstarch with ¼ cup water and stir this into simmering stock. Add salt, sugar, and reserved chicken. Add cream, heat through, cut do not boil. Adjust seasoning to taste. Garnish each serving with an apple slice. Yields 4–6 servings.

From Elsah's Landing Restaurant, 18 La Salle Street, Elsah, Illinois.
Best Recipes of Illinois Inns and Restaurants (Illinois)

Mulligatawny Soup

This soup is a second cousin to Indian Curry. While not as hot as a curry, it does have the distinctive taste.

¼ cup butter
1 medium onion, sliced
1 medium carrot, sliced
1 stalk celery, diced
1 green bell pepper, diced
 coarsely
1 medium apple, pared, cored,
 sliced
1 cup cooked chicken, cut up

⅓ cup all-purpose flour
1 teaspoon curry powder
⅛ teaspoon mace
2 whole cloves
1 sprig parsley
2 cups stock (chicken broth)
1 cup tomatoes, cooked
Salt and pepper to taste

In deep kettle, in butter, sauté onion, carrot, celery, green pepper, apple, and chicken. Stir frequently until onions are tender. Gradually stir in remaining ingredients. Simmer, covered ½ hour. Serve. Makes about 6 servings.

The Cookery Collection (Indiana)

Chicken Velvet Soup

This recipe was a standard at the famous Tea Room of L. S. Ayres' Department Store in Indianapolis. Ayers' opened for business in 1905, and Riley probably shopped there. In the store's early years, it was thought that food was served from informal food stands before the Tea Room opened.

6 tablespoons butter or
 margarine
6 tablespoons flour
½ cup milk
½ cup light cream

3 cups chicken broth
1 cup finely chopped cooked
 chicken
Dash of pepper

In saucepan, melt butter or margarine. Blend in flour, then stir in milk, light cream, and chicken broth. Cook over medium heat, stirring constantly, till mixture thickens and comes to a boil. Reduce heat. Stir in finely chopped cooked chicken and a dash of pepper. Return soup to boiling and serve immediately. Makes about 5 cups soup.

The James Whitcomb Riley Cookbook (Indiana)

Spaetzle

SOUP:

1½ cups finely diced celery
1½ cups grated carrots

¾ cup finely chopped onion
3 quarts rich chicken broth

Cook vegetables in chicken broth until tender, 15–20 minutes. Keep Soup simmering while adding Batter.

BATTER:

2 eggs, beaten
½ teaspoon salt

1 cup all-purpose flour
⅓–½ cup milk

Beat eggs; add salt and flour; add milk gradually. Batter should be about the consistency of pancake batter. Pour Batter into Soup from pitcher onto a wire whisk (keep turning the whisk). This will break up the spaetzle into small pieces. Simmer until pieces are tender. Serve with sprinkles of chopped parsley. This is a good hearty soup. Serves 10–15.

Feeding the Flock—Trinity United Methodist Women (Ohio)

Salmon Chowder

Keep an open mind when you see all the canned products in this recipe. It's a winner! Trust the food editor who mode it for a friend recovering from surgery—she was almost like new the next day.

1 (15-ounce) can red salmon
1 small onion, chopped
2 celery ribs, diced
2 tablespoons butter
2 (10¾-ounce) cans cream of
  celery soup

2 soup cans milk
1 (12-ounce) can cream-style
  corn
1 (12-ounce) can whole-kernel
  corn
1 tablespoon dill weed

Remove skin and center bone from salmon. Sauté onion and celery in butter until soft. Add remaining ingredients and heat soup. Do not boil.

Aren't You Going to Taste It, Honey? (Ohio)

Onion Bisque

Our most requested soup, Murphin Ridge's Onion Bisque was awarded "Best Soup" by Cincinnati magazine. On top of that, it's easy to make. Feel free to substitute vegetable stock or even water for the unsalted chicken stock.

6 onions, or 1 sweet or Vidalia
  onion per person, sliced
½ cup butter
2 tablespoons sugar
Unsalted chicken stock to cover
  (at least 4 cups)

½ cup heavy cream
1½ cups grated Parmesan cheese
Bowl-sized croutons, toasted with
  butter and sprinkled with
  Parmesan cheese

In a large saucepan, sauté onions in butter until they become limp; sprinkle onions with sugar while they sauté. Cover onions with stock and cook slowly, 30–45 minutes, watching to see that the stock does not boil away. Turn off heat, and taste soup for seasoning. Purée soup in batches in food processor, or blend soup in saucepan with an immersion blender. Leave some small bits of onion for texture. Return soup to saucepan, if necessary. Add cream and cheese and heat soup through slowly. Serve with croutons on side. Yields 8–10 servings.

A Taste of the Murphin Ridge Inn (Ohio)

Stormy Weather Chili

2 medium onions, diced
1 cup diced celery
2 tablespoons cooking oil
1½ pounds ground beef
4 cups canned tomatoes
1 (15½-ounce) can chili beans

1–2 (15-ounce) cans red kidney
  beans
Salt and pepper to taste
1 tablespoon sugar
1 bay leaf
2–3 teaspoons chili powder

Sauté onions and celery in cooking oil in large kettle or pressure pan. When golden, stir in ground beef and brown until red is gone. Stir in remaining ingredients, and simmer 1 hour. A pressure pan will lower the cooking time. Cook for about 20 minutes at 10 pounds pressure. Put pan under cold running water until pressure is down before trying to open lid. Remove bay leaf before serving.

Up a Country Lane Cookbook (Iowa)

Cincinnati Chili

The first chili parlor opened its doors next to the Empress Burlesque (later named the Gaiety) in downtown Cincinnati in 1922, naming itself The Empress Chili Parlor. This establishment was owned by Greek Tom Kiradjieff who banked on the city sharing his taste for the unusual blend of spices. The rest is history. The original recipe which has always been mixed secretly at home, was never revealed. Yet chili restaurants sprang up all over town, including Skyline and Gold Star. Local chili aficionados developed preferences for their favorites. Al Heitz, a Camp Washington devotee, liked the old recipe best because it left his lips numb; old timers say that the chiles have indeed "cooled off" through the years. Inevitably, various chili recipes were published in cookbooks. Recently, a packaged Cincinnati Chili Mix has appeared on supermarket shelves. Whether the chili is hot or not, Cincinnati prides itself on being a true chili capital.

2–3 pounds ground beef
1 quart cold water
1 (6-ounce) can tomato paste
2 large onions, chopped
  (about 1½ cups)
1½ tablespoons vinegar
1 teaspoon Worcestershire
1 garlic clove, chopped fine
2 tablespoons chili powder
5 bay leaves
2 teaspoons cinnamon
1 teaspoon allspice
2 cayenne peppers (more to
  taste)
1½ tablespoons unsweetened
  cocoa
Salt and pepper to taste
1½ pounds cooked spaghetti
1 pound Cheddar cheese, grated
1 box oyster crackers
1 (16-ounce) can kidney beans
1 onion, chopped fine (optional)

Crumble raw ground beef into water. Add all ingredients except spaghetti, cheese, crackers, beans, and onions, and bring to a boil. Stir well, breaking all the meat up before it cooks. Cover and simmer 2 or more hours, stirring occasionally. Yields 8–10 servings.

The proper way to serve this chili is over spaghetti on an oval dish. (There should be a piece of pepper for every serving for absolute authenticity.) For "3-Way," top it off with a pile of grated cheese with a dish of crackers on the side. To make a "4-Way," add a spoonful of onions before the cheese is placed on top. For a "5-Way," add warmed beans in addition to onions and cheese.

Cincinnati Recipe Treasury (Ohio)

White Chili

Chili-heads, those guys who live for a bowl of red, keep their recipes a secret and wear outlandish clothes when they enter chili contests, probably don't have much to do with even the name White Chili, let alone the taste of it. But for the rest of the world, it has been a real "WOW!" since it arrived on the chili scene. White beans, chicken breasts, and broth keep the name honest.

1 pound Great Northern beans
2 pounds boneless chicken
  breasts
1 tablespoon olive oil
2 medium onions, chopped
4 garlic cloves, minced
2 (4-ounce) cans chopped mild
  green chiles
2 teaspoons ground cumin
1½ teaspoons dried oregano,
  crumbled

¼ teaspoon ground cloves
¼ teaspoon ground red pepper
5 cups canned chicken broth
1 (7-ounce) bottle beer
½ teaspoon each: white, lemon
  and black pepper (optional)
3 cups grated Monterey Jack
  cheese (optional)
Sour cream and salsa (optional)

Cover beans with water and soak overnight; drain. Place chicken in a large saucepan. Add cold water to cover and bring to a simmer. Cook until just tender, about 15 minutes. Drain; cool. Remove skin; cut into small pieces.

Drain beans. In same pot, sauté onion in oil until translucent; stir in garlic, chiles, cumin, oregano, cloves, and ground red pepper; sauté 2 minutes. Add beans, broth, and beer. If desired, stir in optional peppers. Bring to a boil; reduce heat and simmer until beans are very tender, about 2 hours. Stir occasionally.

Add chicken and 1 cup cheese, if desired; stir until cheese melts. Season with salt and pepper to taste. Serve with remaining cheese, sour cream, and salsa for guests to spoon onto chili if they wish.

Aren't You Going to Taste It, Honey? (Ohio)

Mom Unser's "Indy" Chili

1 pound lean pork, tenderloin or
  chops
1 medium onion, chopped
1 clove fresh garlic, chopped
1 (20-ounce) can tomatoes
1 shake oregano
Salt to taste
3 (4-ounce) cans mild or medium
  green chiles

Remove all fat from pork and cube it. Sauté pork, onion, and garlic together. Squeeze tomatoes through fingers and add to skillet with tomato juice. Add shake of oregano and salt to taste. Add green chiles, and simmer approximately 35 minutes. Add water if necessary. Pinto beans may be added, if desired, or served as a side dish. Serves 4.

Note: Mary "Mom" Unser is mother of Al, Bobby, Louie, and Jerry Unser.

Champions: Favorite Foods of Indy Car Racing (Indiana)

Venison Stew

8 slices bacon, cut up
2 pounds boneless venison,
  cubed
4 cups water, divided
2 cups dry red cooking wine
Salt and pepper to taste
½ teaspoon thyme
¼ cup parsley flakes
½ teaspoon marjoram
4 carrots, sliced
2 cups baby pearl onions
2 large potatoes, cut in
  1½-inch pieces
1 cup cold water
⅓ cup all-purpose flour

Cook bacon in Dutch oven until crisp. Remove bacon with slotted spoon; reserve. Brown venison in bacon grease about 7 minutes. Add 2 cups water, wine, and spices. Heat to boiling. Reduce heat and simmer until tender. Stir in carrots, onions, and potatoes. Heat to boiling. Reduce heat and simmer until vegetables are tender. Shake cold water and flour in tightly covered shaker. Slowly stir into stew. Heat to boiling, stirring constantly. Boil and stir 1 minute. Sprinkle with bacon.

The Great Iowa Home Cooking Expedition (Iowa)

Salads

Located along Lake Michigan's southern shore are two magnificent feats of nature, the Indiana Dunes National Lakeshore and the Indiana Dunes State Park. Together, they boast coastal beaches, tall sand dunes, wetlands, a wooded forest, bogs, and the most diversified plant life in the Midwest.

Cucumbers in Sour Cream

1 cucumber, peeled, sliced
  paper thin
4 onions, thinly sliced
1 teaspoon salt

3 tablespoons sugar
3 tablespoons vinegar
Pepper
2 tablespoons sour cream

Mix together sliced cucumber, onion, and salt. Mix with your hand to coat cucumber completely. Place in refrigerator and let stand at least ½ hour or longer.

Pour off liquid, squeezing pickles in your hand. Add sugar, vinegar, and pepper . Mix thoroughly and taste. If necessary, add a little more sugar and vinegar. Stir in sour cream and serve. You may also add a bit of dill weed, if desired.

Our Best Home Cooking (Illinois)

Artichoke Heart Salad

2 (14-ounce) jars marinated
  artichoke hearts, drained,
  reserve juice
⅔ cup Hellmann's mayonnaise
¾ teaspoon curry powder
1 (4¾-ounce) package
  chicken-flavored rice mix
  (cook ahead and cool)

6 green onions, chopped
½ green bell pepper, chopped
12 stuffed green olives, sliced
1 cup chopped mild green chiles
  (optional)

Combine juice from artichokes with mayonnaise and curry powder. In a large bowl, toss cooked, cooled rice with remaining ingredients. Pour dressing over all; toss well. Serves 12.

The Kettle Cookbook (Ohio)

Thunder & Lightning

Vine-ripened tomatoes are a requisite for this salad.

2 green bell peppers, seeded, cut julienne
4 ripe tomatoes, cut into bite-size pieces

4 ribs celery, sliced
2 medium white onions, cut julienne

DRESSING:

1½ cups cider vinegar
1½ cups sugar
1 cup vegetable oil

1 (2-ounce) bottle hot pepper sauce

Prepare vegetables. Combine Dressing ingredients and pour over vegetables. Chill about 20 minutes before serving. Also good to add sliced cucumbers to this salad.

More to Love . . . from The Mansion of Golconda (Illinois)

Summertime Salad

5 tablespoons butter
¼ cup chopped fresh parsley
2 tablespoons minced chives
1 small clove garlic, pressed
Salt to taste

1 pound fresh peas
1 teaspoon salt
1 tablespoon olive oil or vegetable oil
¾ pound spaghetti or linguini

Make an herb butter by combining butter, parsley, basil, chives, and garlic. Add a little salt to taste. Steam peas until tender, 5–8 minutes. Refresh under cold water and set aside.

Bring a large pot of water to boil. Add 1 teaspoon salt, 1 tablespoon oil, and pasta. Cook 3–5 minutes. Drain and toss into a warm serving dish with herb butter and peas. Serve immediately.

Favorite Herbal Recipes Vol. III (Illinois)

Spaghetti Salad

1 pound thin spaghetti
1 green bell pepper, diced
1 medium tomato, diced
1 small red or white onion, diced
1 cucumber, diced

1 (2¾-ounce) jar Salad Supreme
1 (8-ounce) bottle Italian dressing

Cook spaghetti following directions on package. Toss all vegetables with spaghetti. Add ¾–1 jar of Salad Supreme; toss. Add Italian dressing; toss. Refrigerate at least 4 hours.

Cooking with Class (Ohio)

Corn and Pasta Salad

Cleveland is a city of great ethnic diversity. Most Italian immigrants arrived in the early 1900s. Those who came from Sicily, a fruit-growing region, helped make the neighborhood called Big Italy the center of the city's fruit industry. In turn, Italian merchants like Frank Catalano built Cleveland into the state's center of the produce industry. They gave us our taste for oranges, bananas, garlic, olive oil, and other delicacies.

Like other Americans, many Italians married members of other ethnic groups. This recipe is a marriage, too—it shows what can happen when Italian pasta meets Midwestern produce.

2 cups rotini pasta, cooked, drained
1 (17-ounce) can whole-kernel corn, drained
½ cup each: chopped green bell pepper, red onion, and sliced radishes

½ cup bottled Italian salad dressing
½ cup salsa or picante sauce
¼ teaspoon salt
⅛ teaspoon pepper

In large bowl, combine pasta, corn, green pepper, onion, and radishes. In small bowl, combine dressing, salsa, salt, and pepper. Pour over pasta mixture; toss lightly. Refrigerate at least 2 hours to blend flavors. Makes 6-8 servings.

Bountiful Ohio (Ohio)

Baked German Potato Salad

For a twist on tradition.

2 quarts boiled red potatoes, peeled and sliced

DRESSING:

6 slices bacon, crisp-cooked
1 cup finely chopped celery
1 cup finely chopped onion
1 tablespoon cornstarch
½ teaspoon salt
½ teaspoon pepper

⅔ cup sugar
⅔ cup cider vinegar
1½ cups water
⅓ cup chopped fresh parsley
2 tablespoons celery seeds

Preheat oven to 375°. Place potatoes in greased 9x13-inch baking dish; set aside. Cook bacon until crisp; crumble; set aside. Reserve fat in skillet. If necessary, add additional fat or oil to make ¼ cup. Stir in celery and onion. Add cornstarch, salt, and pepper, and cook 2 minutes. Add sugar, vinegar, and water, and stir with whisk. Bring to a boil and cook 1 minute. Add parsley, celery seeds, and reserved bacon, and combine; remove from heat.

Pour warm Dressing over potatoes in baking dish. Mix gently. Bake 45 minutes. Makes 10–12 servings.

The Des Moines Register Cookbook (Iowa)

Back Home in Indiana Potato Salad

2 pounds potatoes
6 slices bacon, chopped
½ cup minced onions
⅓ cup vinegar

⅓ cup water
1 tablespoon parsley
Salt and pepper to taste

Boil potatoes with skins until slightly tender. Remove from water and slice while still hot into glass baking dish. Sauté chopped bacon and onions, only until onions are almost, but not quite brown. Stir in vinegar, water, parsley, salt and pepper to taste. Pour over potatoes and warm in oven to serve. Sprinkle additional parsley for decoration before serving.

Indiana's Finest Recipes (Indiana)

Deviled Potato Salad

8 hard-boiled eggs
3 tablespoons vinegar
3 tablespoons prepared mustard
1 cup mayonnaise
½ cup sour cream
½ teaspoon celery salt
1 teaspoon salt
2 teaspoons chopped onion
6 medium potatoes, cooked, cubed
Tomato wedges, cucumber slices, egg slices for garnish

Cut eggs in half; remove yolks and mash. Blend yolks, vinegar, mustard, mayonnaise, sour cream, celery salt, and salt. Mix well. Chop egg whites and onions. Combine with mixture and add to potatoes. Chill and garnish with tomato wedges, cucumber slices, and/or hard-boiled egg slices. Yields 6–8 servings.

Sharing Our Best (Elizabeth House) (Ohio)

Greek Roasted Potato Salad

6 medium white potatoes
½ cup lemon juice plus 2 tablespoons, divided
¼ cup water
5 tablespoons olive oil, divided
2 medium garlic cloves, minced
1 teaspoon oregano
½ teaspoon salt
Pepper to taste
3 medium plum tomatoes, cut in small cubes
4 green onions, finely chopped
1 small cucumber, peeled, cut into cubes
2 teaspoons Dijon mustard
½ cup chopped fresh parsley
½ cup feta cheese

Cut potatoes into cubes in large bowl with ½ cup lemon juice, water, and 1 tablespoon olive oil, garlic, oregano, salt, and pepper. Transfer to greased baking dish and bake at 400° for 35–40 minutes or until potatoes are tender. Stir twice while baking, then cool. Combine cooled potatoes with tomatoes, green onions, and cucumber. Mix together the mustard, remaining 2 tablespoons lemon juice, and remaining 4 tablespoons olive oil. Toss into salad. Add parsley and feta cheese. Serve at room temperature.

A Festival of Recipes (Ohio)

Dill Pickle Potato Salad

3 pounds potatoes (about 8 medium)
6 hard-cooked eggs, chopped
3 ribs celery, chopped
6 green onions, chopped
2 medium dill pickles, finely chopped
1½ cups mayonnaise
¼ cup dill pickle juice
4½ teaspoons prepared mustard
1 teaspoon celery seed
1 teaspoon salt
½ teaspoon pepper
Leaf lettuce (optional)

Place potatoes in a Dutch oven or large kettle and cover with water. Bring to a boil. Reduce heat, cover, and simmer for 20–30 minutes or until tender; drain and cool. Peel and cube potatoes. Place in a large bowl; add eggs, celery, onions, and pickles.

In a small bowl, combine mayonnaise, pickle juice, mustard, celery seed, salt, and pepper. Pour over potato mixture; mix well. Cover and refrigerate for at least 4 hours. Serve in a lettuce-lined bowl, if desired. Yields 8–10 servings.

Columbus Colony Creations (Ohio)

Sauerkraut Salad

1 (32-ounce) can sauerkraut
1 cup chopped mango
1 cup chopped celery
1 cup chopped onion
1 cup chopped carrots
1 cup sugar
½ cup white vinegar
¼ cup salad oil

Wash and drain sauerkraut. Add chopped fruit and vegetables. Whip sugar, vinegar, and salad oil until white. Mix with sauerkraut mixture. Refrigerate 2 hours.

Treasures and Pleasures (Ohio)

Spinach Salad

DRESSING:

1 cup oil
¾ cup sugar
⅓ cup ketchup

¼ cup vinegar
1 teaspoon Worcestershire

Mix ingredients and heat to dissolve sugar. Dressing may be warm or at room temperature, but should be poured over Salad ingredients immediately before serving.

SALAD:

6–8 strips crisp bacon, crumbled
2 hard-boiled eggs, chopped
½ cup sliced mushrooms

Fresh spinach and leaf lettuce, torn into bite-size pieces
Small purple onion, sliced

Combine ingredients in large bowl.

Favorite Recipes (Ohio)

Spinach Salad with Bacon and Apple

DRESSING:

¼ cup vegetable oil
Freshly ground pepper, to taste
3 tablespoons tarragon wine vinegar

1 teaspoon sugar
⅛ teaspoon salt
½ teaspoon dry mustard

Combine ingredients and set aside.

SALAD:

1 pound fresh spinach, washed, stemmed
5 slices bacon
⅓ cup sliced almonds

3 green onions, including some greens, thinly sliced
1 red apple, diced

Drain thoroughly and chill spinach. Sauté bacon in skillet; remove and drain on paper towels. Discard all but 1 tablespoon drippings; add almonds and stir over medium heat until browned. Remove and drain on paper towels. Before serving, break spinach into bite-size pieces. Place in bowl. Add green onions, apples, and almonds; crumble bacon on top. Spoon Dressing over Salad. Serves 8.

Lutheran Church Women Cookbook (Iowa)

Spinach and Fruit Salad

1 (1-pound) package fresh
  spinach
3 tart apples, finely cut
1 (11-ounce) can Mandarin
  oranges, drained

½ (6-ounce) can frozen orange
  juice concentrate
½ cup mayonnaise
8 slices bacon, fried, crumbled
Fresh croutons

Wash spinach carefully; remove large stems and break into bite-size pieces. Toss with apples and oranges. Blend orange juice concentrate and mayonnaise. Toss with salad. Add bacon and croutons. Serves 6–8.

Still Gathering (Illinois)

Asparagus, Spinach & Turkey Salad

1 pound turkey breast, thick
  sliced
Olive oil
1–1½ pounds fresh asparagus

2 bunches spinach
4 hard-cooked eggs, chopped
2 green onions, chopped

Sauté turkey slices in oil and cut into cubes. Steam asparagus, then cut diagonally into 1-inch pieces. Wash and stem spinach and coarsely chop. When ready to serve, toss all salad ingredients together in a bowl. Pour Mustard Dressing over salad and serve immediately. Serves 8.

MUSTARD DRESSING:
½ cup Dijon mustard
6 tablespoons water

¾ cup oil
¼ cup red wine vinegar

Place mustard in a bowl, gradually whisking in the water until it is thoroughly blended. Slowly beat in oil. Add vinegar and whisk until well combined.

A Treasury of Recipes for Mind, Body & Soul (Ohio)

Hot Baked Turkey Salad

SALAD:

3 cups cubed turkey or chicken
1 cup diced celery
1 (8-ounce) can water chestnuts
1 (2-ounce) jar chopped pimento
½ cup toasted croutons
½ teaspoon salt

½ cup toasted sliced almonds
¾ cup mayonnaise
¾ cup sour cream
2 tablespoons lemon juice
2 teaspoons grated onion

TOPPING:

½ cup buttered crumbs

¼ cup grated Parmesan cheese

Combine Salad ingredients. Spoon into a greased 2-quart casserole. Combine Topping mixture and sprinkle over top. Bake, uncovered, at 350° for 25–30 minutes until heated through.

Heavenly Dishes (Ohio)

Mary Alice's Hot Chicken Salad

4 cups cubed, cooked chicken
⅔ cup toasted slivered
   almonds
1 cup grated Cheddar cheese
2 cups sliced celery
4 hard-boiled eggs, sliced
¼ cup chopped onion

1 (4-ounce) can pimentos, well
   drained
1 (6- to 7-ounce) can water
   chestnuts, sliced
2 tablespoons lemon juice
¾ cup mayonnaise
1½ cups crushed potato chips

Toss first 8 ingredients together with lemon juice mixed with mayonnaise. Cover with crushed potato chips. Bake at 400° for 25 minutes. Serves 8–12. Prepare one day before serving.

Treasured Recipes (Ohio)

Wong's Chinese Chicken Salad

This ultimate Chinese chicken salad recipe comes directly from Hong Kong.

4 whole chicken breasts, halved
2 quarts cooking oil, preferably
  peanut oil
3¾ ounces cellophane noodles
11 ounces (8 or 9 squares) frozen
  won ton wrappers, cut into
  ⅛-inch strips

1 cup nuts (dry roasted peanuts,
  almonds, or cashews)
1 head iceberg lettuce, shredded
1 cup diagonally-cut scallions
½ cup chopped parsley

Poach or steam chicken breasts 20 minutes or until barely tender. Do not overcook. Discard skin and bones; shred chicken with fingers into 2-inch pieces.

Heat oil to 350°. Test oil temperature by dropping in a cellophane noodle. It should become opaque and "explode" instantly. Drop noodles, in small amounts, into oil. Upon "explosion," remove immediately with slotted spoon to drain on paper towels. Using same oil, cook won ton strips in small amounts until lightly browned. Remove with slotted spoon to drain on paper towels. Drop nuts in same oil; cook until lightly browned. Remove with slotted spoon to drain on paper towels.

MARINADE:

6 tablespoons dry mustard
3 tablespoons Oriental sesame
  oil

1½ cups soy sauce

Place mustard in a small bowl; gradually add sesame oil while stirring to eliminate lumps. Add soy sauce. Mix well. Marinate chicken in 1 cup Marinade for 20 minutes only.

Arrange shredded lettuce on large flat platter. Layer won ton strips over lettuce followed by cellophane noodles. Layer marinated chicken over noodles. Sprinkle with scallions, nuts, and desired amount of remaining Marinade. Garnish with chopped parsley and serve immediately.

Noodles may be prepared several days in advance and stored in airtight container. Serves 8.

Noteworthy (Illinois)

Card Club Chicken Salad

2 cups cooked chicken, diced
2 cups cooked macaroni
6 hard-boiled eggs, diced
1 cup diced, cooked carrots
1 (16-ounce) peas, drained (or frozen, cooked)
2 cups diced celery

1 tablespoon minced onion
¼ cup sliced green pepper (optional)
1 (2-ounce) jar pimentos
1 teaspoon sugar
1 teaspoon salt
½ teaspoon pepper

Combine all ingredients.

DRESSING:
1 pint mayonnaise
¼ cup French dressing

⅔ cup evaporated milk
1 cup diced Cheddar cheese

Combine Dressing ingredients. Pour over salad. Can be made ahead and refrigerated. Serve a cupful of salad on a lettuce leaf along with fancy crackers.

The Berns Family Cookbook (Iowa)

Garden Club Salad

8 cups cooked, cubed chicken or turkey
1 (16-ounce) can sliced water chestnuts
2 pounds grapes, halved
2 cups chopped celery
2 cups slivered almonds

2 cups mayonnaise
1 cup sour cream
1½ teaspoons curry powder
2 tablespoons soy sauce
1 (1-pound, 13-ounce) can pineapple chunks

Combine chicken or turkey, chestnuts, grapes, celery, and almonds. In separate bowl, combine mayonnaise, sour cream, curry powder, and soy sauce. Add to chicken mixture; stir well. Add pineapple and toss lightly. Serve on bed of lettuce. Do not substitute salad dressing for mayonnaise. Serves 12–15 generously.

St. Joseph's Parish Cookbook (Iowa)

Berried Treasure Chicken Salad

½ (16-ounce) package torn
   mixed greens (6 cups)
8 ounces sliced, fully cooked
   chicken breast
2 cups mixed fresh berries
   (sliced strawberries,
   blueberries, raspberries,
   or blackberries)
2 oranges, peeled, sliced, cut
   into quarters

1 (8-ounce) container mixed berry
   or strawberry yogurt
½ cup mayonnaise or salad
   dressing
Dash of ground cinnamon
Orange juice (optional)
½ cup broken walnuts or pecans
   (optional)

Place mixed greens in a large bowl. Stack chicken slices; halve the stack lengthwise. Cut crosswise into ¼-inch strips; add chicken strips to lettuce in bowl. Add fresh berries and orange pieces.

Stir together yogurt, mayonnaise or salad dressing, and cinnamon in a small bowl. If necessary, add orange juice, 1 teaspoon at a time, to make a drizzling consistency. Spoon salad onto 4 dinner plates; drizzle with dressing. If desired, sprinkle with walnuts or pecans.

Franklin County 4-H Favorites (Ohio)

Born in Wapakoneta, Ohio, on August 5, 1930, Neil Alden Armstrong is best known as the first human to set foot on the moon. He was mission commander of the *Apollo 11* moon landing mission on July 20, 1969. Armstrong and Buzz Aldrin descended to the moon's surface in the lunar module *Eagle* ("The *Eagle* has landed."), while Collins orbited above in the command module *Columbia*. Armstrong's first words after touching the moon's surface were, "That's one small step for man, one giant leap for mankind." The Neil Armstrong Air & Space Museum in Wapakoneta tells the thrilling saga through models, aircraft, photos, film footage, and radio transmissions.

Fruit Chicken Salad

6 cups cooked chicken
French dressing
1 cup chopped celery
2 tablespoons lemon juice
½ cup pineapple tidbits
¼ cup whipped cream
  (or more)

3 teaspoons salt
Dash of white pepper
1 cup grapes
1 cup mayonnaise
½ cup slivered almonds
Olives for garnish

Dice chicken in ½-inch pieces and marinate in French dressing 2 hours. Mix all other ingredients together (except almonds). Chill. When ready to serve, sprinkle almonds over top and garnish with olives.

Recipes of the Durbin (Indiana)

Fruited Chicken Salad

1½ cups cut-up chicken or
  turkey
1 cup green seedless grapes,
  halved, drained
1 (8-ounce) can water chestnuts,
  drained, chopped
1 (11-ounce) can Mandarin
  oranges, drained

1½ cups rotini, cooked
½ cup mayonnaise or salad
  dressing
½ teaspoon salt or 1 teaspoon
  soy sauce
¼ teaspoon curry powder

Mix chicken, grapes, water chestnuts, orange segments, and rotini. Mix remaining ingredients; toss with chicken mixture. Serves 6.

Stirring Up Memories (Iowa)

Rhubarb Swirl Salad

3 cups diced, raw rhubarb
¾ cup sugar
1 (3-ounce) package strawberry
   Jell-O

1 (3-ounce) package instant
   vanilla pudding
1½ cups cold milk
1 (8-ounce) carton Cool Whip

Mix rhubarb and sugar in saucepan. Let stand for 1 hour; then over low heat, simmer until rhubarb is tender. Remove from heat; stir in Jell-O until it is dissolved and syrupy. Prepare pudding with milk; beat until thick. Add Cool Whip. Blend in rhubarb and lightly swirl. Refrigerate several hours or overnight.

Our Heritage (Iowa)

Jane's Orange Salad

Great any time of year. A nice presentation for company.

SALAD:

1 head lettuce
1 cup grape halves
1 (11-ounce) can cold Mandarin
   oranges, drained

Chopped red onion to taste
½ cup toasted almonds
1 avocado, diced

DRESSING:

⅔ cup oil
⅓ cup orange juice
¼ cup sugar
3 tablespoons vinegar

Dash dry mustard
1 teaspoon celery seeds
2 tablespoons chopped parsley

Tear lettuce into bite-size pieces. Toss with remaining Salad ingredients. Combine all Dressing ingredients; mix well; chill. Shake well before pouring over salad. Mix Salad and Dressing just prior to serving.

MDA Favorite Recipes (Ohio)

Pineapple & Mango Salad

1 medium half-ripe fresh
  pineapple
2 half-ripe mangoes
3 tablespoons red wine vinegar

1 tablespoon Dijon rough
  mustard
1 tablespoon paprika
1 teaspoon sugar

Discard crown of pineapple. Cut off skin. With point of knife, remove eyes and discard. Cut pineapple in half and into quarters. Discard hard core. Cut pineapple into bite-size pieces. Transfer to glass salad bowl. Peel mangoes; slice and cut into bite-size pieces. Transfer to salad bowl. Discard seeds or if preferred add to bowl. Add vinegar, mustard, paprika, and sugar. With wooden spoon, toss and mix well. Chill and serve.

Easy Cooking with Herbs & Spices (Ohio)

Pear and Brie Salad

RASPBERRY PURÉE:
¼ cup raspberry vinegar
¾ cup sour cream

1 cup raspberries

Mix vinegar, sour cream, and raspberries in a blender or food processor. Process to blend. Strain through a fine mesh colander if you wish to remove seeds. Set aside.

SALAD:
1 head Bibb lettuce, washed,
  dried, chilled
1 small head romaine lettuce,
  washed, dried, chilled
4 pears

Juice of 1 lemon
¼–½ pound Brie, thinly
  sliced, bite-size
¼ cup raspberries, washed,
  drained

Arrange chilled greens on serving plates. Peel, quarter, core, and slice pears. Brush lightly with lemon juice. Arrange pears on greens in a decorative pattern. Top with 3–4 bite-size Brie pieces. Drizzle with Raspberry Purée and accent with whole berries to serve. Serves 4–6.

Back Home Again (Indiana)

Taffy Apple Salad

Use both red and green apples for a more colorful salad. Garnish the top with additional peanuts.

1 (16-ounce) can crushed
   pineapple
4 cups miniature marshmallows
1 tablespoon flour
½ cup sugar
1 egg, beaten

1½ tablespoons white vinegar
8 ounces whipped topping
2–3 cups coarsely chopped
   unpeeled apples
1 cup chopped Spanish peanuts

Drain pineapple, reserve the juice. Combine pineapple with marshmallows in a bowl; set aside.

   Combine reserved juice with flour, sugar, egg, and vinegar in a saucepan; mix well. Cook until slightly thickened, stirring constantly. Cool to room temperature. Fold in whipped topping, marshmallow mixture, apples, and peanuts. Chill several hours. Serves 6–8.

Generations (Illinois)

Apple Salad

DRESSING:
1 cup sugar
4 tablespoons flour
2 tablespoons butter

⅛ teaspoon salt
2 eggs, beaten
Juice from pineapple

In a saucepan, combine sugar, flour, butter, salt, eggs, and pineapple juice; cook until thick; cool.

SALAD:
4–6 apples, peeled, diced
Juice from 1 lemon
1 (15-ounce) can pineapple
   tidbits, reserve juice for
   Dressing

1 cup white or red grapes
1 cup chopped celery
1 cup mini marshmallows
1 cup Cool Whip
1 cup chopped nuts

In large bowl, combine fruits and marshmallows. Pour Dressing over mixture. When ready to serve, add Cool Whip and nuts.

Ohio State Grange Cookbook (Blue) (Ohio)

Apple Salad

Makes an appetizing and attractive salad.

DRESSING:

1 cup Miracle Whip Salad
  Dressing

2 tablespoons sugar
2 cups Cool Whip

SALAD:

3 large apples, chopped (leave
  skins on/preferably red
  apples)
1 cup chopped celery

1 cup finely grated carrots
1 cup chopped nuts
1 cup raisins

Mix Dressing ingredients together. Add to mixed Salad. Serve immediately or refrigerate.

Home Cooking II (Indiana)

Golden Raisin Coleslaw

VINAIGRETTE:

4 tablespoons golden raisins
3 tablespoons red wine vinegar
2 tablespoons olive oil
½ cup water

2 tablespoons finely chopped
  onion
1 teaspoon Dijon mustard
Salt and pepper to taste

In a small saucepan, combine the above ingredients and boil mixture, stirring, for 30 seconds. In a blender purée the Vinaigrette until smooth.

COLESLAW:

2 cups grated cabbage
1 carrot, coarsely grated

½ cup golden raisins

Combine cabbage, carrot, and raisins. Pour Vinaigrette over Coleslaw and toss. Serves 6.

Light Kitchen Choreography (Ohio)

Mild Tomato Aspic Salad

1 (3-ounce) package lemon
  Jell-O
¾ cup boiling water
1 cup tomato juice
1 teaspoon lemon juice
1 cup finely chopped celery

1 cup finely chopped green
  pepper
½ cup sliced stuffed olives
Mayonnaise and hard-cooked egg
  slices for garnish

Dissolve Jell-O in boiling water; add juices. Refrigerate until mixture begins to thicken, then add remaining ingredients. Pour into mold or pan. Chill until set. Garnish with egg slices and dabs of mayonnaise.

Variation: For luncheon salad, add 1½ cups cleaned, cooked small shrimp (or 2 [4½-ounce] cans).

The American Gothic Cookbook (Iowa)

Roasted Beet Salad

Roasting beets takes advantage of their naturally high sugar content and creates a rich, caramelized flavor that makes this salad special. Even people who think they don't like beets, love roasted beets.

4 large raw beets
2 tablespoons olive oil, divided
¾ teaspoon salt, divided
1 tablespoon balsamic vinegar
¼ cup chopped fresh basil

¼ cup chopped fresh parsley
⅛ teaspoon black pepper
2 ounces feta or goat cheese,
  crumbled

Preheat oven to 400°. Cut leaves off the top of beets. Scrub beets with vegetable brush. Place beets on a piece of aluminum foil; drizzle with 1 tablespoon olive oil and ½ teaspoon salt. Roll beets around to be sure beets have a light coating of oil and salt. Wrap with foil; bake in 400° oven for 30 minutes. Allow beets to cool, then remove skin.

Cut beets into ½- to 1-inch chunks. Place in large bowl. Add remaining 1 tablespoon oil, balsamic vinegar, basil, parsley, remaining ¼ teaspoon salt, and black pepper; mix. Add crumbled cheese; stir gently. Chill at least 30 minutes before serving. Makes 6 (¾-cup) servings.

More Nutritious Still Delicious (Ohio)

Sliced Zucchini Pickles

They make hamburgers taste better. Also try the dilled version.

1 quart vinegar
2 cups sugar
½ cup salt
2 teaspoons ground turmeric
1 teaspoon dry mustard

2 teaspoons celery seeds
4 quarts sliced, unpeeled
   zucchini
1 quart sliced onions

Bring vinegar, sugar, salt, and spices to a boil. Pour over zucchini and onions, and let stand one hour. Bring to a boil and cook 3 minutes. Pack in hot jars and adjust lids. Process in boiling water bath (212°) for 5 minutes. Remove jars and complete seals until closures are self-sealing type. Makes 6–7 pints.

Variation: Dilled Zucchini Pickles: Substitute 2 teaspoons dill seeds for turmeric.

500 Recipes Using Zucchini (Ohio)

Idiot Pickles

1 (32-ounce) jar Kosher dills
1¾ cups sugar

¼ cup vinegar
¼ cup water

Drain and rinse pickles. Cut pickles into ¾-inch pieces and put back in pickle jar. Heat sugar, vinegar, and water together until sugar melts, about 3½ minutes. Pour mixture over pickles and seal. Put in refrigerator. Ready in 3 days.

Cooking with Class (Ohio)

Abraham Lincoln began his political career in Springfield, Illinois, where he served in the House of Representatives. He was elected sixteenth president of the United States in 1860, and has been ranked by scholars as one of the greatest U.S. presidents. Lincoln's Tomb in Springfield is the final resting place of Lincoln, his wife, Mary Todd Lincoln, and three of their four sons.

Garlic Roasted Potatoes

4 large baking potatoes, peeled
4 cloves garlic
6 tablespoons butter

¾ cup Parmesan cheese
Salt and pepper to taste

Cut potatoes in half lengthwise; slice ¼-inch thick. Rinse in cold water; drain thoroughly on paper towels. Mince garlic or put through press. Melt butter in small saucepan; add garlic and cook on medium heat for 1 minute. Place potatoes in large bowl; add butter/garlic, half the cheese and seasonings. Stir until potatoes are well coated; pour into shallow pan. Top with remaining cheese; bake at 400°, uncovered, until golden brown, about 30 minutes. Do not stir or turn during baking. Yields 8 servings.

175th Anniversary Quilt Cookbook (Ohio)

Parmesan Potato Rounds

⅓ cup butter or margarine,
  melted
¼ cup all-purpose flour
¼ cup grated Parmesan cheese

Salt and pepper to taste
6 medium baking potatoes, each
  sliced into 4 rounds
Italian seasoning to taste

Pour butter into a 10x15-inch baking dish. In a plastic bag, combine flour, cheese, salt, and pepper. Shake a few potato slices at a time in the bag to coat with flour mixture. Place potatoes in a single layer over butter. Bake at 375° for 30 minutes. Turn slices and sprinkle with Italian seasoning. Bake 30 minutes more or until tender. Yields 6 servings.

Hopewell's Hoosier Harvest II (Indiana)

US MARINE CORPS

Held to raise money for family farmers in the United States, Farm Aid started as a benefit concert on September 22, 1985, in Champaign, Illinois. The concert was organized by musicians Willie Nelson, John Mellencamp, and Neil Young. Nelson and Mellencamp then brought family farmers before Congress to testify about the state of family farming in America. Congress subsequently passed the Agricultural Credit Act of 1987 to help save family farms from foreclosure. Today, Farm Aid is an organization that works to increase awareness of the importance of family farms.

Potato Latkes I

4 large potatoes
2 eggs, beaten
1 teaspoon salt
Dash of pepper

1 teaspoon grated onion
½ cup all-purpose flour (scant)
½ teaspoon baking powder
Vegetable oil for frying

Peel potatoes and grate on a fine grater. Pour off half the liquid that accumulates and add rest of ingredients; mix well. Drop batter by tablespoonfuls onto a well greased hot frying pan. Fry, browning both sides. Serve hot with applesauce, sugar, or sour cream. Serves 4.

C-U in the Kitchen (Illinois)

Farmhouse Potatoes 'n Ham

5–6 large russet potatoes,
    peeled, thinly sliced
¼ cup butter or margarine
3 tablespoons flour
1⅓ cups milk
2 teaspoons prepared mustard
⅓ cup minced sweet red onion

1⅓ cups shredded Cheddar
    cheese, divided
1½ cups diced, cooked ham
¼ teaspoon salt
⅛ teaspoon pepper
⅓ cup seasoned dry bread
    crumbs

Preheat oven to 350°. Arrange sliced potatoes in 2- to 3-quart oblong oven-safe casserole dish; set aside. Put butter in 4-cup glass measure or microwave-safe bowl. Microwave in HIGH about 45 seconds to melt. Blend in flour, milk, and mustard. Microwave on HIGH 3 minutes. Stir and add onion. Microwave on HIGH until sauce thickens. Add 1 cup cheese and stir until melted. Fold in ham, salt, and pepper. Pour sauce over potatoes. Sprinkle with remaining ⅓ cup cheese and top with bread crumbs. Bake 50–60 minutes, until potatoes are tender. Makes 6–8 servings.

The Des Moines Register Cookbook (Iowa)

Holiday Mashed Potatoes

1 (8-ounce) package cream
  cheese, cut in chunks
¼ cup margarine
12 medium potatoes, cooked,
  mashed

½ cup sour cream
½ cup milk
2 eggs, slightly beaten
1 teaspoon salt
¼ cup finely chopped onion

Add cream cheese and margarine to mashed potatoes. Combine sour cream and milk; add to potato mixture. Add beaten eggs, salt, and onion. Put in greased casserole dish. (May be prepared the day before serving and refrigerated in greased casserole dish.) Bake, uncovered, at 350° for 45 minutes.

A Cause for Applause (Illinois)

Whipped Mashed Potatoes

These are too light and creamy to be called mashed. There are small pieces of potato in each bite. No one will ever know you didn't have to peel potatoes. It seems like too many servings of potatoes, but they are so good you will want to have extra for second helpings.

2 (30-ounce) bags frozen fat-free
  shredded hash browns
2 (14.5-ounce) cans fat-free
  chicken broth

¼ cup imitation butter-flavored
  sprinkles
1 cup fat-free evaporated milk

In a large saucepan or Dutch oven, place hash browns and chicken broth. Cover and heat on high until it comes to a full boil. Remove pan from heat and let sit, covered, for 5 minutes. Drain potatoes and discard chicken broth. Place potatoes back into pan and stir in butter-flavored sprinkles and milk until well mixed.

In food processor, whip half of potato mixture at a time for 3–4 minutes and place into a large serving bowl. These may seem too runny, but they will thicken as they sit for a minute. Cover bowl with plastic wrap and wrap bowl in a large bath towel to keep warm until dinner is served. Yields 22 (½-cup) servings.

Busy People's Fun, Fast, Festive Christmas Cookbook (Ohio)

My Version of McDonald's Fries

2 large russet potatoes   **Salt to taste**
1 (48-ounce) can shortening

Peel potatoes, dry them, and slice using a mandoline or other slicer with a setting as close to ¼-inch square strips as you've got. If your fries are a little thicker than ¼ inch, the recipe will still work, but it won't be an exact clone, and you definitely don't want super thick steak fries here.

Rinse fries in a large bowl filled with around 8 cups cold water. The water should become milky. Dump water out and add another 8 cups cold water plus some ice and let fries sit for an hour. Spoon shortening into deep fryer and set it to 375°. On many fryers, this is the highest setting. Remove fries from water and spread them out to dry for 10–15 minutes. Don't let them sit much longer than this, or they will begin to turn brown. The oil should now be hot enough for blanching stage. Split up fries and add them in batches to oil for 1½ minutes at a time. Watch them carefully to be sure they don't begin to brown. If they start to brown on edges, take them out.

Remove fries to paper towels to drain and cool. When fries have cooled, put them into a resealable bag or covered container and freeze for 4–5 hours or until potatoes are completely frozen. As fries freeze, turn off fryer, but turn it back on and give it plenty of time to heat up before the final frying stage for your fries. Split up frozen fries and add one-half at a time to hot oil. Fry for 4½–6 minutes or until fries have become a golden brown color and are crispy on outside when cool. The second batch may take a tad longer than the first, since the oil may have cooled. Drain fries on paper towels and salt generously. Makes 4 servings.

Sharing the Best from Our Kitchen (Ohio)

The Midwest is headquarters for several hamburger chains. McDonald's is in Oak Brook, Illinois. Though founded in California, Ray Kroc turned it into a franchise beginning with a still-standing store in Des Plaines, Illinois. The Midwest is also home to Wendy's in Dublin, Ohio, White Castle in Columbus, Ohio, and Steak 'n Shake, which was founded in Normal, Illinois, and is now based in Indianapolis, Indiana.

Lemon Dill Potatoes

4 large baking potatoes
¼ cup margarine or butter, melted
⅓ cup sour cream
2 tablespoons fresh dill, finely snipped, or 1½ teaspoons dried dill weed

4 teaspoons lemon juice
⅛ teaspoon garlic salt
⅛ teaspoon pepper
Paprika (optional)

Scrub potatoes and prick with fork. Bake in a 425° oven for 40–60 minutes or until tender. Let stand 5 minutes. Cut potatoes in half lengthwise. Gently scoop out each potato half, leaving a thin shell. Place potato pulp in a large bowl. Add 3 tablespoons melted butter, sour cream, dill or dill weed, lemon juice, garlic salt, and pepper. With electric mixer on low speed, beat until smooth. Pile mixture into potato shells. Place in a 7x12-inch baking dish. Brush potatoes with remaining melted butter. Sprinkle with paprika, if desired. Bake in a 425° oven about 20 minutes , or until light brown. Makes 8 servings.

Stirring Up Memories (Iowa)

For 50 years, Winnebago Industries has been giving people reasons to travel farther, stay longer, and enjoy their vacations like never before. The company was founded in Forest City, which is located in Winnebago County, Iowa. Winnebago has become the leading manufacturer of motor homes and related products in the United States. The brand name has become synonymous with "motor home" and is commonly used as a generic term for such vehicles, whether they were produced by the company or not.

Baked Sweet Potatoes and Apricots

Anyone with a "sweet tooth" will love this dish!

6 fresh medium sweet potatoes,
   or 2 (20-ounce) cans sweet
   potatoes, drained
1 (17-ounce) can apricot halves
   in light syrup, cut into thirds
1½ tablespoons brown sugar

1 tablespoon cornstarch
¼ teaspoon salt
½ teaspoon cinnamon
⅓ cup golden raisins
¼ cup dry sherry
1 teaspoon grated orange peel

Cook fresh sweet potatoes in boiling water until tender, 30–35 minutes. Peel and halve potatoes lengthwise. Place in a 9x13-inch baking dish.

   Drain apricots, reserving syrup; add water to syrup, if necessary, to equal 1 cup liquid; set aside. Arrange apricots over potatoes.

   In saucepan, combine brown sugar, cornstarch, salt, and cinnamon. Stir in apricot syrup and raisins. Cook and stir over HIGH heat until mixture comes to a boil. Stir in sherry and orange peel. Pour mixture over potatoes and fruit. Bake, uncovered, in 350° oven, basting occasionally for 20 minutes or until well glazed. Serves 6.

Light Kitchen Choreography (Ohio)

Stuffed Sweet Potatoes

6 medium sweet potatoes
Vegetable oil
2 cups firmly packed brown
   sugar, divided
2 eggs

¼ cup milk
1 teaspoon vanilla
1 cup butter, divided
1 cup walnuts
⅓ cup all-purpose flour

Rub potatoes with oil. Bake at 400° for 1 hour. Let stand until cool enough to handle. Cut slice from top of each potato and carefully scoop out pulp, leaving shells intact. Mash pulp until smooth. Add 1 cup brown sugar, eggs, milk, vanilla, and ½ cup butter, mixing well. Spoon mixture into potato shells.

   Combine remaining 1 cup brown sugar, walnuts, flour, and remaining ½ cup butter, mixing to form crumbs. Sprinkle on stuffed potatoes and place in baking dish. Bake at 350° for 20 minutes. Serves 6.

I'll Cook When Pigs Fly (Ohio)

Oven-Roasted Vegetables

Quick and easy to prepare!

10 unpeeled new potatoes, cut
   into quarters
1 cup peeled baby carrots
1 small onion, cut into wedges
¼ cup olive oil
3 tablespoons lemon juice
3 cloves garlic, minced
1 tablespoon minced fresh
   rosemary or 1 teaspoon dried

1 teaspoon salt
½ teaspoon pepper
½ small eggplant, cut into
   ½-inch slices
1 medium red or green bell
   pepper, cut into ½-inch strips

Arrange new potatoes, carrots, and onion in a 9x13-inch baking dish. Drizzle with a mixture of olive oil, lemon juice, garlic, rosemary, salt, and pepper. Bake at 450° for 30 minutes, stirring occasionally. Stir in eggplant and bell pepper. Bake 15 minutes.

Generations (Illinois)

Garden Casserole

4 medium-size potatoes, peeled
2 onions, sliced
1 medium-size zucchini
4 or 5 tomatoes
3 carrots, pared

1 cup chicken broth
Salt and pepper
¼ cup butter, melted
1 cup small bread cubes
2 cups grated Cheddar cheese

Slice potatoes thin and spread over bottom of a medium-size, ungreased casserole dish. Place onions, in rings, over potatoes. Cut zucchini in half, remove seeds, and cut in small chunks. Spread over previous layer. Cut tomatoes in small chunks. Place over squash. Slice carrots thin and place throughout casserole. Pour chicken broth over entire casserole. Add salt and pepper to taste. Cover dish and bake at 375° for 1 hour or until vegetables are softened, but crisp. Mix bread cubes with melted butter until all are coated. Sprinkle grated cheese and bread cubes over entire casserole. Return to oven. Bake, uncovered, for 15 minutes longer. Serves 8.

Five Loaves and Two Fishes II (Illinois)

Neapolitan Vegetable Cheesecake

Far from being a dessert, this "cheesecake" is an excellent accompaniment to broiled meat or chicken. The name is derived from the texture, which resembles the dessert.

3 cups packed coarsely grated zucchini
1 teaspoon salt, divided
1 onion, chopped
1 tablespoon butter
3 cloves garlic, finely minced
1 cup coarsely grated carrots
3 tablespoons flour
½ teaspoon basil
½ teaspoon oregano
¼ cup packed chopped parsley
1½ tablespoons lemon juice

4 eggs
3 cups ricotta cheese
½ pound mozzarella cheese, grated
¾ cup grated Parmesan cheese, divided
Salt to taste
Freshly ground pepper to taste
⅓ cup fine bread crumbs
5–6 plum tomatoes, thinly sliced
Rolled anchovies (optional)

Sprinkle grated zucchini with ½ teaspoon salt. Place in sieve and let drain 15 minutes. Squeeze out all moisture.

In large skillet combine onion, butter, and remaining ½ teaspoon salt. Sauté 3–4 minutes. Add zucchini, garlic, carrots, flour, basil, and oregano. Stir over medium heat 5–6 minutes. Remove from heat. Add parsley and lemon juice.

In large bowl combine eggs, ricotta, mozzarella, and ⅔ cup Parmesan cheese. Beat well. Add vegetable mixture and blend thoroughly. Stir in salt and pepper.

Butter a 10-inch springform pan and sprinkle a few bread crumbs on bottom. Pour mixture into pan. Bake uncovered in preheated 375° oven 30 minutes. Remove from oven. Decorate with tomato slices; dredge in remaining bread crumbs and optional anchovies. Sprinkle with remaining Parmesan cheese.

Reduce oven temperature to 350° and bake additional 30 minutes. Turn oven off, open door, and leave "cake" inside 15 minutes. Remove from oven. Cool on rack 10 minutes before serving. Serves 8.

Noteworthy (Illinois)

Spiced Red Cabbage

From the Strawtown Inn, Pella, Iowa.

1 large head red cabbage, very
    finely sliced (about 5 cups)
1 cup chopped, unpeeled, crisp
    tart apples (such as Jonathan,
    Winesap, or McIntosh)
1 tablespoon whole allspice
½ teaspoon salt
¼ teaspoon grated nutmeg

¼ teaspoon ground cinnamon
¼ teaspoon freshly ground
    black pepper
¼ cup red wine vinegar
⅓ cup brown sugar
2 tablespoons butter, or more as
    desired

Place cabbage in large sauté pan and add enough water to cover. Bring to a boil; lower heat and simmer, covered, until cabbage is limp and soft, about 5 minutes. Drain off all but ½ cup water. Add apples; toss and continue cooking until apples are tender, about 15 minutes. Add spices, vinegar, and brown sugar and continue cooking until cabbage and apple mixture is tender and most of liquid is gone. Add butter and serve. Makes 6 servings.

The Des Moines Register Cookbook (Iowa)

Cabbage Lasagne

1 pound lean ground beef
1 cup chopped onion
½ cup chopped green bell
    pepper
1 medium cabbage
½ teaspoon oregano

1 teaspoon salt
⅛ teaspoon pepper
1 (18-ounce) can tomato paste
8 ounces mozzarella cheese,
    sliced

Sauté ground beef, onion, and bell pepper until meat is brown. Boil cabbage until tender. Save 2 cups liquid from cabbage and drain off excess. Combine 2 cups of the reserved cabbage liquid, oregano, salt, pepper, and tomato paste; simmer over low heat for 4 minutes. Add cooked meat mixture to tomato mixture. Pour ½ of this mixture into a 9x13-inch pan. Layer cabbage, then remaining tomato mixture. Top with slices of cheese to cover. Bake at 400° until cheese is browned, 30-40 minutes. Serves 8.

Taste & See (Indiana)

Creamed Spinach

Popeye would have gone nuts over this smooth and creamy spinach.

2 tablespoons cornstarch
1 tablespoon sugar
1 envelope Butter Buds, or 1
    tablespoon Butter Buds
    Sprinkles
1 (5-ounce) can evaporated
    skim milk

2 (10-ounce) packages frozen
    chopped spinach, excess water
    squeezed out
⅓ cup grated fat-free Parmesan
    cheese

In a large nonstick skillet, dissolve cornstarch, sugar, and Butter Buds in milk. Turn heat to medium. Add spinach; stir constantly and bring to a boil. Sprinkle with Parmesan cheese. Reduce heat to low; cover; let simmer 10 minutes. Yields 7 servings.

Busy People's Low-Fat Cookbook (Ohio)

Berghoff Creamed Spinach

3 slices bacon, diced
2 tablespoons butter
1½ tablespoons flour
1 cup half-and-half, scalded
1 large onion, diced, sautéed
    until soft, but not brown

1 pound cooked spinach, chopped
    fine
Salt, pepper, and nutmeg to taste

Sauté bacon in Dutch oven till crisp. Reduce heat to medium low and add butter. When melted, whisk in flour to make roux. Cook 2 minutes, stirring constantly. Mixture should be golden. Be sure not to overcook. Slowly add hot half-and-half, whisking constantly till sauce is smooth and thickened. Blend in remaining ingredients and heat through, adding salt, pepper, and nutmeg to taste.

Note: May use frozen spinach, just thaw.

Grand Detour Holiday Sampler (Illinois)

Skillet Sweet Corn

Cream corn right off the cob.

6 ears fresh corn
6 tablespoons butter
½ cup light cream

½ teaspoon salt
½ teaspoon granulated sugar
Ground pepper to taste

Husk corn and remove silks. Slice off kernels with a long sharp knife or electric knife. Using the back of a dinner knife, scrape the milky substance from the cob into the corn. Heat butter in a skillet, add corn and milky substance, and cook and stir 3–4 minutes or until desired tenderness. Add cream and seasonings. Stir over low heat 2–3 minutes. Makes 4 servings.

A Cook's Tour of Iowa (Iowa)

Easy Corn on the Cob

For cooking small batches of corn on the cob, no method is easier than microwaving; and it allows the corn to retain its flavor and crispness. Plan on 2–3 minutes for each ear of corn—less time if corn is very tender, a little more if it's not as fresh. As Iowans will tell you, it's important to get the corn from the field to the table as quickly as possible. Also, buy corn still in the husks, because the husks help retain flavor and freshness.

2 large ears of corn, husks and
silks removed

1 teaspoon water

Place corn in a microwave-safe dish. Add water and cover with wax paper or plastic film. Pierce paper several times and microwave in HIGH for 5–6 minutes. Let stand in microwave for 1 minute to complete cooking. Remove wax paper or plastic wrap carefully to prevent being scalded by the steam.

Variation: Many corn lovers believe that microwaving corn in the husks brings out more of the natural corn flavor. Just remove any outer husks that are wilted or soiled and follow the above instructions. The silks will pull away easily after cooking. Serves 2.

New Tastes of Iowa (Iowa)

Corn & Tomato Casserole

3 strips bacon
½ medium onion, finely
   chopped
¼ cup finely diced green bell
   pepper
3 large ears sweet corn or 1
   (16-ounce) package frozen sweet
   corn

2 tablespoons brown sugar
½ teaspoon salt
Dash of pepper
1 teaspoon dried sweet basil
2–2½ cups canned tomatoes,
   drained, chopped

TOPPING:

¾ cup herb-flavored stuffing
   mix or ¾ cup crushed
   tortilla chips

2 cups shredded Cheddar
   cheese

In large skillet, fry bacon until crisp. Save drippings in skillet. Crumble bacon into greased 1½-quart casserole dish. Set aside. Sauté onion and green pepper in bacon drippings until tender.

   Cut corn off cobs; add to onion mixture along with brown sugar, salt, pepper, basil, and tomatoes. Cook 10–15 minutes. Pour over bacon in casserole. Top with stuffing mix or crushed tortilla chips and cheese. Bake at 350° for 25–30 minutes. Makes 6 servings.

Cookin' with Friends (Illinois)

Cream Cheese and Corn

¼ cup milk
1 (3-ounce) package cream
   cheese
1 tablespoon butter

½ teaspoon salt
⅛ teaspoon pepper
3 cups frozen corn, cooked,
   drained

Combine milk, cream cheese, butter, salt, and pepper in saucepan. Cook over low heat, stirring constantly until cheese melts and is blended. Add drained corn and warm.

Note: 2 (12-ounce) cans whole-kernel corn may be used in place of frozen corn.

Home Cooking II (Indiana)

Onion Patties

Tastes just like onion rings!

¾ cup all-purpose flour
1 tablespoon sugar
1 tablespoon cornmeal
2 teaspoons baking powder

2 teaspoons salt
¾ cup milk
2½ cups finely chopped onions

Mix dry ingredients together; then add milk. Batter should be fairly thick. Add onions; mix thoroughly. Drop by tablespoonfuls into ½ inch hot oil in skillet. Flatten slightly when you turn them. Brown on both sides until crisp. Drain on paper towels.

The Amish Way Cookbook (Ohio)

Broccoli Soufflé Restaurateur

Very elegant.

¼ cup butter
¼ cup all-purpose flour
½ cup whipping cream,
  scalded
½ cup rich chicken broth
3 egg yolks
1 teaspoon grated onion

1 teaspoon chopped parsley
1 teaspoon Worcestershire
1 teaspoon finely chopped chives
Salt, pepper, nutmeg
1½ cups cooked broccoli
⅓ cup grated Cheddar cheese
4 egg whites, stiffly beaten

Melt butter; stir in flour. Gradually stir in scalded cream mixed with chicken broth. Cook, stirring constantly, until mixture thickens. Remove from heat. Beat egg yolks with onion, parsley, Worcestershire, and chives. Add salt, pepper, and nutmeg to taste. Stir a little hot mixture into egg yolks; combine with remainder. Add broccoli and cheese. Fold in egg whites. turn into 2-quart buttered soufflé dish. Bake at 400° for 25 minutes. Makes 6 servings.

SoupÇon II (Illinois)

Fried Cauliflower with Cheese Sauce

1 large head cauliflower
1 (12-ounce) can beer, at room temperature

1¼ cups all-purpose flour
Vegetable oil for deep frying

Wash cauliflower; cut into small flowerets. Cook, covered, in a small amount of water in saucepan 8–10 minutes or until tender-crisp; drain.

Combine beer and 1¼ cups flour in bowl; mix well. Dip cauliflower in batter. Deep-fry in 375° oil until golden brown; drain. Serve Cheese Sauce with cauliflower. Yields 6 servings.

CHEESE SAUCE:
2 tablespoons butter
2 tablespoons flour
1 cup milk

1½ cups shredded Cheddar cheese

Melt butter in heavy skillet. Add flour, stirring until smooth. Cook 1 minute, stirring constantly. Add milk gradually. Cook over medium heat until thickened, stirring constantly. Remove from heat. Add cheese, stirring until melted.

Pioneer Pantry (Illinois)

Mushrooms Florentine

1 clove garlic, chopped
½ cup margarine, divided
1 pound sliced mushrooms
3 packages frozen chopped spinach, thawed, drained

1 large onion, chopped
Salt to taste
Pepper to taste
1 cup shredded Cheddar cheese

Sauté garlic in ¼ cup margarine; remove garlic and sauté mushrooms. Combine spinach, onion, and remaining margarine. Salt and pepper to taste. Place in a shallow baking dish. Sprinkle with half the cheese. Cover with mushrooms and then sprinkle with remaining cheese. Bake at 350° for 30 minutes. Serves 6–8.

A Taste of the World (Iowa)

Baked Sweet Sauerkraut with Tomatoes and Bacon

The Ohio Sauerkraut Festival is held in Waynesville, population 2,000, the second week of October, and attracts thousands of people. Remember, this state was settled by Germans; they flock to sample food and buy crafts at the festival's five hundred booths. It is sort of like a krauty Mardi Gras.

This old, old recipe is a real treasure. The few ingredients—all listed in the title—would have been in any Ohio kitchen at the turn of the century. The dish is baked quite a long time, until the top caramelizes, the liquid cooks away, and the kraut is nearly transparent.

1 (14½-ounce) tomatoes, coarsely chopped, undrained
1 (16-ounce) can sauerkraut, undrained
1 cup sugar
6 slices raw bacon, cut in ½-inch pieces
½ teaspoon freshly ground pepper

Preheat oven to 325°. Grease a flat (see Note) 2-quart glass baking dish. Place all ingredients in the dish and combine thoroughly. (You may have to use your hands to distribute bacon evenly.) Bake, uncovered, for 2 hours and 15 minutes, or until top begins to brown deeply and most of the liquid has cooked away.

Note: It is important to use a flat dish so the liquid evaporates as it cooks.

Heartland (Ohio)

Sauerkraut and Sausage

1 (27-ounce) can sauerkraut, rinsed
1 medium apple, peeled, chopped
1 small onion, chopped or use minced onion
1 tablespoon caraway seeds
2 tablespoons brown sugar or more according to taste
Several shakes coarsely ground pepper
½ package smoked sausage cut in small chunks

Cook over low to medium heat on top of stove, or bake at 350° for an hour.

Recipes from "The Little Switzerland of Ohio" (Ohio)

White Bean Bake

What can represent southern Illinois better than white beans?

8 cups seasoned cooked navy
  beans
1 cup golden raisins
2 cups chopped onions
1 cup sour cream
1 cup light brown sugar, packed
2 (3-ounce) packages cream
  cheese, softened

2 (4-ounce) cans chopped mild
  green chiles
8 cooked sausage patties,
  crumbled (1 pound)
2 cups grated provolone cheese
4 green onions, chopped fine (use
  some green tops)
½ cup seasoned bread crumbs

Place navy beans, raisins, and onions in large bowl. Combine sour cream, brown sugar, and cream cheese, and blend well. Add to beans. Add chiles, sausage, and mustard, and mix well. Pour into 10x15-inch baking pan. Bake at 350° about 45 minutes, until bubbly. Remove pan from oven and top with provolone cheese, green onions, and bread crumbs. Return to oven and bake 5 minutes more to melt cheese. Serve at once.

More to Love . . . from The Mansion of Golconda (Illinois)

Baked Beans with Garlic

1 (29-ounce) can Bush's
  Homestyle Baked Beans
2 (15-ounce) cans pork and
  beans
1 medium onion, chopped

½ heaping teaspoon minced
  garlic
½ cup ketchup
½ cup brown sugar

Use a 3-quart crockpot. Open beans and drain as much liquid off as possible. Put beans, onion, garlic, ketchup, and brown sugar in crockpot and cook on high for about 3 hours. Turn down to low for an additional hour. Caution: keep an eye on the liquid; don't let it go dry. Add a little water only if they look dry. Yields 15–20 servings.

Favorite Recipes–First Church of God (Ohio)

Amish-Style Baked Beans

1 (16-ounce) can kidney beans
1 (16-ounce) can butter beans
1 (16-ounce) can pork and beans
4 slices bacon

2 small onions, chopped
1 cup brown sugar
1 cup ketchup
1 teaspoon prepared mustard

Drain beans and mix together. Fry, but don't brown bacon. Add bacon and remaining ingredients to beans. Bake 1 hour at 350°.

Taste & See (Indiana)

Barbecued Green Beans

A real crowd pleaser.

6 slices bacon, diced
1 onion, chopped
4 (1-pound) cans cut green
  beans, drained (fresh do not
  work well)

1 cup firmly packed brown
  sugar
1 cup ketchup

Preheat oven to 250°. Cook bacon and onion together in medium-size skillet over medium heat until bacon is crisp. Remove with slotted spoon and place in ungreased 2-quart baking dish. Add green beans.

Mix brown sugar and ketchup in medium-size bowl. Fold into green beans. Bake, covered, at 250° for 3 hours. Serves 6–8.

Winners (Indiana)

Gilbert Van Camp, Sr. is thought to be the originator of canned food as we know it today. In 1861, Van Camp, who once was a tin-smith, and thus familiar with the technology of making tin cans, came up with the idea of putting vegetables and fruit in tin cans, so they could be preserved for later use. At that time, Van Camp and his wife Hester, ran a grocery store in Indianapolis, Indiana, where they sold the canned goods. He opened up a canning company and by 1909, Van Camp's Pork and Beans became an American staple. Over the years, a number of canned goods have been sold under the Van Camp's name, but now it only sells canned cooked beans.

Green Beans Italiano

I got this idea from Kenny Roger's Restaurant. I'm not sure what he has in his recipe, but this is a pretty close match and just as good. And I can almost bet that mine is a lot less fattening. These beans are popular primarily with adults.

2 medium onions, thinly sliced
  (about 1½ cups)
¾ cup fat-free Italian dressing
1 (14½-ounce) can diced
  tomatoes, drained

2 (16-ounce) bags frozen green
  beans
½ tablespoon lite salt (optional)

In a large nonstick skillet, approximately 12 inches in diameter, sauté onions in salad dressing over medium heat until tender, about 2–3 minutes. Add tomatoes and green beans. Increase heat to medium high. Stir until well coated. Salt, if desired. Cover and cook 5–7 minutes until beans are tender. Serve hot. Yields 12 (⅔-cup) servings.

Busy People's Low-Fat Cookbook (Ohio)

Green Beans with
Hot Bacon Dressing

1 (10-ounce) package frozen
  green beans
¼ cup mayonnaise
1 tablespoon sugar
¼ cup chopped onion

1 tablespoon butter, melted
2 tablespoons vinegar
6 slices bacon, fried crisp,
  crumbled

Cook beans according to package directions. Drain and set aside. Combine mayonnaise, sugar, onion, cutter, and vinegar in a small bowl. Microcook for 30 seconds, or combine these ingredients in a small saucepan and heat. Pour over hot cooked beans. Top with crumbled bacon and serve immediately. Serves 4.

Nutbread and Nostalgia (Indiana)

Sue's Carrot Casserole

1 pound carrots	½ teaspoon salt
¼ cup carrot liquid	½ teaspoon pepper
2 tablespoons grated onion	½ cup seasoned bread crumbs
¾ tablespoon horseradish	¼ cup butter, melted
½ cup mayonnaise	

Scrape carrots and cut on the diagonal, making slices about ¼-inch thick. Cook in salted water until tender-crisp. Drain, reserving ¼ cup cooking liquid. Mix onion, horseradish, mayonnaise, salt, pepper, and carrot liquid. Combine with carrots in a buttered casserole. Mix bread crumbs with melted butter and spread over carrots. Bake at 375° for 15–20 minutes, or until bubbling. Serves 6.

A Taste of Fishers (Indiana)

Tally Ho Tomato Pudding

Toledo claims this sweet pudding to be its very own and traces it to the Tally Ho Restaurant. It is customary for Toledo hosts to prepare it for out-of-town dinner guests, and the tradition continues at the Columbian House, an 1827 stagecoach inn, in Waterville, Ohio. The buttered bread cubes bake through the pudding and turn a golden brown when it is completed. Then it must be served quickly before it falls.

1 cup brown sugar	2 cups dry bread cubes, crusts
1 cup tomato purée	removed
¼ cup water	½ cup butter, melted

Combine brown sugar, tomato purée, and water. Cook 5 minutes. While tomato mixture is cooking, put bread cubes in casserole and pour melted butter over. Pour on hot tomato mixture. Do not stir. Bake 50 minutes in a 325° oven. The drier the bread cubes, the more crusty the pudding will be.

Aren't You Going to Taste It, Honey? (Ohio)

Pasta, Rice, Etc.

The only natural population of the Lakeside Daisy in the United States grows on the Marblehead Peninsula in Ottawa County, Ohio. In 1988, the Lakeside Daisy was listed as a federally threatened species. In early to mid-May, its bright yellow flowers adorn the otherwise bleak landscape of the Marblehead quarry.

Stuffed Manicotti

1 pound mild bulk pork sausage
1 (6-ounce) can tomato paste
2 (15-ounce) cans Italian tomato
   sauce
¼ cup water
½–¾ tablespoon light brown
   sugar
1 (15-ounce) carton ricotta
   cheese
3 cups shredded mozzarella
   cheese, divided
1 egg
1 teaspoon parsley flakes
8 manicotti noodles, cooked,
   rinsed, drained
Grated Parmesan cheese
   (optional)

In large saucepan, brown sausage; drain. Remove half and set aside. Stir tomato paste, sauce, water, and brown sugar into sausage; simmer 15 minutes. Meanwhile, in medium bowl, combine remaining sausage, ricotta, 2 cups mozzarella cheese, egg, and parsley. In a 9x13-inch pan, pour ⅓ of sauce mixture. Stuff noodles with cheese and sausage mixture, and place on top of sauce. Pour rest of sauce over noodles. Sprinkle remaining cup of mozzarella cheese and Parmesan on top. Bake uncovered at 350° for 20 minutes.

Oeder Family & Friends Cookbook (Ohio)

Chicken Lasagna

1 (10¾-ounce) can cream of
   mushroom soup
1 (10¾-ounce) can cream of
   chicken soup
1 cup grated Parmesan cheese
1 cup sour cream
1 small onion, chopped
¼–½ teaspoon garlic powder
Pepper to taste
2–3 cups cooked, diced chicken
8 ounces lasagna noodles, cooked,
   drained
2 cups shredded Cheddar cheese

Mix together soups, Parmesan cheese, sour cream, onion, garlic powder, pepper, and chicken. Spread ¼ of the mixture in the bottom of a 9x13-inch pan. Alternate layers of noodles, chicken mixture, and shredded cheese 3 times, ending with cheese. Bake at 350° for 40–45 minutes or until heated through. Let stand 10 minutes before cutting.

Hopewell's Hoosier Harvest II (Indiana)

Rookwood Pottery Pasta Alla Roma

4 ounces spinach noodles, cooked
1½ ounces mushrooms, diced
2 ounces diced tomatoes
2 ounces cauliflower florets
2 ounces broccoli florets

3 ounces diced ham
¾ teaspoon minced garlic
Butter for sautéing
4 ounces tomato sauce
1 ounce heavy cream
Parmesan cheese for topping

In large skillet, sauté noodles, mushrooms, tomatoes, cauliflower, broccoli, ham, and garlic in butter. Blend in tomato sauce and cream. Place on oven-proof serving dish, top with Parmesan cheese, and run under broiler to brown. Makes 1 serving. Recipe from Rookwood Pottery, Cincinnati, Ohio.

Dining in Historic Ohio (Ohio)

Seafood Fettuccine

This is a pure, unadulterated pasta dish–just like you might have in a fine Italian restaurant.

About 1 pound fettuccine noodles
2 tablespoons butter
1 small onion, chopped fine
2 or 3 gloves garlic, chopped fine

1 pound fresh seafood (shrimp, scallops, crab, etc.; use one or a combination)
2 cups whipped cream
½ cup grated Romano cheese
½ cup grated Parmesan cheese

Cook fettuccine to al dente stage (just done—not overcooked) in boiling salted water. Rinse well; set aside. In a heavy large sauté pan, melt butter. Sauté onion and garlic until onion is transparent. (Do not brown.) Stir all the time. Add seafood and sauté. Add whipping cream and stir until cream is warm. Add grated cheeses and heat over low heat until cheese melts and sauce thickens. You can increase heat a little, but you must stir all the time. Add cooked fettuccine and lift and toss until noodles are coated with sauce. Serve to 4 or 5 lucky people.

It's About Thyme (Indiana)

Pasta Scampi

4 tablespoons olive oil
4 cloves garlic, minced
2 pounds shrimp, peeled, deveined
1 each medium red and green bell peppers, cut into strips
1 cup dry white wine
4 tablespoons lemon juice
1 teaspoon dried basil or oregano
4 tablespoons chopped fresh parsley
6 ounces spaghetti
6 quarts boiling water
1 tablespoon cornstarch
¼ cup water
Grated Parmesan cheese

Heat oil in a nonstick frying pan. Add garlic, shrimp, and pepper strips; sauté stirring frequently, until shrimp are pink. Add liquids and spices and cook several minutes longer.

Meanwhile, prepared spaghetti in boiling water and drain when tender. Mix cornstarch with ¼ cup water and add to shrimp mixture stirring until mixture thickens. Serve spaghetti topped with shrimp mixture. Sprinkle with grated Parmesan cheese.

Note: Scallops may be used in place of shrimp, if preferred.

Tried and True by Mothers of 2's (Ohio)

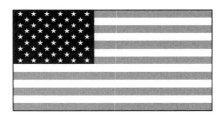

In 1958, seventeen-year-old high school student Robert Heft from Lancaster High School, Ohio, designed a fifty-star flag to represent the new states of Hawaii and Alaska. It was accepted by Congress as the new U.S. flag. He originally received a "B-" for the project, but after discussing the grade with his high school teacher, Stanley Pratt, it was agreed that since the flag was accepted by Congress, his grade should be changed to an "A."

Italian Shrimp and Pasta Toss

1 cup sliced fresh mushrooms
½ cup chopped onion
2 cloves garlic, minced
1 teaspoon chopped basil leaves
2 tablespoons olive oil
½ cup water
2 tablespoons lemon juice
2 teaspoons chicken bouillon

1 pound medium raw shrimp, peeled, deveined
1 cup chopped green bell pepper
1 large tomato, seeded, chopped
8 ounces angel hair pasta, cooked
2 tablespoons grated Parmesan cheese

In large skillet, cook mushrooms, onion, garlic, and basil in oil until tender. Add water, lemon, and bouillon; bring to a boil. Reduce heat; add shrimp and pepper. Simmer, uncovered, 5–8 minutes or until shrimp are pink. Stir in tomato. In large bowl, toss shrimp mixture with hot, drained noodles and cheese. Serve with additional cheese, if desired.

Cook, Line & Sinker (Ohio)

Greek-Style Shrimp with Pasta

1 teaspoon finely chopped garlic
5 tablespoons olive oil, divided
2 cups cubed peeled tomatoes
½ cup dry white wine
Salt and black pepper to taste
¾ cup finely chopped fresh basil
1 teaspoon dried crumbled oregano

1½ pounds medium shrimp, peeled, deveined
⅛ teaspoon hot red pepper flakes
8 ounces crumbled feta cheese
6 ounces rigatoni, cooked, drained

Sauté garlic in 2 tablespoons olive oil in a skillet. Add tomatoes. Cook 1 minute. Add wine, salt, pepper, basil, and oregano. Cook over medium heat 10 minutes. Season shrimp with salt and pepper. Heat remaining 3 tablespoons olive oil in large skillet. Add shrimp. Sauté 1 minute or until shrimp turn pink. Sprinkle with red pepper flakes. Spoon into a small, greased baking dish. Sprinkle with feta cheese. Spoon tomato sauce over top. Bake at 400° for 10 minutes or until bubbly. Spoon over hot pasta on a serving platter. Yields 4 servings.

America Celebrates Columbus (Ohio)

Johnny Marzetti

Whether it's spelled Moussetti, Marziette, Mouzetti, Mousette, or Mousset, this dish is a basic guide for whipping up a quick casserole dinner from items you have on hand. Who is the infamous Johnny? No one seems to know, but he certainly got around.

2 cups chopped green bell
  peppers
1 cup chopped celery
2 cups chopped onions
1 pound ground beef
1 pound ground pork
¼ cup butter or margarine
2 teaspoons salt
½ cup chopped stuffed olives

1 (4-ounce) can sliced
  mushrooms, with liquid
1 (10½-ounce) can tomato soup
1 (8-ounce) can tomato sauce
1 (8-ounce) can tomato-
  mushroom sauce
1 pound broad noodles
2 cups grated American cheese

In a large skillet, sauté green peppers, celery, onions, and meats in hot butter. Add salt, reduce heat, and cook about 5 minutes. Stir in olives, mushrooms, and liquid, soup, and sauces. Cook another 5 minutes. Cook noodles according to package directions, undercooking them slightly. Drain. Turn noodles into a greased 10x14-inch roasting pan. Add meat mixture. Stir gently until well mixed. Sprinkle cheese on top. Bake 35 minutes at 350°. Yields 8 servings.

Cincinnati Recipe Treasury (Ohio)

Spaghetti Pie

6 ounces spaghetti
2 tablespoons margarine
⅓ cup grated Parmesan cheese
2 eggs, well beaten
1 cup cottage cheese
1 pound ground beef or bulk
  pork sausage
½ cup chopped onion
¼ cup chopped green bell
  pepper

1 (8-ounce) can tomatoes, cut up
6 ounces tomato paste
1 teaspoon sugar
1 teaspoon crushed dried
  oregano
½ teaspoon garlic salt
½ cup shredded mozzarella
  cheese

Cook spaghetti according to directions and drain. (Should have about 3 cups cooked spaghetti.) Stir in margarine until melted. Stir in Parmesan cheese and eggs. Form spaghetti mixture into a "crust" in a buttered 10-inch pie plate. Spread cottage cheese over bottom of spaghetti crust.

In a skillet, cook meat, onion, and green pepper until cooked. Drain off fat. Stir in undrained tomatoes, tomato paste, sugar, oregano, and garlic salt. Heat through. Add meat mixture over cottage cheese in "crust." Bake uncovered at 350° for 20 minutes. Add mozzarella cheese on top and bake 5 minutes longer. Serves 6.

Amish Country Cookbook III (Indiana)

Raggedy Ann, a rag doll with red yarn for hair, was created by writer Johnny Gruelle of Arcola, Illinois. The character was created in 1915 as a doll, and was introduced to the public in the 1918 book *Raggedy Ann Stories*. A sequel, *Raggedy Andy Stories* (1920) introduced the character of her brother, Raggedy Andy. Raggedy Ann was inducted into the National Toy Hall of Fame in 2002. Raggedy Andy joined her in 2007. Gruelle also provided color illustrations for a 1914 edition of *Grimm's Fairy Tales*.

Vegetable Pasta Pie

2⅔ cups cooked spaghetti
  (small box)
1½ ounces grated Parmesan
  cheese

1 tablespoon plus 1 teaspoon
  margarine
1 teaspoon parsley

Combine ingredients in a medium bowl; mix well. Press spaghetti mixture into bottom and up the sides of a 9-inch pie pan to form a crust; set aside.

FILLING:
1 cup chopped zucchini
½ cup chopped green pepper
⅓ cup chopped onion
½ cup sliced mushrooms
2 tablespoons water
1 clove garlic, minced

1 cup tomato sauce
½ teaspoon oregano
½ teaspoon marjoram
½ cup tomato paste
¼ teaspoon salt
½ teaspoon basil

In a large nonstick skillet combine vegetables, water, and garlic; cook over medium heat, stirring often, about 10 minutes or until vegetables are tender-crisp. Stir in remaining ingredients and simmer 5 minutes. Place over spaghetti pie crust.

TOPPING:
2½ ounces grated Cheddar
  cheese

1⅓ cups cottage cheese

Combine Cheddar and cottage cheeses and top vegetable mixture. Bake at 350° for 30 minutes or until heated throughout and cheese is melted.

Enjoy (Iowa)

Betty's Tomato, Basil and Brie Sauce

6–8 tomatoes, peeled, cubed
  in small pieces
½ pound Brie, cubed in small
  pieces
¼ cup olive oil

1 cup chopped fresh basil
3–4 cloves garlic, minced
½ teaspoon oregano
Salt and pepper to taste
1 tablespoon red wine vinegar

Put all ingredients in a large bowl and let stand in a warm place (outside on a warm day) for several hours. Serve over cooked pasta.

Jubilee (Illinois)

Roasted Red Pepper Sauce with Pine Nuts

8 large sweet red peppers
½ cup olive oil
4 cloves garlic, sliced thin
¾ pound thin spaghetti
1½ tablespoons coarse salt for
   pasta water
½ cup chopped fresh basil, or 2
   teaspoons dried

3 tablespoons pine nuts, roasted
   10 minutes at 350°
Freshly ground black pepper
Freshly grated
   Parmigiana-Reggiano cheese

Roast peppers for about an hour at 400°. Turn a few times. When skins are blistered and blackened, remove from oven and place in a paper bag for 20 minutes. Take out, peel, core, and discard seeds. Cut into strips, saving juices that run off.

Put oil and garlic in a large fry pan. Sauté garlic until just before golden. In a separate pot, heat 5 quarts water for pasta. Add pepper pieces to fry pan and cook for an additional few minutes. Cook pasta until al dente, and toss with sauce in fry pan. Add basil and pine nuts, and grind some black pepper over all. Serve with grated cheese. Serves 4–6.

Viva Italia (Ohio)

Freezer Tomato Sauce

Delicious on spaghetti!

20 large tomatoes
4 large onions
4 large carrots
1 mango
1 (6-ounce) can tomato paste
   (optional)

4 tablespoons sugar
2 tablespoons salt
¾ teaspoon pepper
4 tablespoons oregano

Peel and cut up tomatoes. Peel and cut up onions. Wash and cut up carrots. Chop mango. Put in large kettle. Add sugar, salt, pepper, and oregano. Cook until vegetables are tender and thick (about 1 hour). Stir often. Blend slightly in blender. Blending too long will cause air bubbles. Put into containers and freeze.

Recipes & Remembrances (Ohio)

Ham Casserole

1 (12-ounce) package noodles
1 cup whole-kernel corn,
  drained
½ cup chopped green pepper
⅓ cup milk

1 cup chopped cooked ham
¾ cup diced cheese
1 (10¾-ounce) can cream of
  mushroom soup

Cook noodles according to package directions. Combine well with remaining ingredients. Turn into greased baking dish. Bake at 375° for 45 minutes.

Celebrating Iowa (Iowa)

Polish Reuben Casserole

2 (10¾-ounce) cans cream of
  mushroom soup
1⅓ cups milk
½ cup chopped onion
1 tablespoon prepared mustard
2 (16-ounce) cans sauerkraut,
  rinsed, drained
1 (8-ounce) package uncooked
  medium-wide noodles

1½ pounds Polish sausage, cut
  in ½-inch pieces
2 cups shredded Swiss cheese
¾ cup whole-wheat bread
  crumbs
2 tablespoons butter, melted

Combine soup, milk, onion, and mustard. Blend well. Spread sauerkraut in greased 9x13-inch pan. Top with uncooked noodles. Spoon soup mixture evenly over top. Top with sausage; then cheese. Combine crumbs and butter in bowl. Sprinkle over top. Cover pan tightly with foil. Bake at 350° for 1 hour or until noodles are tender.

Favorite Recipes (Ohio)

Cowboy Goulash

The whole family loves this one.

1 (family-size) package macaroni
  and cheese dinner
1 pound hamburger meat
½ cup chopped green pepper
¼ cup chopped onion
1 (15-ounce) can whole corn,
  drained

1 (6-ounce) can tomato paste
½ cup water
1 teaspoon salt
Dash of pepper

Prepare macaroni and cheese as directed. Brown meat, green pepper, and onion. Stir in corn, tomato paste, water, salt, and pepper. Add macaroni and cheese and mix well. Simmer 5 minutes. Serves 4–5.

125 Years—Walking in Faith (Iowa)

Harvest Rice

This is a great addition to a Thanksgiving dinner, but great served any-time with roast chicken, turkey, or pork.

2 cups chicken broth
½ cup brown rice
½ cup wild rice
2 tablespoons butter
3 medium onions, sliced into
  small wedges (or green
  onions for additional color,
  if desired)

1 tablespoon brown sugar
1 cup dried cranberries
⅔ cup sliced mushrooms
½ cup toasted almond slivers
½ teaspoon finely grated orange
  zest
Salt and pepper to taste

Combine broth and rice in saucepan and bring to a boil. Reduce heat to low; cover and simmer 35–45 minutes until rice is tender and broth is absorbed.

In medium skillet, melt butter over medium heat. Add onions and brown sugar. Sauté until butter is absorbed and onions are translucent and soft. Lower heat and continue to cook onions until they caramelize. Stir in cranberries and mushrooms. Cover skillet and cook 10 minutes, or until berries start to swell. Stir in nuts and orange zest, then fold this mixture into cooked rice. Salt and pepper to taste, and serve.

The "Friends" Cookbook (Ohio)

Chicken Spectacular

3 cups cooked chicken (1 whole chicken)
1 box wild rice, prepared
1 small onion, chopped
1 (8-ounce) can water chestnuts, drained, chopped

1 (16-ounce) can French-style green beans, drained
1 cup mayonnaise
1 (10¾-ounce) can cream of celery soup

Combine chicken and cooked rice. Add onion, chestnuts, and green beans. Add mayonnaise and soup; mix well. Bake 30–40 minutes at 350°, or until browned and bubbly.

Country Cooking (Indiana)

Chicken with Spanish Rice

1 tablespoon plus 1 teaspoon oil
2 pounds skinless, boneless chicken breasts
1 teaspoon paprika
8 ounces uncooked rice
½ cup sliced scallions
1½ cups chicken broth

1 cup canned whole tomatoes with liquid
2 tablespoons chopped parsley
⅛ teaspoon ground black pepper
1½ cups green beans, halved

In a large skillet, heat oil. Cut chicken in squares. Season with paprika on both sides. Cook until golden brown on both sides, 7–8 minutes. Remove chicken and put in covered dish to keep warm. Add rice and scallions to skillet. Cook; stir frequently until rice is golden, 2–3 minutes. Stir in broth, tomatoes with liquid, parsley, and pepper. Crush tomatoes with spoon. Bring to a boil. Return chicken and any liquid in bowl. Cover; cook over low heat 15 minutes. Add green beans and cover; cook an additional 15 minutes.

The PTA Pantry (Ohio)

Tea Room Chicken

1 (6-ounce) package wild rice
  mix, cooked
1 (16-ounce) package frozen
  chopped broccoli
3 cups cooked, diced chicken
1 cup shredded Velveeta cheese
1 cup sliced fresh mushrooms
½ cup mayonnaise

1 (10¾-ounce) can cream of
  mushroom soup
¼ teaspoon dry mustard
¼ teaspoon curry powder
Parmesan cheese
½ cup cracker crumbs
1 tablespoon butter

In a 9x13-inch pan, layer rice, broccoli, chicken, cheese, and mushrooms. In a separate bowl, combine mayonnaise, soup, mustard, and curry powder. Pour over chicken mixture. Sprinkle with Parmesan cheese. Sauté crackers with butter and sprinkle over cheese. Bake at 350° for 30–45 minutes, or until bubbly.

Madison County Cookbook (Iowa)

Skillet Chicken Risotta

1 (3-pound) chicken, cut up
2 tablespoons oil
½ cup rice
½ cup chopped onion
2 teaspoons salt or to taste

½ teaspoon poultry seasoning
1 (4-ounce) can mushroom pieces
3 carrots, peeled, sliced on bias
1 cup chopped tomatoes
1½ cups water

Brown chicken in oil. Remove chicken pieces from skillet. Drain all but 2 tablespoons fat from skillet. To skillet add rice, onion, salt, and poultry seasoning. Cook and stir until rice is lightly browned. Add mushrooms, carrots, tomatoes, and water. Place chicken atop rice mixture. Cover and simmer 45 minutes or until chicken and rice are done.

Herrin's Favorite Italian Recipes Cookbook (Illinois)

Cheesy Turkey Bake

3 cups diced cooked turkey
2 cups cooked rice
1 medium onion, chopped
½ cup chopped celery
1 (10¾-ounce) can cream of
　mushroom soup
1 cup mayonnaise
1 (15-ounce) can mixed
　vegetables, drained

4 tablespoons lemon juice
2 teaspoons salt
1 cup grated smokey Cheddar
　cheese
2 (9-inch) deep-dish pie shells
4 tablespoons butter, melted
2 cups crushed cornflakes

In large bowl, mix all ingredients except pie shells, cornflakes, and butter. Refrigerate overnight or several hours.

Precook pie shells 10 minutes at 400°. Fill pie shells with turkey mixture and bake 40 minutes at 350°. Melt butter and sauté cornflakes. Sprinkle this topping over pies and bake 5 more minutes. Each pie serves 6.

Dawn to Dusk (Ohio)

Shrimp-Rice Marguerite

4 pounds shrimp, cooked,
　cleaned
3 tablespoons lemon juice
5 tablespoons oil
½ cup minced onion
½ cup chopped green pepper
3–4 tablespoons butter
1½ cups raw rice, cooked
　as directed
1½ teaspoons salt

½ teaspoon pepper
½ teaspoon mace
Dash of cayenne pepper
2 (10¾-ounce) cans condensed
　tomato soup
2 cups heavy cream
1 cup slivered almonds, divided
1 cup sherry
Paprika

Marinate shrimp in lemon juice and oil for 2 hours. Drain. Sauté onion and green pepper in butter; add all ingredients except ¼ cup almonds, and sprinkle with paprika. Bake at 350° approximately 45 minutes until bubbly.

Note: This dish is best if made and let stand overnight or 12 hours before baking, for flavors to blend.

Woodbine Public Library Community Cookbook (Iowa)

Swiss Alpine Quiche

2 cups shredded Swiss cheese
2 tablespoons flour
1 (10-ounce) package chopped broccoli, thawed, drained
2 cups chopped cooked ham
3 tablespoons chopped onion
1 unbaked pie shell (10-inch deep plate)
1¼ cups milk
3 eggs, slightly beaten
½ teaspoon salt
⅓ teaspoon pepper

Combine cheese and flour. Layer ½ broccoli, ½ ham, ½ onion, and ½ cheese mixture in pie shell. Repeat layers. Combine milk and eggs and seasonings. Pour over mixture in shell. Bake at 350° for 40–45 minutes until lightly browned. Let stand 5 minutes before slicing.

Recipes from Jan's Cake & Candy Crafts (Indiana)

Cheesy Green Onion Quiche

Pastry for bottom of quiche dish
8 slices bacon, cooked, crumbled
¾ cup shredded Swiss cheese
4 eggs, beaten
1 (8-ounce) carton sour cream
½ cup half-and-half
¼ cup sliced green onions
1 tablespoon all-purpose flour
¾ teaspoon salt
⅛ teaspoon pepper
Dash of dried crushed red pepper

Line a 9-inch quiche dish or pie plate with pastry. Trim excess pastry around edges. Prick bottom and sides of pastry with fork. Bake at 400° for 3 minutes. Remove from oven and gently prick with fork. Bake 5 minutes longer.

Sprinkle bacon and cheese into pastry shell. Combine remaining ingredients; mix well. Pour into pastry shell and bake at 375° for 40–45 minutes until set.

Treasured Recipes (Ohio)

Zucchini Quiche

1 tablespoon canola oil
4 cups thinly sliced, unpeeled
   zucchini (about 1½ pounds)
1 cup chopped onion, fresh or
   frozen
2 tablespoons dried parsley
   flakes
½ teaspoon black pepper
¼ teaspoon salt
¼ teaspoon garlic powder
½ teaspoon dried basil
¼ teaspoon dried oregano
2 large eggs
1½ cups shredded reduced-fat
   Muenster or mozzarella cheese
1 (9-inch) Brown Rice Crust
2 teaspoons Dijon mustard

Preheat oven to 375°. Spray a large skillet with cooking spray. Add oil to skillet; heat 1–2 minutes. Add zucchini and onion; cook until tender, about 10 minutes. Add parsley, pepper, salt, garlic powder, basil, and oregano; stir to mix.

In a large mixing bowl, blend eggs and cheese. Add zucchini mixture to egg-cheese mixture; stir to combine. Spread prepared Brown Rice Crust with mustard. Pour zucchini mixture evenly into crust. Bake in 375° oven for 18–20 minutes or until knife inserted in center comes out clean. Let stand 10 minutes before cutting into wedges to serve. Serve hot. Serves 6.

BROWN RICE CRUST:
2 cups cooked brown rice, or 1
   (8.8-ounce) package 90-second
   prepared brown rice
1 large egg, beaten
1 tablespoon grated Parmesan
   cheese

In mixing bowl, combine rice, egg, and Parmesan cheese; stir to mix. Press firmly into prepared 9-inch pie plate. Bake in 375° oven for 3 minutes. Fill with desired filling and continue baking according to recipe instructions.

More Nutritious Still Delicious (Ohio)

Gnocchi

4 pounds potatoes (must be Idaho)
2 tablespoons salt
1 stick butter
2 eggs, beaten

4 cups all-purpose flour
Salt to taste
2 tablespoons salt
Parmesan cheese, grated
Meat sauce

Cook potatoes with jackets on in salted water. Peel and mash while hot. Place butter in center of hot mashed potatoes. When butter has melted (about 15 minutes) mix potatoes thoroughly. Cover with dish towel and allow to cool.

Make small well in center of potatoes and pour eggs in and mix well. Gradually add flour and salt, to taste. Knead well to form dough. Separate mixture into 4 equal parts. Sprinkle each with flour. Roll each portion into a roll the thickness of a sausage. Slice in pieces slightly thicker than ½ inch. Gently roll each piece on flat grater, slightly curling each piece. Pieces should resemble macaroni shells.

Cook in 4 quarts boiling salted water (cook about ⅓ of total amount at one time) about 20–30 seconds. Gnocchi will rise to top of boiling water when done. Gently scoop out with slotted spoon as they rise to top. Sprinkle Parmesan cheese on top of cooked Gnocchi and top with generous amounts of meat sauce. Serves 8.

Herrin's Favorite Italian Recipes Cookbook (Illinois)

The Springfield Horseshoe

The sauce is the thing. . . .

Frozen French fries
8 slices toasted white bread

Sliced, baked ham, or
8 hamburger patties

Prepare fries per package directions. Place 2 slices bread side by side on plate. Top with ham slices or 2 hamburger patties. Cover with Sauce. Top with a mound of fries, drizzled with more Sauce.

SAUCE:

2 egg yolks
½ cup beer
2 tablespoons butter
3 cups grated sharp Old English
  Cheddar or Colby Longhorn
  cheese

1 teaspoon Worcestershire
¼ teaspoon dry mustard
½ teaspoon salt
Dash of cayenne pepper

Beat egg yolks and beer together. Melt butter and cheese over boiling water, stirring in one direction only with a wooden spoon.

Add seasonings. Stirring constantly, add beer and egg mixture a little at a time. Keep mixture piping hot as you stir; but don't let it bubble. Constant stirring and the very best cheese will yield a smooth, uncurdled mixture. Serves 4.

Cook Book: Favorite Recipes of Our Best Cooks (Illinois)

The horseshoe sandwich was first made by Joe Schweska and Steve Tomko at the Leland Hotel in Springfield, Illinois, in 1928. Steve Tomko then took the recipe to Wayne's Red Coach Inn, where it was served until the restaurant closed in 2006. The recipe lives on at the Godfather's Pizza which opened in the spot of the old Red Coach. There you may still get an original Red Coach recipe horseshoe. Although widely debated by locals, the sandwich is said to have originally been served as a tribute to the many horsemen that frequented these hotels. The original horseshoe was served on a sizzling metal platter that represented the anvil; the shape of the ham serves as the shoe with the fries representing the nails. The horseshoe has been featured on Al Roker's *Roker on the Road* and Guy Fieri's *Diners, Drive-Ins and Dives* on the Food Network.

Stromboli

1 pound ground beef
½ cup diced onion
½ cup diced green pepper
2 medium cloves garlic, minced
1 (15½-ounce) jar spaghetti
  sauce with mushrooms

2 (8-ounce) packages refrigerated
  crescent rolls
4 slices mozzarella

Cook beef, onion, and green pepper with garlic until beef is browned and vegetables are tender. Spoon off fat. Stir in spaghetti sauce. Cool to room temperature.

On floured surface, roll each package of rolls to 9x11-inch rectangle. Arrange 2 slices cheese in center of each and ½ beef mixture. Starting at long edge, roll up. Pinch seams. Place both rolls 3 inches apart on cookie sheet. Bake at 350° for 30 minutes. Let stand 5 minutes for easier slicing. Makes 6 servings.

Trinity Lutheran Church Centennial Cookbook (Iowa)

Almost Pizza

7 cups thinly-sliced potatoes,
  about 3 pounds
1 pound lean ground beef
1 (10¾-ounce) can condensed
  nacho cheese soup
1 (10¾-ounce) can condensed
  tomato soup

½ onion, chopped
1 teaspoon sugar
½ teaspoon crushed dried
  oregano
1 (3½-ounce) package pepperoni
  or your favorite topping
1–2 cups mozzarella cheese

Place sliced potatoes in greased 9x13-inch baking dish; set aside. Cook ground beef. Drain off fat. Combine cheese soup and milk in saucepan; cook and stir over medium heat until heated through. Mix together tomato soup, onion, sugar, and oregano. Sprinkle meat over potatoes. Pour cheese mixture over all. Top with tomato soup mixture, favorite topping, and mozzarella cheese. Cover; bake at 375° for 1¼–1½ hours. Let stand 5 minutes before serving. Serves 8–10.

Our Heritage (Iowa)

Chicago-Style Pizza

Chicago is famous for its wonderful, thick, gooey, deep-dish pizzas. The special method was developed by Uno's Pizzeria in the 1950s.

CRUST:

1 package dry yeast
1¼ cups warm water
1 tablespoon sugar
1½ teaspoons salt

2 tablespoons oil
3 cups all-purpose flour
2 tablespoons cornmeal

Dissolve yeast in water. Add sugar, salt, and oil. Stir in flour to make a soft dough. turn out onto well-floured board. Knead about 3 minutes. Put in greased bowl; cover and let rise in warm place until doubled in bulk, about 1½ hours.

SAUCE AND TOPPING:

1 (28-ounce) can Italian pear
  tomatoes, well drained,
  chopped
1 tablespoon oregano
1 teaspoon sugar
2 tablespoons oil

1 pound mozzarella or Scamorza
  cheese, thinly sliced
1 pound mild Italian sausage,
  broken up, cooked, drained
½ cup grated Parmesan cheese

Combine tomatoes, oregano, and sugar. Set aside.

Brush a 14-inch, deep-dish pizza pan with oil; sprinkle with cornmeal. Punch dough down; press in bottom of pan. Let rise about 30 minutes. Arrange cheese over dough. Place sausage over cheese. Spread with tomato sauce. Sprinkle with Parmesan cheese. Place pizza in a 500° oven. Immediately reduce heat to 450° and bake 20–25 minutes or until cheese is melted and Crust is golden. Makes 4 (2-slice) servings.

SoupÇon II (Illinois)

CHICAGO OFFICE OF TOURISM

Chicago lays claim to a number of regional specialties, all of which reflect the city's ethnic and working class roots. Included among these are its nationally renowned deep-dish pizza and the Chicago-style hot dog. The grand tour of Chicago cuisine culminates annually in Grant Park at the Taste of Chicago, the largest food festival in the world, which runs from the final week of June through Fourth of July weekend.

Meats

Buckingham Fountain is a prominent Chicago landmark and the centerpiece of Grant Park. Dedicated in 1927, it was modeled after Latona Fountain at Versailles, France. During good weather a water display begins every hour on the hour and the center jet shoots up to 150 feet. At dusk, a light and music show coincides with the display.

Italian Beef

3 ½ pounds rump roast
4 cups hot water
4 beef bouillon cubes
1 ½ teaspoons salt
1 teaspoon pepper

2 dashes garlic salt
1 ½ teaspoons oregano
2 green bell peppers, cut into
   strips
2 tablespoons butter

Brown roast at 450° for 30 minutes. Mix remaining ingredients except peppers and butter. Pour mixture over browned meat. cover and bake 3 hours at 350°. Refrigerate in pan overnight.

Brown green peppers in butter. After browning cover and steam for about 20 minutes. Pour green peppers into juice around meat and slice meat very thinly and put into juice. Reheat and serve on buns. Makes about 15 sandwiches. If there are leftovers, you may have to add 1 cup beef bouillon when reheating.

Five Loaves and Two Fishes II (Illinois)

Peppery Brisket Roast

1 teaspoon garlic salt
1 teaspoon onion salt
2 teaspoons celery salt
2 teaspoons Worcestershire
1 ½ teaspoons salt
2 teaspoons black pepper
1 tablespoon liquid smoke
1 (3- to 4-pound) well-trimmed
   boneless brisket

3 tablespoons brown sugar
1 tablespoon dry mustard
1 tablespoon soy sauce
1 tablespoon lemon juice
3 drops Tabasco
½ cup ketchup
Dash of nutmeg

Combine garlic salt, onion salt, celery salt, Worcestershire, salt, pepper, and liquid smoke.

Spread brisket evenly with above mixture. Place in greased roasting pan or baking dish. cover and chill overnight. Allow brisket to come to room temperature. Preheat oven to 300°. Cover brisket and bake 30 minutes.

Combine brown sugar, dry mustard, soy sauce, lemon juice, Tabasco, ketchup, and nutmeg. Mix well. Pour over brisket. Cover and bake 1–1½ hours, or until tender. Makes 6–8 servings.

Elsah Landing Heartland Cooking (Illinois)

Barbeque Brisket

1 (5- to 6-pound) beef brisket,
  not corned
Dash of liquid or dry smoke
Dash of celery salt
Dash of garlic powder
Dash of onion powder
Dash of Worcestershire
Dash of seasoned salt
Water, enough to cover bottom of
  pan

Place brisket in roasting pan. Sprinkle smoke, celery salt, garlic powder, and onion powder on both sides of brisket. Marinate in refrigerator overnight or 12 hours.

After marinated, sprinkle on Worcestershire and seasoned salt. Add enough water to cover bottom of pan about ½ inch deep. Cover with foil and bake at 250° for 8–12 hours, until tender. Slice and remove fat before serving. Serve with Barbeque Sauce.

BARBEQUE SAUCE:
1 cup drippings from brisket
1 (8-ounce) can tomato sauce
2 tablespoons brown sugar
4 tablespoons water
2 tablespoons flour

Combine drippings, tomato sauce, and brown sugar in a saucepan. Boil. Whisk together water and flour. Pour flour mixture into boiling drippings. Cook until thickened. Serve with brisket.

Favorite Recipes–First Church of God (Ohio)

Best Meat in Iowa

Sirloin or chuck roast
1 teaspoon ginger
1 teaspoon dry mustard
2 tablespoons dark molasses
½ cup soy sauce
¼ cup oil
3 cloves garlic, cut up (or
  2 teaspoons garlic salt)

Cut meat into cubes. Mix remaining ingredients and place cubes of meat in mixture. Let stand in refrigerator 24 hours or at least 5 hours if in a huffy. Broil or grill 6–12 minutes, or to desired doneness.

A Taste of Grace (Iowa)

Sweet and Sour Pot Roast

Outstanding—this one will catch your fancy.

1 tablespoon oil
1 (4-pound) chuck roast
1 (10½-ounce) can beef
  bouillon
1 (16-ounce) can jellied
  cranberry sauce

1 (5-ounce) bottle prepared
  horseradish
8 carrots, peeled, cut into 2-inch
  pieces
2 onions, quartered

Preheat oven to 350°. Heat oil in Dutch oven and brown roast. Add bouillon, cranberry sauce, and horseradish. Cover and bake at 350° for 1½ hours. Add carrots and onions to roast. Bake an additional 1½ hours.

Reserve pan juices and pour over meat. Serve with buttered noodles, if desired. Serves 6–8.

Winners (Indiana)

Bourbon-Marinated Flank Steak

You don't have to grill this steak on an outdoor grill. It has a great flavor when broiled under a very hot, preheated broiler. The time would be approximately the same as the grilling time.

1 large (2-pound) flank steak
½ cup light soy sauce
3 tablespoons vegetable oil
2 medium onions, sliced
3 large cloves garlic, chopped

2 tablespoons minced fresh
  gingerroot
2 tablespoons dark brown sugar
¼ teaspoon hot pepper sauce
½ cup bourbon

Trim all visible fat from flank steak. In a heavy-duty, gallon-size plastic bag with a zip top, mix together all marinade ingredients. Add steak. Refrigerate for at least 8 hours or as long as 24 hours.

Cook on a hot grill 8 minutes on the first side and 5 minutes on the second side for a medium-rare steak. Increase cooking time if a more well-done steak is desired. To serve, cut across the grain into 1-inch-wide strips. Serves 4–6.

Cooking with Marilyn (Ohio)

Easy Swiss Steak

2½ pounds round steak,
 ½-inch thick, cut in serving-
 size pieces
1 medium onion, cut into rings
2–3 cloves garlic, minced or
 sliced
2 tablespoons butter
Salt and pepper to taste
1 (10¾-ounce) can cream of
 celery soup
1 (10¾-ounce) can cream of
 mushroom soup
1 soup can water

In frying pan, brown meat, onion, and garlic in butter. Place meat in a casserole dish. Salt and pepper lightly. Mix soups and water; pour over steak. Cover and bake in 350° oven for 2½ hours. Serve over mashed potatoes. Makes 4–6 servings.

The PTA Pantry (Ohio)

Dad's Favorite Steak

1 top round steak, Swiss steak,
 or arm roast
½ cup water
¼ cup oil
2 tablespoons brown sugar
1 clove garlic, minced
½ cup soy sauce
¼ cup lemon juice
½ teaspoon ginger
10 drops hot sauce

Chill beef. Cut 1½–1¾ inches thick. Score both sides in diamond pattern, ⅛ inch deep.

Cook remaining ingredients for marinade slowly for 10 minutes; chill. Place steak in plastic bag, add marinade, press out air, tie securely, and place in pan in refrigerator for 6–8 hours or overnight.

Remove steak from marinade, reserving marinade, and place on grill over ash covered coals or on a rack in broiling pan so surface meat is 4–5 inches from heat. Broil at moderate temperature, rare or medium (25–30 minutes, depending on thickness of steak and doneness desired), brushing with marinade and turning occasionally. Carve in thin slices, diagonally, against the grain.

Amish Country Cookbook III (Indiana)

Pepper Steak

1½ pounds round steak,
  cut into thin strips
¼ cup oil
2 cloves garlic
1 cup chopped onion
1 tablespoon soy sauce
1 tablespoon Worcestershire

1 teaspoon salt
¼ teaspoon pepper
1 cup chopped green pepper
½ cup chopped celery
1½ tablespoons cornstarch
1¼ cups water

Brown beef in hot oil; add onion, garlic, soy sauce, Worcestershire, salt, and pepper. Cook 20 minutes, or until vegetables are tender. Combine cornstarch and water and add to meat mixture until thickened. Serve over hot rice.

Spitfire Anniversary Cookbook (Iowa)

Sirloin Supreme

1 large sweet onion
1 large green pepper
2 pounds sirloin steak

2 tablespoons cooking oil
1 (8-ounce) can sliced
  mushrooms, drained

Cut onion and green pepper into ¼-inch rings; set aside. Cut steak into strips 2 inches long and ½-inch wide. Brown meat in hot oil in heavy saucepan or Dutch oven; set aside.

SAUCE:
¾ cup ketchup
¾ cup beef broth
3 tablespoons flour

4 tablespoon soy sauce
Freshly ground pepper

In saucepan, blend ketchup and beef broth. Blend flour, soy sauce, and pepper and stir into ketchup and broth mixture. Heat until bubbling, stirring constantly.

Return meat to heat and add Sauce and onion rings. Cover and simmer ½ hour, stirring occasionally to prevent sticking. Add green pepper rings and mushrooms, and simmer an additional 10 minutes. Serve with hot, fluffy rice. Serves 6–8.

Note: If a lesser cut of meat is used, such as round steak, increase cooking time to allow meat to become tender.

Plain & Fancy Favorites (Ohio)

Newman's Own Marinated Steak

Paul Newman, academy award-winning motion picture actor, was owner of the Newman-Hass racing team.

½ cup Newman's Own Olive
   Oil and Vinegar Dressing
2 cloves garlic, crushed
1 large onion, cut up
Salt and pepper
1 large sirloin steak, about 1½
   inches thick

Combine dressing, garlic, onion, dash of salt and pepper in a shallow glass dish. Add steak; turn to coat with marinade. Refrigerate several hours, turning steak occasionally. Just before serving, preheat broiler or grill. Drain steak; broil or grill to preferred doneness. Slice and serve. Serves 4.

Champions: Favorite Foods of Indy Car Racing (Indiana)

Glazed Country Steak

1½ pounds boneless beef
   chuck shoulder steak, cut in
   serving-size pieces
¼ cup all-purpose flour
½ teaspoon salt
¼ teaspoon pepper
2 tablespoons vegetable oil
¼ cup dry white wine
1 clove garlic, finely chopped
¼ cup tomato juice
1 teaspoon parsley flakes
½ cup beef broth
1 small onion, chopped
2 cups cubed raw potatoes
1 cup carrot chunks
2 tablespoons brown sugar
1 cup raisins

Combine flour, salt, and pepper; pound into steak. In skillet, brown steak pieces on both sides in oil. Pour off drippings. Add wine, garlic, tomato juice, parsley flakes, beef broth, and onion. Cook, covered, over low heat for 30 minutes. Add potatoes and carrots; cook 30 minutes more. Sprinkle with brown sugar and raisins; simmer 15 minutes, or until meat is tender. Serve on platter encircled with vegetables. Makes 4–6 servings.

Lehigh Public Library Cookbook (Iowa)

Country Fried Steak

¾ cup all-purpose flour
½ teaspoon salt
½ teaspoon pepper
4 (5-ounce) beef cube steaks
¼ cup plus 1 tablespoon
  vegetable oil

1 cup chopped onion
1 cup water
1 cup milk

Combine flour, salt, and pepper; measure out and reserve ¼ cup flour mixture. Place remaining ½ cup flour mixture in a shallow dish. Pound steaks to ¼-inch thickness; dredge in flour mixture, coating well on both sides and pressing flour into meat.

Heat 3 tablespoons oil in a large heavy skillet over medium-high heat. Dredge steaks again in any remaining flour mixture and fry until browned on both sides, adding 1 or 2 tablespoons additional oil to skillet if needed. Remove steaks and set aside. Add onion to skillet and sauté until lightly browned. Add water, stirring to loosen clinging particles.

Return steaks to skillet; cover and simmer 30 minutes or until tender. Remove steaks, reserving drippings in skillet. Add reserved ¼ cup flour mixture, stirring until smooth. Cook until lightly browned, stirring constantly. Stir in milk with a wire whisk. Cook, stirring constantly, until thickened. Return steaks to skillet, turning to coat with sauce; simmer until hot.

Thank Heaven for Home Made Cooks (Illinois)

Pasties

4 cups all-purpose flour
2 teaspoons salt
1½ cups shortening
10 tablespoons ice water
1 pound lean beef, cut into small cubes
1 pound coarsely ground lean beef
1 pound lean pork, cut into small cubes
5 large potatoes, peeled, chopped
1½ cups small cubes rutabaga
2 large onions, chopped
1 tablespoon salt
1 teaspoon ground pepper

Mix flour and salt in large chilled bowl. Cut in shortening with pastry blender until mixture is crumbly. Add ice water all at once. Mix well, adding additional water, if needed, to hold dough together. Divide dough into portions. Combine beef cubes, ground beef, pork, potatoes, rutabaga, onions, salt, and pepper in a bowl and mix well.

Roll each portion of dough into a ¼-inch thick circle on a lightly floured surface (approximately 8-inch diameter). Place 1 cup mixture in center of each dough circle. Fold up sides of dough to enclose filling, overlapping edges and pressing together to seal. Crimp edge and cut a vent. Place on a baking sheet. Bake at 400° for 45–50 minutes, or until golden brown. Serve with ketchup and dill pickles.

Note: May bake, cool, individually wrap, and freeze. May serve with beef gravy. One Pastie and a salad makes a great meal.

Variation: May add 2 or 3 chopped carrots to meat and vegetable mixture—adds color and flavor.

The "Friends" Cookbook (Ohio)

Beef Roll-Ups

1 box beef flavor stuffing mix
6–8 thin slices beef
2 tablespoons olive oil
1 (14-ounce) can beef consommé
½ can water

Prepare stuffing mix as directed on package. Place ⅓ cup stuffing mix on each slice of beef. Roll up, tuck ends under, and secure with toothpicks. Heat oil in heavy skillet. Brown roll-ups in oil, then cover with consommé and water. Any extra stuffing can be mounded on top of beef. Cover skillet and bake in 350° oven for 1–1½ hours.

Columbus Colony Creations (Ohio)

Italian "Carne Pane"
(Meatloaf)

⅓ cup olive oil
1 cup chopped onion
1 cup chopped sweet Italian
  peppers
7 garlic cloves, minced
½ teaspoon basil
½ teaspoon oregano
½ teaspoon thyme
1 teaspoon Sweet Italian
  Seasoning
1 pound Italian sausage
1 pound lean ground beef

1 teaspoon salt
1 teaspoon black pepper
½ cup spaghetti sauce
3 eggs, beaten
½ cup Italian-style bread
  crumbs
½ cup grated Italian Parmesan
  cheese
½ cup Italian tomatoes, drained,
  or ½ cup dried tomatoes
Mozzarella cheese, shredded

In a large non-reactive skillet, warm olive oil over medium heat. Add onions, sweet pepper, green peppers, garlic, basil, oregano, thyme, and Italian seasoning; cover and cook 10 minutes, stirring once or twice. Remove from heat and set aside to cool.

Preheat oven to 350°. Meanwhile in large bowl, combine Italian sausage, ground beef, salt, pepper, spaghetti sauce, eggs, bread crumbs, Parmesan cheese, and tomatoes, and mix thoroughly. Combine onion-seasoning mixture and mix. Place in meatloaf pan and top with mozzarella cheese.

Bake meatloaf for about 1½ hours at 350°, or until an instant-reading thermometer inserted into center of loaf registers 160°. Let meatloaf rest on a rack for 10 minutes before slicing.

Note: May wish to drain fat by removing meatloaf from baking dish.

Enjoy (Iowa)

German Meatloaf

With Ohio having such a high percentage of citizens with a German heritage, you can expect all sorts of good dishes made with sauerkraut. This meat loaf is seasoned with both kraut and rye bread crumbs—an inspired combination. Serve the moist and sassy meatloaf with mashed potatoes and a glass of beer. Meatloaf has never been so good!

2 cups soft unseeded rye bread
  crumbs
1 (16-ounce) can sauerkraut,
  drained
2 eggs, lightly beaten
½ cup milk

½ cup chopped onion
1 teaspoon caraway seeds
½ teaspoon ground pepper
2 tablespoons ketchup or chili
  sauce
2 pounds lean ground beef

Preheat oven to 350°. In a large bowl, combine all ingredients except meat and mix well. Add ground beef and mix thoroughly. Pat into a thick, flat loaf approximately 10 inches long and 8 inches wide and place on a rack in a greased or foil-lined 9x13-inch pan. Bake 1¼ hours, or until nicely browned. Let stand 10 minutes before slicing.

Heartland (Ohio)

Shepherd's Pie

1 tablespoon vegetable oil
1 medium onion, chopped
1 pound lean ground beef
1 teaspoon dried basil
½ pound fresh green beans,
  steamed until tender

1 cup chopped canned tomatoes
2 medium-size potatoes, cooked
  until tender
1 egg, beaten
½ cup water

Heat oil in large skillet and sauté onion until golden. Add beef and basil; cook until browned. Stir in green beans and tomatoes, then turn mixture into casserole dish. Preheat oven to 350°. Mash potatoes together with egg and water; spoon evenly over meat mixture and bake for 15 minutes.

Down Home Cooking from Hocking County (Ohio)

Swedish Meatballs

½ cup chopped onion
1 tablespoon butter
½ cup bread crumbs
1 cup milk
1 pound ground beef
¼ pound ground pork

1 egg
½ teaspoon sugar
1½ teaspoons salt
¼ teaspoon ginger
Dash of pepper and nutmeg

Brown onion in butter. Soak bread crumbs in milk. Mix onion and milk mixture with meats, egg, sugar, salt, ginger, pepper, and nutmeg. Form into meatballs and brown in skillet. When brown, put in casserole.

GRAVY:
2 tablespoons flour
1 (10½-ounce) can beef
  consommé soup

¼ cup water
¼ teaspoon instant coffee

After all the meatballs are browned, add flour to drippings in skillet; add soup, water, and instant coffee. Pour Gravy over meatballs and bake in oven until bubbly.

Community Centennial Cookbook (Iowa)

Brown Beef over Pasta

1 pound ground beef
2 bay leaves
1 small carrot, diced
1 teaspoon crushed parsley
  flakes
1 teaspoon crushed dried
  chives
1 tablespoon minced garlic

¼ head cabbage, shredded
1 stalk celery, diced
1 small onion, diced
1 (16-ounce) can bean sprouts,
  drained, cut
2 cups tomato juice, no salt
  added

Brown beef in skillet with bay leaves; wash with hot water, and drain well. Grind herbs in a pestle and mortar. Combine all ingredients in a wide oven-proof dish. Bake in 350° oven until vegetables are tender, about one hour. Serve over cooked pasta. Serves 4.

Heartline Cookbook (Ohio)

Easy Barbecued Hamburger

Prepare a salad, bring out the potato chips, and make this hot sandwich for a quick evening meal.

2½ pounds hamburger meat
1 cup ketchup
2 cups chopped green bell
  pepper
2 onions, chopped

1 tablespoon dry mustard
3 tablespoons sugar
2 tablespoons vinegar
1 teaspoon salt

Cook first 4 ingredients together until meat is browned and vegetables are tender. Add remaining ingredients; cook ½ hour on low heat. Serve on warm hamburger buns.

Sharing Our Best (Indiana)

Grant Wood's Cabbage Rolls

Grant Wood's own recipe, a favorite.

8 large cabbage leaves
1 pound bulk, ground sausage
2 cups cooked rice (or mashed
  potatoes)
1 teaspoon salt

½ cup tomato juice
2 cups boiling water
3 tablespoons vinegar
2 tablespoons sugar

Pour boiling water over cabbage leaves and let stand about 4 minutes, then drain. Mix well the sausage, rice (or potatoes), and salt. Place meat mixture in equal portions on each cabbage leaf. Roll from stem end, folding in the sides, to wrap meat in leaf. Tie each bundle with string or fasten with toothpicks. Place rolls in kettle and cover with tomato juice, boiling water, and vinegar. Add sugar. Simmer until tender, about 1 hour.

The American Gothic Cookbook (Iowa)

Artist Grant Wood was born in Anamosa, Iowa. He is best known for his paintings depicting the rural American Midwest, particularly the painting *American Gothic,* an iconic image of the 20th century. Wood is considered the patron artist of Cedar Rapids, Iowa, and one of his designs is depicted on the 2004 Iowa State Quarter. The Cedar Rapids Museum of Art houses the largest collection of Grant Wood artwork.

Beef Stick
(Summer Sausage)

5 pounds ground beef
5 heaping teaspoons Morton
   Tenderquick Salt
2½ teaspoons salt
1 teaspoon liquid smoke
½ teaspoon sage
1 heaping teaspoon Italian
   seasoning

2½ teaspoons garlic salt
   or powder
2½ teaspoons whole
   mustard seeds
2 teaspoons coarse pepper
½ teaspoon ground red
   pepper
Pinch of ground cloves

Mix all ingredients together well. Refrigerate 48 hours; mix well every day. Shape into 2-inch diameter rolls. Put on broiler pan or racks in pan. Bake 150° for 4 hours.

Hoosier Heritage Cookbook (Indiana)

Beef or Deer Jerky

1 pound very lean steak
4 tablespoons soy sauce
4 tablespoons Worcestershire
1 tablespoon ketchup or BBQ
   sauce

¼ teaspoon garlic powder
½ teaspoon salt
½ teaspoon ground pepper
¼ teaspoon onion salt

Cut steak into ¼-inch strips with the grain. Marinate overnight in mixture of remaining ingredients; drain. Lay flat on trays (cookie sheets). Don't overlap. Bake at 145° for 6–10 hours. Turn at least once while drying. Ready when it bends like green willow without breaking.

Trinity Lutheran Church Centennial Cookbook (Iowa)

Veal Française

Try this for your next dinner party.

1½ pounds veal, cut in
   medallions, pounded flat
1 cup all-purpose flour

1 egg, beaten
¼ pound butter

Dip veal in flour, next in egg, then in flour again; shake off excess flour. Sauté in butter turning once, until cooked (about 5 minutes) over medium heat. Remove meat to platter and keep warm.

SAUCE:

½ cup chicken broth
¼ cup white wine
⅛ cup lemon juice
¼ cup butter

1 cup whipping cream
1 tablespoon chopped fresh
   parsley
Lemon slices

Mix all ingredients together in fry pan and bring to a boil. Add veal and heat for 5 minutes. Arrange veal on a serving platter and garnish with thin slices of lemon. Serves 4.

Angels and Friends Cookbook II (Ohio)

Wiener Schnitzel

Breaded veal cutlets, Vienna style.

4 boneless veal cutlets (pork
   may be substituted)
Paprika
Salt and pepper to taste
Flour

1 egg
1–2 tablespoons water or milk
Bread crumbs
Butter for frying
Lemon slices for garnish

If there is a skin around meat, cut it in several places so it won't curl while frying in pan. Pound meat a little. Sprinkle with paprika, salt and pepper. Coat with flour. Beat egg and water (or milk) and dip cutlets in it. Coat with bread crumbs on both sides. Heat butter in fry pan and add meat. Let cook to a golden brown over medium heat, about 5 minutes on each side. Serve with lemon slices.

Guten Appetit (Indiana)

City Chicken

It is believed this is strictly a Cincinnati recipe that came about because "some butcher probably had a pile of pork and veal scraps left over one day," according to Russ Gibbs, Findlay Market's "oldest" proprietor with 40 years of Butter and Egg Stand #28. City chickens are available ready-made at most of the meat stands, which number over half of the 32 stands inside the market building.

1 pound lean pork	¼ cup cornmeal
½ pound veal	Salt and pepper to taste
6 wooden skewers	Frying oil
½ cup flour	

Cut meat into bite-size cubes. Thread pork and veal onto wooden skewers, 2 pieces of pork and 1 of veal, until all the meat is gone and each skewer has an equal amount. Place flour, cornmeal, and seasonings into a bag and toss in the city chickens. Shake until meat is well covered with mixture. Fry at a medium heat, turning occasionally, until browned on all sides. This should take approximately 20–30 minutes so that the pork will be cooked through. Drain on absorbent paper. Afterward, wash skewers and use them again. Yields 2–3 servings.

Note: The city chicken can be flour and dipped in an egg batter if so desired. Of course, Russ recommends this alternative.

Cincinnati Recipe Treasury (Ohio)

The Second City is a long-running improvisational theatre based in Chicago's Old Town neighborhood. Since 1959, The Second City has established itself as a Chicago landmark and a national treasure. The troupe chose the self-mocking name "The Second City" from the title of an article about Chicago by A. J. Liebling that appeared in *The New Yorker* in 1952. The theatre has launched the careers of such comic greats as Dan Aykroyd, John Belushi, John Candy, Steve Carell, Stephen Colbert, Chris Farley, Tina, Fey, Bonny Hunt, Tim Meadows, Mike Myers, Bill Murray, Catherine O'Hara, Gilda Radner, Joan Rivers, and Martin Short. *Saturday Night Live* and *SCTV* borrowed many of the writing and performing techniques pioneered by The Second City.

Grilled Pork Chops

½ cup soy sauce
½ cup cooking sherry
2 teaspoons seasoned salt
1 teaspoon ginger
½ teaspoon dry mustard
6 pork chops about 1¼ inches
  thick

Combine all ingredients except chops. Use this to marinate chops.
Cover and refrigerate 4–6 hours or overnight. Turn several times.
Remove from marinade and place on grill. Cook 20–30 minutes or
until meat is not pink in the center. Remove from grill immediately.
Do not overcook.

Women's Centennial Cookbook (Ohio)

Iowa Chops
(Stuffed)

½ cup whole-kernel corn
½ cup bread crumbs
Pinch of salt and pepper
¾ tablespoon parsley
Pinch of sate
½ tablespoon chopped onion
½ cup diced apple
1 tablespoon whole milk
2 Iowa pork chops, thick cut

In a bowl, combine ingredients, except chops, till well mixed. Cut a
slit in the side of chops and stuff with mixture. In a separate bowl,
combine basting ingredients and blend until smooth. In frying pan,
brown stuffed chops and then bake in a 350° oven for about an hour,
basting chops often with sauce.

BASTING SAUCE:
¼ cup honey
¼ cup mustard
¼ teaspoon rosemary leaves
½ teaspoon salt
Pinch of pepper

Combine ingredient well.

Spanning the Bridge of Time (Iowa)

BBQ Pork Chop Casserole

4 loin pork chops
¼ cup diced onion
¾ cup chili sauce
¼ cup ketchup
1 teaspoon dry mustard
¼ teaspoon garlic powder

2 tablespoons brown sugar
½ cup water
3 tablespoons cider vinegar
1 beef bouillon cube
Salt and pepper to taste

Brown chops. Place in a 1½-quart casserole. Sauté onion until soft in pan drippings. Add remaining ingredients and bring to a boil. Pour over pork chops. Bake at 350° for 1½ hours, covered.

Firebelles Cookbook (Ohio)

Harvest Barbecued Pork Roast

1 (4- to 5-pound) pork roast
¾ cup barbecue sauce

1 (10-ounce) jar pure apple jelly

Roast meat approximately 3 hours. Heat sauce and jelly. Stir to blend well. Baste meat with half of the sauce during last half hour of roasting time. Serve remaining sauce with sliced meat. Takes 2½–3 hours at 325°. Serves 8–10.

Cook of the Week Cookbook (Iowa)

Pork Cutlets & Sour Cream Sauce

A 1960's recipe.

1 pork tenderloin, sliced about
   ½-inch thick
Salt and pepper to taste
1 teaspoon sweet or medium
   paprika
2 tablespoons butter

2 tablespoons oil
¼ cup finely chopped onion
½ cup dry white wine
½ cup chicken broth
½–¾ cup sour cream

Pound meat; sprinkle with salt, pepper, and paprika. Sauté in butter and oil until browned and cooked. Transfer meat to platter. Pour off excess fat in skillet and add onions. Cook until wilted. Add wine and deglaze pan. Add chicken broth and simmer 5 minutes. Remove sauce from heat and add sour cream. Put through a fine sieve and pour over meat. Serves 4-6.

Aspic and Old Lace (Indiana)

Sweet and Sour Pork with Rice

2 tablespoons cooking oil
1 pound boneless pork, cut up
   in 1-inch cubes
1 (15-ounce) can pineapple
   chunks
½ cup light corn syrup
¼ cup vinegar

2 tablespoons soy sauce
1 clove garlic, minced
2 tablespoons cornstarch
2 tablespoons water
½ cup red and green pepper
   slices

Heat oil in skillet; brown pork. Add next 5 ingredients. Bring to a boil, simmer 10 minutes, or until done. Mix cornstarch and water; add to pork with peppers. Boil 2 minutes stirring constantly. Serve over rice. Serves 4.

Amish Country Cookbook I (Indiana)

Apricot Baked Ham

Ham is a great choice for the Christmas Eve meal, because once it goes in the oven, it practically takes care of itself until dinnertime. The sugary crust makes the ham beautiful to serve.

1 (10- to 14-pound) whole ham, fully cooked, bone-in
Whole cloves
⅓ cup dry mustard

1 cup apricot jam
1 cup light brown sugar, firmly packed

Trim skin and excess fat from ham. Place ham on a rack in a large roasting pan. Insert cloves in ham every inch or so. Be sure to push cloves into ham surface as far as they'll go.

Now combine dry mustard and jam. Spread over entire surface of ham. Pat brown sugar over jam mixture. Bake uncovered at 325° for 2½–3½ hours, or until meat thermometer registers 140°. Count on 15–18 minutes per pound. The sugary crust that forms on the ham keeps the juices in. When ham is done, remove from oven and let set 15–20 minutes before carving. Will serve 15 or more.

Christmas Thyme at Oak Hill Farm (Indiana)

Hot Ham Buns

Poppy seeds give them a special flavor; try to use rye buns.

¼ cup butter or margarine, softened
2 tablespoons prepared horseradish mustard
2 teaspoons poppy seeds

2 teaspoons finely chopped onion
4 rye hamburger buns, split
4 thin slices boiled ham (can use baked)
4 slices Swiss cheese

Mix butter, mustard, poppy seeds, and onion; spread generously on both cut surfaces of buns. Tuck a slice of ham and cheese in each bun. Arrange on baking sheet. Do not wrap in foil. Bake at 350° for about 15 minutes or until sandwiches are hot. Makes 4 sandwiches.

Note: Do not wrap in foil. Baking the sandwiches unwrapped results in a deliciously crisp outside with a tasty filling.

Singing in the Kitchen (Iowa)

Ham Loaf

2¼ pounds ground ham
½ pound sausage
¼ cup minced onion
⅛ cup minced green pepper
1 tablespoon minced parsley

3 eggs, beaten
1 cup milk
½ teaspoon white pepper
1¼ cups dry bread crumbs

Mix together all ingredients. Shape into loaf and bake in a 350°–375° oven for 30 minutes. Pour Basting Sauce over loaf and bake 30 minutes longer or until loaf is done. Makes 10–12 servings.

BASTING SAUCE:

2 tablespoons prepared
   mustard

6 tablespoons water
½ cup brown sugar

Stir until sugar is dissolved. Pour ¾ over ham loaf after first 30 minutes. Thicken remaining ¼ of sauce with a small amount of cornstarch and serve with loaf.

Recipes of the Durbin (Indiana)

Ham Loaf

MEAT MIX:

1 pound ground smoked ham
1½ pounds ground lean pork
2 eggs
1 cup cracker crumbs
1 cup milk

½ teaspoon salt
Pepper to taste
6 slices pineapple
10 maraschino cherries

Mix together meats, eggs, crumbs, milk, salt, and pepper. Place pineapple in the bottom of a baking dish and put cherries in the center.

SAUCE MIX:

¾ cup brown sugar
1 teaspoon dry mustard

¼ cup vinegar

Mix ingredients, and spread ½ of Sauce Mix over pineapples. Over this, spread Meat Mix. Spread remaining Sauce Mix over top. Bake at 375° for 1½–2 hours. Serves 10.

Cooking Along the Lincoln Highway in Ohio (Ohio)

Mini Ham Loaves

Your guests will enjoy these.

3 pounds ground ham
2 pounds lean ground pork
4–5 eggs

2 cups crushed cornflakes
2 cups milk

Mix ham, pork, eggs, cornflake crumbs, and milk; shape into small loaves, using about a rounded ½ cup meat mixture. Bake, uncovered, on a greased jellyroll pan at 325° for 30 minutes. Meanwhile, prepare sauce.

RAISIN SAUCE:

2 tablespoons cornstarch
¼ cup cold water
1 (6-ounce) can frozen orange
   juice concentrate, thawed

1½ cups brown sugar
1 tablespoon dry mustard
2 tablespoons cider vinegar
1½ cups golden raisins

Dissolve cornstarch in cold water. Combine with remaining sauce ingredients in a saucepan. Bring to a boil and cook several minutes. Baste ham loaves with Raisin Sauce; reduce heat to 300° and continue baking for an additional 30 minutes. (For a family-size ham loaf, use half of ingredients. Bake at 300° for 1½–2 hours.) You can prepare ahead and bake just before serving.

Angels and Friends Cookbook II (Ohio)

Lamb in Gingered Cranberry Sauce

2 pounds cubed lean lamb
½ cup diced onion
2 teaspoons seasoned salt
¼ teaspoon pepper
¼ teaspoon garlic powder
¼ teaspoon ground oregano

¼ teaspoon ground ginger
1 (6-ounce) can tomato paste
1 cup red Burgundy
½ cup water
1 (16-ounce) can whole cranberry
   sauce

In a large skillet, brown lamb; pour off fat. Add onion, seasonings, tomato paste, wine, and water; cover and simmer 45 minutes. Add cranberry sauce and simmer an additional 45 minutes more. Serve hot over rice. Yields 4–6 servings.

Holy Cow, Chicago's Cooking! (Illinois)

Brain Sandwiches

About 12 ounces cleaned pork
  brains
3–4 heaping tablespoons
  all-purpose flour

1 level teaspoon baking powder
1 large egg
Salt and pepper to taste

Wash brains in pieces under cold running water, removing as much of the thin covering membrane as possible. With hands, knead brains to break up into small lumps. Combine with remaining ingredients in a large mixing bowl; beat with electric mixer on medium-low speed until batter is very nearly smooth; do not over beat.

Heat about ¼ inch vegetable oil in a large skillet until bubbling hot, but not smoking. Drop batter by spoonfuls (allowing about 3 tablespoons per fritter) and fry until batter bubbles and begins to look dry. Turn and fry on other side until edges are crispy and golden brown. It should take about 5–6 minutes per side. Serve on hamburger buns with sliced onion, pickle, and other hamburger-type toppings and garnishments, as desired. Yields 6–8 sandwiches.

Festival Foods and Family Favorites (Indiana)

Bratwurst Noodle Casserole

2 pounds bulk Carle's
  Bratwurst
1 medium onion, diced
12 ounces noodles, boiled,
  drained

1 pound sauerkraut, drained
2 (10¾-ounce) cans cream of
  mushroom soup
¼ cup grated Cheddar cheese
1 cup bread crumbs

Brown bratwurst in skillet until fully cooked, but still juicy. Add onion and sauté. In a bowl, mix bratwurst, onion, noodles, sauerkraut, and mushroom soup. Place into greased 9x13-inch baking pan or 2-quart casserole dish. Top with cheese and bread crumbs. Bake at 350° for 45 minutes.

Cooking Along the Lincoln Highway in Ohio (Ohio)

Hot Dog!

8 hot dogs
8 cheese slices

1 (8-ounce) package crescent
rolls

Split hot dogs and fill with folded cheese slice. Wrap this in a crescent dough roll and bake 10–13 minutes in 375° oven. Serve with mustard to dip them in. Yummy!

The Indiana Kid's Cookbook! (Indiana)

Country Sausage Gravy

This gravy can be served over biscuits or potatoes. It has a hearty flavor and is easy to prepare.

1 pound bulk sausage
1 (10¾-ounce) can cream of
  chicken soup
1 can milk

½ teaspoon dry mustard
¼ teaspoon seasoned salt
¼ teaspoon pepper
1 cup sour cream

In a heavy skillet, crumble sausage and cook over medium heat until browned; drain and set aside. In the same skillet, blend soup and milk together. Add mustard, salt, and pepper, and bring to a boil. Reduce heat and stir in sausage and sour cream. Simmer until heated through, but do not boil. Serves 4–6.

Ohio Cook Book (Ohio)

Poultry

"The Greatest Spectacle in Racing," the Indianapolis 500-Mile Race is one of the oldest motor sport events. The first "Indy 500" was held in 1911, with American Ray Harroun piloting a Marmon "Wasp" to victory—outfitted with his invention, the rear-view mirror. The race, held each year at Indianapolis Motor Speedway near Indianapolis, Indiana, attracts drivers from around the world.

Best Roast Chicken

1 (5- to 6-pound) roasting
  chicken
Kosher salt to taste
Freshly ground pepper to taste
1 large bunch fresh thyme
1 lemon, halved

1 head garlic, cut in half
  horizontally
2 tablespoons butter, melted
1 Spanish onion, thickly sliced
1 cup chicken stock
2 tablespoons all-purpose flour

Preheat oven to 425°. Remove giblets and any excess fat from chicken. Rinse chicken inside and out and pat dry on outside. Place chicken in a roasting pan and liberally salt and pepper inside cavity. Stuff cavity with thyme, lemon halves, and garlic. Brush outside of chicken with butter and season with salt and pepper. Tie legs together with kitchen string and tuck wing tips under body of chicken. Scatter onion slices around chicken.

Roast at 425° for 1 hour and 30 minutes or until juices run clear when cut between leg and thigh. Transfer chicken to a cutting board and cover with foil to keep warm.

Remove fat from bottom of roasting pan, reserving 2 tablespoons in a small cup. Add chicken stock to pan and cook over high heat, scraping bottom of pan, for 5 minutes, or until reduced. Combine reserved 2 tablespoons chicken fat and flour and add to pan. Boil a few minutes or until gravy thickens. Strain gravy into a small saucepan and season to taste. Keep warm over very low heat. Carve chicken, placing meat on a serving platter. Serve chicken with gravy.

Crowd Pleasers (Ohio)

Oven Fried Chicken

1 frying-size chicken
⅓ cup plain flour
1 teaspoon salt
Dash of pepper
1 egg

2 tablespoons water
¾ cup cornflake crumbs
¼ cup grated Parmesan cheese
¼ cup margarine, melted

Coat chicken with combined flour and seasoning. Dip chicken in combined egg and water; coat with combined crumbs and cheese. Place in a 9x13-inch baking pan, drizzle margarine over chicken. Bake at 375° for 1 hour, or until tender.

Our Favorite Recipes II (Indiana)

Shaker Fried Chicken

2 (2½-pound) frying chickens
1 tablespoon minced parsley
¼ teaspoon dried marjoram
6 tablespoons butter, melted
Salt and pepper to taste

2 tablespoons flour
2 tablespoons butter
4 tablespoons bacon drippings or
    lard
1 cup light cream

Wash and dry chickens. Cut into 16 pieces. Mix herbs with melted butter and coat chicken thoroughly. Let stand at room temperature for 1 hour. Mix salt and pepper with flour and dredge chicken in this to coat thoroughly. In a Dutch oven, over moderate heat, melt 2 table-spoons butter and add bacon drippings. Add coated chicken and cook to brown well. Pour cream over and let simmer, covered, for 20 minutes. Garnish with watercress and serve with a green salad. Serves 6–8.

The Shaker Cookbook (Ohio)

Harry's Chicken Vesuvio

This recipe is a specialty of Chef Abraham Aguirre, chef at Harry Caray's restaurant, "Holy Cow!!!"

½ chicken, cut into 4 pieces	Boiling water
½ teaspoon salt	1 baking potato, peeled, cut into
½ teaspoon pepper	quarters
2 teaspoons oregano	7 tablespoons olive oil, divided
2 teaspoons granulated garlic	2 large cloves garlic
2 ounces frozen peas	½ cup dry white wine
1 teaspoon sugar	2 teaspoons chopped parsley

Rinse chicken and pat dry. Season with salt, pepper, oregano, and garlic.

Combine peas, sugar, and enough boiling water to cover in bowl; mix well. Let stand 1 minute; drain. Sauté potato in 1 tablespoon olive oil in skillet until golden brown; drain. Heat 6 tablespoons olive oil to 300° in 10-inch skillet. Add garlic cloves. Cook 2 minutes, stirring occasionally. Add chicken. Sauté until brown on both sides. Add potato; mix well.

Deglaze skillet with white wine. Spoon into baking pan. Bake in 400° oven for 20–30 minutes or until chicken is tender. Transfer chicken to serving platter. Arrange potato and peas around chicken. Pour sauce over top. Sprinkle with parsley. Yields 4 servings.

The Cubs 'R Cookin' (Illinois)

Parmesan Oven-Fried Chicken

½ cup bread crumbs	¼ teaspoon minced garlic
2 tablespoons parsley	6 chicken breast halves, skinless,
¼ teaspoon pepper	boneless
⅓ cup grated Parmesan cheese	¼ cup French salad dressing

Combine all ingredients, except chicken and dressing, in a bag large enough to shake chicken breasts in. Dip clean breasts into salad dressing and shake in mixture in bag. Place in a 9x13-inch pan. Bake 1 hour at 350°, uncovered.

A Taste of Fishers (Indiana)

Oven-Fried Parmesan Chicken

1½ tablespoons canola oil
6 ounces plain nonfat yogurt
4 boneless, skinless chicken
   breasts (about 1¼ pounds)
½ cup plain dry bread crumbs
4 tablespoons grated Parmesan
   cheese
2 tablespoons all-purpose flour
2 teaspoons chili powder
½ teaspoon onion powder
¼ teaspoon garlic powder
⅛ teaspoon cayenne pepper

Preheat oven to 425°. Spray a 9x13x2-inch baking pan with cooking spray. Drizzle canola oil over bottom of pan.

In a medium bowl, mix yogurt and chicken until chicken is coated. Cover bowl with plastic wrap; refrigerate until needed.

In a gallon-size, resealable plastic bag, combine bread crumbs, cheese, flour, chili powder, onion powder, garlic powder, and cayenne pepper; seal. Shake gently to combine. Remove chicken from yogurt. Place chicken in bag one piece at a time. Shake gently to coat. Place coated chicken in prepared baking pan. Bake uncovered in 425° oven for 20 minutes or until chicken is cooked through and juices run clear. Makes 4 servings.

More Nutritious Still Delicious (Ohio)

Chicken Parmigiana

4 boneless, skinless, chicken
   breast halves
2 eggs, beaten
1 cup Italian-style bread crumbs
¼ cup olive oil
1 (15½-ounce) jar meat flavored
   spaghetti sauce
½ cup grated Parmesan cheese
1 cup shredded mozzarella
   cheese

Preheat oven to 400°. Dip chicken into eggs, then bread crumbs. Coat thoroughly. In medium skillet, heat olive oil. Cook chicken in oil until done and well browned. Pour spaghetti sauce in 7x11-inch pan. Place chicken on sauce and top with cheeses. Bake 15 minutes or until cheese is melted and lightly browned. Makes 4 servings.

Favorite Recipes of Collinsville Junior Service Club (Illinois)

Chicken Nuggets

4 chicken breasts   ½ cup butter, melted

CRUMB MIXTURE:
½ cup bread crumbs   ¼ cup grated Cheddar cheese
¼ cup grated Parmesan cheese   1 teaspoon basil
¼ teaspoon pepper   ½ teaspoon salt

Cut chicken into 1½-inch pieces or smaller. Dip chicken in melted butter, then roll in crumb mixture. Place on a cookie sheet covered with lightly greased aluminum foil. Bake in 400° oven for 10–15 minutes.

175th Anniversary Quilt Cookbook (Ohio)

Orange Chicken

12 pieces chicken, cut up (4 breasts, 4 thighs, 4 drumsticks)
Flour
Oil for frying
Salt and pepper to taste
2 large onions, sliced
1 cup orange juice
¼ cup orange marmalade
1 teaspoon celery seeds
¼ cup orange liqueur
1 orange

Dust chicken pieces with flour. Put 2 tablespoons oil in a large frying pan on medium heat and brown chicken pieces 4 at a time. Add salt and pepper and remove to a plate. Lower heat.

Put onions into pan and sauté gently without browning. Add orange juice, marmalade, and celery seeds, and bring to a simmer. Add liqueur and ignite with a match. Place chicken and sauce in a Dutch oven or large covered casserole. Add 1 orange cut into wedges. Cover and bake at 325° for 1–1½ hours. Serves 6.

Note: Excellent party dish, as it tastes even better the second day.

C-U in the Kitchen (Illinois)

Broiled Apricot Chicken

1 cup apricot nectar
3 tablespoons brown sugar
1 teaspoon grated orange peel
2 tablespoons ketchup
2 tablespoons cornstarch
1 tablespoon horseradish
   mustard
½ teaspoon salt
6 chicken breasts
1 (15-ounce) can apricot halves
   (drained)

Preheat broiler. Combine apricot nectar, brown sugar, orange peel, ketchup, corn starch, horseradish mustard, and salt. Stir until cornstarch is fully dissolved. Bring to a boil and hold for 1 minute. Remove from heat.

Broil chicken breasts 4–5 minutes on each side. Brush often with apricot sauce during broiling and before serving. Garnish with apricot halves. Makes 6 servings.

The French-Icarian Persimmon Tree Cookbook (Illinois)

Chicken Breasts with Red Grapes

2 tablespoons unsalted butter
1 tablespoon olive oil
6 chicken breast halves, boned,
   skinned
⅓ cup white zinfandel or other
   blush wine
1 cup heavy cream
1 tablespoon fresh whole lemon
   thyme leaves or 1 teaspoon
   dried finely crumbled thyme
Salt and freshly ground black
   pepper
½ pound seedless red grapes

Heat butter and oil in a sauté pan or skillet over medium-high heat; add chicken and sauté until meat is lightly browned on all sides, about 5 minutes. Add wine to pan and bring to a boil, loosening browned bits from bottom of pan with wooden spoon. Stir in cream, thyme, and salt and pepper to taste. Reduce heat to a simmer, cover, and cook until sauce thickens slightly, about 5 minutes. Stir in grapes and simmer until grapes are heated through and chicken is tender but still moist inside, about 5 minutes.

Angels and Friends Cookbook II (Ohio)

Chicken Cordon Bleu

1 cup bread crumbs
⅛ teaspoon basil
⅛ teaspoon garlic salt
¼ teaspoon pepper, divided
¼ teaspoon salt
12 ounces breast of chicken
   pounded out to make
   8 fillets ½ stick butter
1 cup milk, divided

8 ounces ham (1 or 2 slices
   per serving)
8 ounces Swiss cheese (1 or
   2 slices per serving)
2 tablespoons flour
1 (8-ounce) can sliced
   mushrooms
⅛ teaspoon thyme

Blend together bread crumbs, basil, garlic salt, pepper, and salt, and toast in oven at 350° for 6 minutes. Dip chicken in a little milk, then dip in bread crumb mixture; cover completely. Place chicken in pan and fry to light brown. Place 1 or 2 slices ham and cheese between 2 pieces of chicken; continue to make 4 servings. Place chicken in pan and cook at 350° for 20–30 minutes.

Heat butter until melted, stir in flour, add remaining milk and heat. Stir until thickened. Add additional flour as necessary to thicken. Add mushrooms, pepper, and thyme; mix and heat until warm. When chicken is done, pour sauce over it and serve. Serves 4.

Sharing Traditions from People You Know (Iowa)

The abbreviation "ORD" for Chicago's O'Hare International Airport comes from its original name, Orchard Field. In 1949, the name was changed in honor of Lieutenant Commander Edward H. "Butch" O'Hare, the Navy's first flying ace and Medal of Honor recipient in World War II. To honor its namesake, the airport displays a Grumman F4F-3 aircraft replicating the one flown by Butch O'Hare during his Medal of Honor flight. The restored Wildcat is exhibited in Terminal Two at the west end of the ticketing lobby. O'Hare International Airport is the second busiest airport in the world, behind Hartsfield-Jackson Atlanta International Airport with 69,353,654 passengers passing through the airport in 2008. The same year, O'Hare had 881,566 aircraft operations, an average of 2,409 per day.

Spinach Stuffed Chicken Breasts

1 (10-ounce) box frozen chopped
  spinach, thawed, drained
4 ounces canned water
  chestnuts, drained, finely
  chopped
1 (8-ounce) package cream
  cheese or low-calorie cream
  cheese

¾ cup sour cream or sour
  half-and-half
1⅝ ounces dry vegetable soup
  mix
4 boneless chicken breasts, split
  (skin on)

Combine all ingredients except chicken. Mix well. Divide mixture into eights. At neck end of each piece of chicken, carefully lift skin. With long handled spoon, fill space between skin and meat with ⅛ spinach mixture, taking care not to break membrane connecting skin to meat. Tuck ends of chicken under and place in oven-proof baking dish. Repeat process with remaining chicken. Bake covered in preheated 350° oven 30 minutes. Uncover and bake additional 30 minutes.

    May be served hot or cold. Cold chicken breasts are attractive sliced and arranged on platter. Serves 6–8.

Noteworthy (Illinois)

Curry Chicken Delight

4 whole chicken breasts,
  skinned, boned, halved
  lengthwise
⅓ cup all-purpose flour
4 slices bacon, cooked, crumbled

¼ cup honey
2 tablespoons mustard
½ teaspoon salt
½ teaspoon curry powder

Rinse chicken; pat dry. Coat with flour. Brown chicken in bacon drippings about 10 minutes. Transfer chicken to an 8x8x2-inch baking dish. Bake at 350°, uncovered, about 30 minutes. Combine honey, mustard, salt, and curry powder; drizzle over chicken. Bake, uncovered, 15 minutes longer. Top with crumbled bacon. Serve with cooked rice.

Indiana's Finest Recipes (Indiana)

Grilled Breast of Chicken with Fresh Basil Tomato Sauce

3 garlic cloves, minced
16 large, fresh basil leaves

4 chicken breasts, boned, halved

Slip ⅛ of the minced garlic and fresh basil leaves under the skin of each chicken breast. Place breasts in a nonreactive pan.

MARINADE:

½ cup white wine vinegar
5 tablespoons olive oil
½ teaspoon salt

¼ teaspoon pepper
1½ teaspoons minced garlic

Combine ingredients and pour over chicken breasts. Marinate 4–6 hours or overnight.

Remove chicken breasts from Marinade. Grill over hot coals 8–10 minutes on each side. Serve with Tomato Basil Sauce.

TOMATO BASIL SAUCE:

¼ cup chopped onion
¼ cup chopped green bell
   pepper
½ teaspoon minced garlic
2 tablespoons butter

2 (8-ounce) cans tomato sauce
½ teaspoon salt
¼ teaspoon pepper
½ cup chopped fresh basil
   leaves

Sauté onion, green pepper, and garlic in butter until onion is tender. Stir in tomato sauce. Add salt and pepper. Simmer 10 minutes. Add chopped basil right before serving. Yields 8 servings.

Recipe from The Heritage Restaurant, Cincinnati, Ohio.
Best Recipes of Ohio Inns and Restaurants (Ohio)

The state of Iowa gets considerable attention every four years because it holds the first presidential caucuses, gatherings of voters to select delegates to the state conventions. Along with the New Hampshire primary the following week, Iowa's caucuses have become the starting points for choosing the two major-party candidates for president. The caucuses, held in January of the election year, involve people gathering in homes or public places and choosing their candidates, rather than casting secret ballots as is done in a primary election. The national and international media give Iowa (and New Hampshire) much of the attention accorded the national candidate selection process, which gives Iowa voters enormous leverage. Those who enter the caucus race often expend enormous effort to reach voters in each of Iowa's 99 counties.

Chicken with Feta and Tomatoes

¼ pound plain, dried bread crumbs
2 tablespoons fresh oregano leaves, chopped, divided
¾ teaspoon salt, divided
¾ teaspoon pepper, divided
4 (5-ounce) boneless, skinless chicken breast halves

2 tablespoons olive oil, divided
½ cup diced red onion
2 teaspoons chopped garlic
¼ cup ouzo (or dry white wine)
2 pounds plum tomatoes, peeled, seeded, cut into ¼-inch strips
½ cup crumbled feta cheese
2 tablespoons chopped fresh dill

In food processor, process bread crumbs, 1 tablespoon oregano, and ¼ teaspoon salt and pepper. Place mixture on wax paper and coat chicken breasts on both sides. In large skillet, heat 1 tablespoon olive oil over medium-high heat. Add chicken and cook for 7 minutes, turning once. Remove chicken to plate.

In same skillet, add remaining 1 tablespoon olive oil, onion, and garlic, and sauté 1 minute. Pour in ouzo. Raise heat to high. Add tomatoes and remaining ½ teaspoon salt and pepper. Cook until tomatoes are soft, about 3 minutes. Stir in remaining oregano. Spoon sauce over 4 dinner plates. Slice chicken, place on top of sauce, and sprinkle with feta cheese and chopped dill. Serves 4.

A Festival of Recipes (Ohio)

Crispy Herb Baked Chicken

⅔ cup Idaho "Spuds" potato flakes
¼ cup grated Parmesan cheese
2 teaspoons dried parsley flakes
¼ teaspoon garlic salt
⅛ teaspoon paprika

Dash of pepper
3–3½ pounds chicken, cut-up, skinned, rinsed, patted dry
⅓ cup butter or margarine, melted

Heat oven to 375°. Grease or line with foil a 10x15-inch baking pan or a 9x13-inch pan. In medium bowl, combine dry ingredients. Stir until well mixed. Dip chicken pieces into margarine. Roll in potato flake mixture to coat. Place in greased pan. Bake at 375° for 45–60 minutes or until chicken is tender and golden brown. Makes 4–5 servings.

Amish Country Cookbook III (Indiana)

Easy Grilled Chicken

Marinate skinless chicken pieces in Wishbone Italian Dressing for 4 hours or longer. Grill chicken 15 minutes on each side.

Recipes from "The Little Switzerland of Ohio" (Ohio)

Provolone Chicken

An impressive dish for a buffet dinner.

5 whole chicken breasts,
   deboned, cut in bite-size
   pieces, flattened
3 eggs, beaten
Seasoned bread crumbs
Butter

8 ounces fresh or canned
   mushrooms, sliced
1 cup chicken broth
6 ounces white wine
½ pound provolone cheese,
   grated

Marinate chicken in eggs while getting the rest of recipe together; drain each piece of chicken and roll in bread crumbs. Brown in butter until lightly brown on both sides. Transfer into a 9x13-inch casserole, layering in rows, overlapping pieces. Sauté mushrooms and arrange over chicken. Add chicken broth and wine. Cover and arrange over chicken. Add chicken broth and wine. Cover with grated cheese. Bake, covered, at 350°, for 30 minutes. Uncover and bake 15 minutes longer. Serve immediately. You can freeze, but add chicken broth, wine, and cheese just before baking.

Angels and Friends Cookbook II (Ohio)

Swiss Chicken Bake

This is great for company! Men love it!

WHITE SAUCE:

3 tablespoons butter
¼ cup all-purpose flour

½ cup white wine
1½ cups milk

Melt butter; add flour, and stir; gradually add milk and cook until thickened, then add wine.

CHICKEN:

5 whole chicken breasts,
   deboned
½ teaspoon salt
⅛ teaspoon pepper
2 eggs, beaten

1 cup bread crumbs
¼ cup oil
1 tablespoon butter
1 cup shredded Swiss cheese
Avocado and tomato slices

Pound out chicken ¼-inch thick; sprinkle with salt and pepper. Dip in beaten eggs, then crumbs. Brown in 2 tablespoons oil and 1 tablespoon butter, 2 minutes on each side, adding additional oil as needed. Arrange chicken in a 9x13-inch pan. Pour White Sauce over. Cover and chill several hours or overnight. Bake covered 50 minutes at 350°; sprinkle with cheese and arrange avocado and tomato slices on top. Bake 10 minutes more, uncovered. Serves 10.

Angels and Friends Cookbook I (Ohio)

Oven-Fried Chicken with Honey Butter Sauce

HONEY BUTTER SAUCE:

¼ cup butter, melted
¼ cup lemon juice

¼ cup honey

Melt butter in saucepan; blend in honey and lemon juice. Do not boil; set aside.

½ cup butter or margarine
1 cup all-purpose flour
2 teaspoons salt

¼ teaspoon pepper
2 teaspoons paprika
1 frying chicken, cut up

Melt butter in a shallow baking pan. Combine flour, salt, pepper, and paprika; dip chicken into flour mixture and then in butter, turning each piece. Arrange, skin-side down in a single layer; bake at 400° for 30 minutes. Turn and pour Honey Butter Sauce over all; bake another 30 minutes at 350° until chicken is tender.

Neighboring on the Air (Iowa)

Crispy Sesame Chicken

1¼ cups cornflake crumbs
¼ cup sesame seeds
¾ teaspoon paprika
¼ teaspoon salt
¼ teaspoon ground ginger

½ cup plain nonfat yogurt
2 tablespoons honey
8 skinned chicken breast halves
Vegetable cooking spray
2 tablespoons melted margarine

Combine first 5 ingredients in a large zip-lock plastic bag; set aside. Combine yogurt and honey in a shallow dish; stir well. Coat chicken pieces with yogurt mixture. Place chicken in zip-lock bag and shake to coat. Remove chicken from bag and place on baking sheet coated with vegetable spray. Drizzle with melted margarine. Bake at 400° for 45 minutes or until done.

Applause Applause (Iowa)

Ratatouille with Chicken and Pesto

The smell while this is cooking is almost as wonderful as the taste.

2 whole chicken breasts, boned,
  skinned
1 medium red onion, thinly
  sliced
1 medium green bell pepper,
  chopped
4 cloves garlic, crushed
¼ cup olive oil
1 small eggplant, chopped
Salt and black pepper to taste
2 small zucchini, cut into
  bite-size pieces

3 tablespoons chopped fresh basil
  or 1 tablespoon dried basil
2 teaspoons oregano
1 teaspoon thyme
4 medium tomatoes, peeled,
  seeded, chopped
8 ounces mushrooms, sliced
1 (8-ounce) can tomato sauce
Cayenne pepper to taste
½ cup orzo, cooked, drained

Rinse chicken and pat dry. Cut into thin slices. Sauté red onion, green pepper, and garlic in olive oil in a skillet for 2 minutes. Stir in eggplant. Sauté several minutes. Season with salt and black pepper. Stir in zucchini. Sauté 2 minutes.

Add chicken, basil, oregano, thyme, and additional black pepper; mix well. Cook over high heat until chicken is tender, stirring constantly. Stir in tomatoes, mushrooms, tomato sauce, and cayenne pepper. Adjust seasonings. Simmer, covered, until of desired consistency. Stir in orzo. May be prepared in advance, chilled until serving time and reheated on the stove or in the oven. Serves 6.

Generations (Illinois)

Easy Chicken à la King

An easy ladies' luncheon.

2 tablespoons butter
½ cup chopped onion
¼ cup chopped green bell
  pepper
1 (10¾-ounce) can cream of
  mushroom soup
1 (8-ounce) cream cheese,
  softened
Dash of pepper
1½ cups cubed, cooked
  chicken

1 (3-ounce) can mushrooms,
  sliced, undrained
2 tablespoons chopped canned
  pimento
2 tablespoons dry sherry
Pepperidge Farm frozen patty
  shells (baked according to
  directions)

In saucepan, cook onion and green pepper in butter until tender. Blend in soup, cheese, and pepper. Stir in chicken and mushrooms. Heat to boiling. Add pimento and sherry. Serve immediately in prepared patty shells. Garnish with fresh parsley. Serves 6.

Angels and Friends Cookbook I (Ohio)

Grandma Ratliff's Chicken & Dumplings

1 (5-pound) stewing chicken
1 teaspoon salt

1 cup milk

Place whole chicken in a large soup kettle and cover with water; add salt. Cook over low heat for approximately 3 hours or until meat is tender; remove chicken, reserving broth, and let chicken cool; debone. Heat chicken broth over medium heat; add milk and enough water to equal 2 gallons; bring to a boil. Carefully drop dumpling dough by large spoonfuls into boiling broth and cook for 20 minutes, stirring frequently. Reduce heat to low, add chicken back to kettle, and continue to cook for 5–10 minutes, or until broth thickens into a gravy. Serves 8–10.

GRANDMA'S DUMPLINGS:

4 cups self-rising flour
3 cups milk
1 cup chicken broth

¼ cup cooking oil
12 drops yellow food coloring
Salt and pepper to taste

In a mixing bowl, combine all ingredients. Mix well, then let rise for 5 minutes before adding to broth.

Ohio Cook Book (Ohio)

Chicken Pot Pie
with Cornbread Crust

1 (10-ounce) package frozen
  peas and carrots
½ cup chopped onion
½ cup chopped fresh or
  canned mushrooms
¼ cup margarine or butter
⅓ cup all-purpose flour
½ teaspoon salt
½ teaspoon crushed dried
  sage, marjoram, or thyme

⅛ teaspoon pepper
2 cups chicken broth
¾ cup milk
3 cups cubed cooked chicken
  or turkey
¼ cup snipped parsley
¼ cup chopped pimento
  (optional)
1 (7½-ounce) package corn
  muffin mix

Cook peas and carrots according to package directions; drain. In a saucepan, cook onion and mushrooms in margarine or butter until tender. Stir in flour, salt, sage, marjoram, or thyme, and pepper. Add chicken broth and milk all at once. Cook and stir until thickened and bubbly. Stir in drained peas and carrots, chicken or turkey, parsley, and pimento. Heat until bubbly. Pour chicken mixture into 6 round 10-ounce casseroles or a 7½x12-inch baking dish. Mix corn muffin mix according to package directions. Spoon mixture on top of casserole. Bake in 450° oven for 12–15 minutes or until muffin mix appears done.

Recipes & Remembrances (Ohio)

WWW.WIKIPEDIA.COM

The "Y" Bridge in Zanesville, Ohio, was proclaimed by "Ripley's Believe It or Not" as the only bridge in the world that you can cross and still be on the same side of the river. And it's the only bridge in the country with three ends. First built in 1814 to span the confluence of the Licking and Muskingum rivers, the structure has had several iterations that were washed away by serious floods before the U.S. Army Corps of Engineers constructed a series of dams and locks that now regulate the flow of the two rivers. The current concrete and steel bridge is the fifth built on the same location. It opened in 1984. The bridge is listed on the National Register of Historic Places.

Hash Brown Chicken Casserole

1 cooked chicken, boned, cut in
   bite-size pieces
1 (32-ounce) package hash
   brown potatoes
1 (10¾-ounce) can cream of
   chicken soup
1 pound Cheddar cheese,
   shredded

1 pint sour cream
1 small onion, diced
Salt and pepper to taste
1 stick margarine
2 cups crushed cornflakes

Mix together chicken and potatoes, soup, cheese, sour cream, onion, salt and pepper; place in a 9x13-inch baking pan. Melt margarine and mix with cornflake mixture. Bake at 350° for 1–1½ hours or until bubbly. Serves 12.

Celebrating Iowa (Iowa)

Lincoln Logs

1½ cups diced, cooked chicken
1½ cups bread crumbs
1 cup finely chopped walnuts
¼ cup finely chopped celery

¼ cup finely chopped onion
½ teaspoon salt
¼ teaspoon paprika
Bread crumbs

WHITE SAUCE:
½ cup chicken stock

½ cup cream

Mix chicken, bread crumbs, walnuts, celery, onion, salt, and paprika. Moisten with sauce. Form mixture into logs 3 inches long. Roll in bread crumbs and fry in oil. Drain and serve with White Sauce.

Cook Book: Favorite Recipes from Our Best Cooks (Illinois)

Iowa's Grilled Turkey Tenderloin

State Fair recipe from Iowa Turkey Foundation.

¼ cup soy sauce	¼ teaspoon ginger
¼ cup vegetable oil	Dash of black pepper
¼ cup dry sherry	Dash of garlic powder
2 tablespoons lemon juice	1 pound turkey tenderloins
2 tablespoons dehydrated onion	(¾- to 1-inch thick)

Blend all ingredients except turkey together in shallow pan for marinade with turkey tenderloins or steaks. Add turkey, turning to coat both sides. Cover and marinate in refrigerator several hours, turning occasionally. Grill over hot coals, 6–8 minutes per side depending on thickness.

Turkey steaks are done when there is no pink in center of meat. Do not overcook. Serves 3–4. Serve on fresh buns.

SEP Junior Women's Club 25th Anniversary Cookbook (Iowa)

Glazed Turkey Breast

This is the easiest way I know to have beautiful slices of moist turkey breast for a delicious low-fat main course.

1 (6- to 7-pound) turkey breast	1 (6½-ounce) can frozen apple
⅓ cup honey	juice (undiluted)
1 tablespoon dry mustard	

Preheat oven to 325°. Remove skin from turkey breast and insert meat thermometer into center of breast. Combine honey, dry mustard, and apple juice. Place turkey breast in a large roasting pan. Baste entire breast generously with apple juice mixture. Cover turkey breast and bake for one hour. Uncover and bake another hour or until meat thermometer registers 180°. Baste frequently after removing cover from turkey. Remove from oven and allow to cool 15–20 minutes before slicing. Serves 8–10.

New Tastes of Iowa (Iowa)

Almond Turkey Casserole

1 cup shredded Cheddar cheese,
  divided
1 tablespoon flour
3 cups chopped, cooked turkey
1½ cups sliced celery
⅔ cup slivered almonds,
  divided
1 cup mayonnaise

1 tablespoon lemon juice
½ teaspoon crushed dried
  oregano leaves
¼ teaspoon salt
¼ teaspoon pepper
1 (15-ounce) can Mandarin
  oranges, drained
Pastry for 2-crust (9-inch) pie

Preheat oven to 400°. Toss ¾ cup cheese with flour. Mix cheese mixture, turkey, celery, ⅓ cup almonds, mayonnaise, lemon juice, seasonings, and oranges. Roll pastry to 11x15-inch square on lightly floured surface. Place in a 9x13-inch baking dish; turn 1 inch beyond edge. Turn under edge; flute. Fill with turkey mixture. Top with remaining ¼ cup cheese and ⅓ cup almonds. Bake 30–35 minutes. Serves 6–8.

A Taste of Fishers (Indiana)

Crock-Pot Dressing

1 cup butter
3 cups chopped onion
3 cups chopped celery
⅜ cup chopped parsley sprigs
3 (4-ounce) cans sliced
  mushrooms
18–20 cups dry bread cubes
2¼ teaspoons sage

2¼ teaspoons salt
1½ teaspoons thyme
¾ teaspoon pepper
¾ teaspoon marjoram
1½ teaspoons poultry
  seasoning
4½–6 cups chicken broth
3 well-beaten eggs

Melt butter in skillet and sauté onion, celery, parsley, and mushrooms. Pour over bread cubes in a large bowl. Add all seasonings and mix well. Pour in enough broth to moisten. Add beaten eggs and mix together well. Pack lightly into a 6-quart slow-cooker. Cover and cook on HIGH for 45 minutes. Reduce to LOW 4–8 hours.

Visitation Parish Cookbook (Iowa)

Seafood

The Chicago Water Tower, built in 1869, was the only public building to survive the Great Chicago Fire of 1871. Though the fire was one of the largest U.S. disasters of the 19th century, the rebuilding spurred Chicago's development into one of the most populous and economically important American cities.

Brett's Dill Broiled Salmon

This is healthy, low in fat, and tastes great!

CUCUMBER-DILL SAUCE:

1 cup sour cream	1 teaspoon fresh dill or
1 cucumber, peeled, grated	2 teaspoons dried dill
1 tablespoon grated onion	½ teaspoon salt (optional)
1 tablespoon lemon juice	Pepper to taste

Combine sour cream, cucumber, onion, lemon juice, dill, salt and pepper to taste in bowl; mix well. Set aside and chill for 1 hour or longer.

1 teaspoon dried dill weed	6 salmon steaks
2 tablespoons white vinegar	Chopped parsley or paprika,
3 tablespoons oil	to taste
1 teaspoon lemon juice	1 lemon, sliced or cut into
1 teaspoon salt	wedges
Dash of pepper	

Combine dill weed, vinegar, oil, lemon juice, salt, and dash of pepper in mixer bowl; mix well. Let stand 1 hour.

Beat vinegar mixture again to mix well. Baste salmon with vinegar mixture; place on preheated greased rack in broiler pan. Broil 2 inches from heat source 5–8 minutes on each side or until fish flakes easily, basting with remaining vinegar mixture.

Serve with chilled Cucumber-Dill Sauce. Top with parsley or paprika and lemon slices. Yields 6 servings.

The Cubs 'R Cookin' (Illinois)

Salmon Patties

1 (16-ounce) can salmon
2 eggs
½ teaspoon salt
⅛ teaspoon pepper

1½ tablespoons grated onion
3 tablespoons sour cream
½ cup bread crumbs

Drain salmon; remove skin. Mash with fork. Add remaining ingredients. Divide into 8 patties and fry until golden brown in hot oil. Serves 6–8.

C-U in the Kitchen (Illinois)

Salmon Grilled with Red Onion Butter

2 (6-ounce) salmon fillets
Salt and pepper to taste

Olive oil

Season fillets. Brush with olive oil. Grill to medium.

RED ONION BUTTER:
1 red onion, sliced
Pinch of salt
1 cup red wine
2 tablespoons cream
1 pound unsalted butter,
  softened

Salt and pepper to taste
Carrot curls for garnish
Zucchini and squash slices
  for garnish
Daikon slices for garnish
  (Japanese mild radish)

Sweat onion in a little butter with a pinch of salt covering pan and cooking 5 minutes. The moisture will be drawn out of the onion without caramelizing onion. Add red wine. Reduce, then add cream; reduce until thick. Whip in softened butter, one chunk at a time. Season with salt and pepper to taste. Place salmon on plate; put Red Onion Butter on side. Garnish with fresh vegetables. Yields 2 servings.

From Melange Restaurant, Wilmette, Illinois.
Best Recipes of Illinois Inns and Restaurants (Illinois)

Red Snapper in Mayonnaise

While waiting for a fishing boat to dock, we heard the woes heaped on those sly fishmongers who dripped blood on the eyes and gills of fish to make them appear fresher—they straightway landed in jail! Against such deception, Greek people market with sharp eyes, looking for the characteristics of fresh fish. Pink eyes, pink gills, firm scales and back, and a fresh sea smell. After cooking, a fresh fish emerges tender and succulent, with white, flaky meat and white bones. And in the city of Chicago, people know and expect to buy "catch" fresh fish—period!

6 pounds whole fresh red snapper	**3 bay leaves**
Salt	**½ teaspoon salt**
Juice of 2 limes	**6 small potatoes**
2 tablespoons olive oil	**Mayonnaise**

Wash fish thoroughly in cold water; pat dry with a paper towel. Rub fish with salt and fresh lime juice, including the cavity. Set aside for ½ hour.

To cook fish, use a flat pot with a rack, or wrap fish in a very porous, clean cheesecloth, and place fish flat in bottom of pot. Pour in enough hot water to barely cover the fish; add olive oil, bay leaves, and salt. Simmer 20–25 minutes, or until cooked. Carefully unwrap fish and gently place on a wide-lipped platter. Set aside to cool.

Boil potatoes, peel, and quarter. Place around fish in platter. Serve with mayonnaise. Makes 6–8 servings.

Garnish: 4 hard-boiled eggs, sliced and placed all over fish. Arrange and decorate fish platter with black olives, sliced gherkins, radishes, chopped parsley, and grated nutmeg.

Opaa! Greek Cooking Chicago Style (Illinois)

Lake Erie Potato-Fried Fish

1½ pounds white bass, yellow
    perch, or other fillets
1 teaspoon salt
¼ teaspoon pepper
1 egg, beaten

1 tablespoon water
1 cup instant mashed potatoes
1 package onion or Italian salad
    dressing mix
Cooking oil

Sprinkle fish fillets with salt and pepper. In a bowl, beat together egg and water. In another bowl, combine potato flakes and dressing mix. Dip fish into egg mixture to coat, then dredge in potato flake mixture. Heat ⅛ inch oil in a skillet. Add fish and over moderate heat, fry for 4–5 minutes per side. Drain on paper towels.

Ohio Cook Book (Ohio)

Butter-Herbed Baked Fish

⅔ cup finely crushed saltines
½ teaspoon each: basil,
    oregano, and salt
¼ teaspoon garlic powder

¼ cup Parmesan cheese
½ cup butter, melted
1 pound white fish fillets such as
    halibut or orange roughy

Preheat oven to 350°. Mix crumbs, herbs, and Parmesan cheese. Dip fish in butter, then in crumbs. Arrange in baking dish and bake 25–30 minutes. Serves 3–4.

Still Gathering (Illinois)

Pan-Fried Halibut à la Sherry

As far as I am concerned, the best way to eat fish is fried. I love the east-ern shore where people don't turn up their noses at frying fish. The fish should be crunchy on the outside and moist and juicy on the inside. Halibut is not usually fried, but I love my recipe for preparing it this way.

4 halibut fillets	¼ cup fresh but dry bread
1 cup white wine	crumbs (or Japanese panko
1 cup heavy cream	crumbs)
1 teaspoon salt	Canola oil
1 teaspoon pepper	Lemon wedges
1 cup all-purpose flour	

Drip fillets in white wine and then cream. Season filets with salt and pepper, then dip in flour and crumbs; shake off any excess breading. Pour ¼ inch canola oil in a pan and fry fillets until golden on both sides. Serve with lemon and tartar sauce. Yields 4 servings.

TARTAR SAUCE:

½ small yellow onion, minced	Dash of Tabasco
2 tablespoons apple cider	1 cup mayonnaise
vinegar	1 teaspoon freshly chopped dill,
3 tablespoons sugar	or ¼ teaspoon dried
½ cup chopped sweet pickles	

Mix onion, vinegar, and sugar in a medium mixing bowl and let it sit for 5 minutes. Stir in rest of ingredients. Season to taste with salt, pepper, and a few drops of Tabasco. Store in refrigerator until fish is ready.

A Taste of the Murphin Ridge Inn (Ohio)

Was Ohio the 17th state or the 48th state to be admitted to the Union? History tells us it was the 17th, but a little digging shows that on the eve of its 2003 bicentennial, Ohio discovered that Congress never officially voted on statehood in 1803, and didn't formally do so until 1953. That makes it the 48th state, not the 17th! Well, Ohio decided to go ahead and celebrate its bicentennial in 2003, rather than wait another 150 plus years.

Foil Wrapped Halibut Steaks

2 (8-ounce) halibut steaks
1 tablespoon margarine
¼ fresh lemon (wedge)
½ teaspoon parsley flakes
½ teaspoon paprika
¼ teaspoon garlic powder
¼ teaspoon lemon pepper

4 slices fresh jumbo mushrooms
1 tablespoon sliced green bell
  peppers
1 tablespoons sliced carrots
1 tablespoon chopped green
  onion

Cut foil large enough to hold each halibut steak individually (2 pieces foil for each steak). This can be cut in the shape of a fish, if you like. Spray each piece of foil with non-stick coating, or just oil each piece of foil lightly. Dot fish with margarine and squeezed fresh lemon wedge. Sprinkle with parsley, paprika, garlic powder, and lemon pepper. Arrange veggies on steak. Seal package tightly with second piece of foil. Bake 30 minutes at 400° or grill 10 minutes per side.

The Fishlady's Cookbook (Illinois)

Best Grilled Tuna

Fresh chopped garlic to taste
1 medium bunch scallions,
  chopped
1½ cups olive oil

½ cup Tamari (light soy)
Juice of 4 limes
4 tuna steaks (the redder, the
  fresher)

Mix chopped garlic and scallions with olive oil, Tamari, and lime juice. Marinate tuna steaks in this for 2–3 hours in refrigerator, turning often. Grill tuna on very hot barbecue grill, basting with reserved marinade. Grill about 2–3 minutes each side for very rare, or about 4 minutes each side for medium. Serves 4.

Champions: Favorite Foods of Indy Car Racing (Indiana)

Thai Crab Cakes
with Cilantro-Peanut Sauce

A new twist on an old standby!

CRAB CAKES:

1¼ cups fresh bread crumbs
1 cup chopped fresh bean
  sprouts
¼ cup finely chopped green
  onions
¼ cup coarsely chopped fresh
  cilantro

2 tablespoons fresh lime juice
⅛ teaspoon cayenne pepper
1 egg, lightly beaten
1 egg white, lightly beaten
1 pound lump crabmeat, picked
  over
2 tablespoons olive oil, divided

Combine bread crumbs, bean sprouts, onions, cilantro, juice, cayenne pepper, egg, egg white, and crabmeat in a medium bowl. Cover and chill 1 hour. Divide mixture into 8 equal portions. Shape each portion into a ½-inch-thick patty. Heat 1 tablespoon oil in a large nonstick skillet over medium heat. Add 4 patties and cook 3 minutes on each side or until lightly browned. Remove patties and keep warm. Wipe skillet clean with paper towels. Re-coat skillet with remaining tablespoon oil and cook remaining 4 patties. Serve with Cilantro-Peanut Sauce.

CILANTRO-PEANUT SAUCE:

¼ cup balsamic vinegar
2½ tablespoons granulated
  sugar
2 tablespoons brown sugar
2 tablespoons low-sodium soy
  sauce
½ teaspoon dried red pepper
  flakes

⅛ teaspoon salt
1 clove garlic, minced
2 tablespoons creamy peanut
  butter
½ cup chopped fresh cilantro
2 tablespoons chopped fresh
  mint

Combine vinegar, sugars, soy sauce, pepper flakes, salt, and garlic in a small saucepan. Bring to a boil, stirring frequently. Remove from heat. Add peanut butter and stir with a whisk until smooth; cool. Stir in cilantro and mint. Yields 4 servings.

Note: Fresh bread crumbs make the difference in this recipe—don't use dried!

Causing A Stir (Ohio)

Baked Shrimp

Quite shrimply, the best! This is one of the easiest and most successful dinner parties to give. Figure at least ½ pound of shrimp per person. Cover your table with newspapers. Use paper plates. Have plenty of paper napkins—people eat so enthusiastically, the sauce runs down to their elbows. Make a simple tossed salad with dressing and chunks of blue cheese. Put pan of shrimp in the middle of the table, flank it with loaves of crusty bread for dipping, and watch people wade in. The shrimp are tender and flavorful, and the sauce is a miracle. There's so much of it, you think it will go to waste. Instead, it goes to waist, because the bread sopped in the sauce is phenomenal.

This can be expensive, but I watch the grocery ads for sales on shrimp. Sometimes you can find a truck on a corner selling fresh shrimp. Put these in clean containers, fill them with water and freeze. When you use the shrimp, they'll taste as if they're only 2 minutes from the ocean.

**2 pounds raw, frozen
  shrimp-in-the-shell
1 cup butter**

**1 cup margarine
¼ cup Worcestershire**

Run shrimp under cold water to remove the frost. Place shrimp and sauce (melted butter and margarine mixed with Worcestershire) in a 9x13-inch pan. Bake uncovered at 350° for 30 minutes.

The Lucy Miele 6-5-4- Cookbook (Illinois)

PHOTO BY RICK DIKEMAN

Built in 1914, Wrigley Field is the oldest National League ballpark and the second oldest active major league ballpark (after Fenway Park which opened on April 20, 1912). Located in Chicago, Illinois, Wrigley is home to the Chicago Cubs. In 1926, the ballpark was renamed from Cubs Park to Wrigley Field in honor of its new owner, William Wrigley, Jr. (of chewing gum fame). Many firsts were started at Wrigley Field, including permanent concession stands and permission for fans to keep foul balls that are hit into the stands. The scoreboard was constructed in 1937 and is still manually operated. After more than 5,000 afternoon games, lights were added, and in August 1988, the first night game was held at the ballpark.

Basil and Garlic Shrimp and Scallops

The mild flavors of these ingredients compliment each other.

1 tablespoon light butter
1 teaspoon Mrs. Dash Tomato
  Basil Seasoning Blend
1 tablespoon minced garlic
1 (20-ounce) bag frozen bay
  scallops, thawed

1 (16-ounce) bag frozen fully
  cooked and cleaned salad
  shrimp, thawed

In large, 12-inch nonstick skillet over medium heat, melt butter with seasoning blend and garlic. Add scallops. Cook 2–3 minutes. Turn scallops; continue cooking another 2–3 minutes or until scallops are white throughout. Add shrimp; cover; reduce heat to low. Cook 1 minute or until shrimp are fully heated. Remove from heat; serve immediately. Yields 4 (⅔-cup) servings.

Busy People's Low-Carb Cookbook

Sandy's Spicy Shrimp

½ teaspoon cayenne
½ teaspoon black pepper
½ teaspoon salt
½ teaspoon crushed red
  pepper
½ teaspoon crushed thyme
  leaves
1 teaspoon crushed dried
  basil leaves

½ teaspoon crushed dried
  oregano
2 dozen large or 1 pound
  medium shrimp
⅓ cup margarine
1½ teaspoons minced garlic
1 teaspoon Worcestershire
¼ cup beer
1 cup diced tomatoes

Combine first 7 spices; mix with shrimp. Melt butter, sauté garlic; add shrimp, Worcestershire, beer, and tomatoes. Cook until shrimp is done and sauce is somewhat reduced. Serve with rice.

I Love You (Iowa)

Cakes

A blimp is an unusual site in most cities. Here, four Goodyear blimps fly in formation over the company's Wingfoot Lake airship hangar near Akron. Goodyear blimps have adorned the skies since 1925 as very visible corporate icons of the world's largest tire and rubber company that began operations in 1898.

Mocha Torte Cake

A family tradition—if you like coffee flavor, you'll like this.

3 eggs, well beaten
1 cup plus 2 tablespoons sugar,
  divided
4 tablespoons coffee, strong and
  cold, divided

1 cup all-purpose flour
1 teaspoon baking powder
Pinch of salt
1 pint cream

Add 1 cup sugar and 2 tablespoons coffee to beaten eggs, beating thoroughly. Add (sifted together) flour, baking powder, and salt. Bake in 2 (8-inch) layer pans at 325° for 22 minutes or longer. When cake is cold, whip cream. Add remaining 2 tablespoons sugar and cold coffee. Spread between layers and on sides and top of cake.

Also, make an icing, using 1 cup powdered sugar mixed with 2 tablespoons coffee and drizzle over all whipped cream areas. It is best placed in freezer, but can be kept in refrigerator. Serve cold.

Sharing Our Best (Indiana)

Cappuccino-Chocolate Coffee Cake

⅓ cup flaked coconut
¼ cup chopped nuts
½ cup sugar, divided
3 tablespoons butter or
  margarine, melted, divided
2 cups Bisquick mix

⅔ cup milk
1 egg
⅓ cup semisweet chocolate
  chips, melted
2 teaspoons powdered instant
  coffee

Heat oven to 400°. Grease an 8x8-inch square pan. Mix coconut, nuts, ¼ cup sugar, and 1 tablespoon butter. Set aside. Beat remaining ingredients, except chocolate chips and coffee, in large bowl on low speed 30 seconds, scraping bowl constantly. Beat on medium speed 4 minutes, scraping bowl occasionally. Pour into pan.

Stir together chocolate and coffee; spoon over batter. Lightly swirl chocolate mixture through batter several times with knife for marbled effect. Sprinkle coconut mixture evenly over top. Bake 20–25 minutes or until golden brown. Serve warm.

Food for Thought (Ohio)

Mocha and Cherry Cake

2 cups granulated sugar
1¾ cups all-purpose flour
¾ cup unsweetened cocoa
   powder
2 teaspoons baking soda
1 teaspoon baking powder
½ teaspoon salt

½ cup egg substitute
1 cup nonfat buttermilk
1 cup strong coffee, cooled
½ cup applesauce
2 teaspoons vanilla
1 can Betty Crocker Light
   Fudge Icing

Preheat oven to 350°. In a very large mixing bowl, combine sugar, flour, cocoa powder, baking soda, baking powder, and salt. Add egg substitute, buttermilk, coffee, applesauce, and vanilla. Beat with electric mixer on low speed 30 seconds until combined, then 2 minutes at medium speed. Spray 2 (9-inch) round cake pans with butter-flavored spray; sprinkle with cocoa powder. Pour batter into pans. Bake 25–30 minutes or until cakes test done. Cool on rack 10 minutes. Remove from pans. Cool. Split each cake horizontally to make 4 layers total.

FILLING:

2½ cups fat-free ricotta
   cheese
½ cup granulated sugar
⅓ cup miniature semisweet
   chocolate chips

½ cup chopped maraschino
   cherries, well drained

Combine ricotta cheese, sugar, and chocolate chips. Gently stir in cherries. Place one cake layer on a serving plate. Spread ⅓ of filling on bottom layer of cake. Top with another cake layer. Continue layering Filling and cake, ending with cake. Ice with Betty Crocker Light Fudge Icing. Makes 14–16 servings.

The Heart of Cooking II (Indiana)

Kahlúa Mousse Cake

CRUST:

½ cup graham cracker crumbs
½ cup finely chopped walnuts
1 cup finely chopped almonds

½ cup sugar
1 stick unsalted butter, melted

Preheat oven to 350°. Lightly oil a 9½ x 2-inch springform pan. In a bowl, stir together ingredients until combined well; press onto bottom of pan. Bake Crust in middle of oven 15 minutes, or until pale golden. Cool in pan on a rack.

CHOCOLATE LAYER:

2 cups heavy cream
16 ounces semisweet chocolate, chopped coarsely

2 tablespoons light corn syrup
1 stick unsalted butter, cut into pieces

In a saucepan, heat cream, chocolate, and corn syrup over moderately high heat, stirring occasionally, until chocolate is melted and mixture just comes to a boil. Remove pan from heat and stir in butter, one piece at a time, until smooth. Pour mixture over Crust in pan and chill, until firm, about 3 hours.

BUTTER CREAM LAYER:

1½ cups sugar
½ cup water
6 large egg yolks
3 sticks unsalted butter, softened

½ cup Kahlúa
4 ounces semisweet chocolate, chopped, melted, cooled

In a saucepan, cook sugar and water over moderately high heat, stirring occasionally, until sugar is melted. Simmer syrup, undisturbed, until a candy thermometer registers 240°.

In a bowl with an electric mixer, beat yolks until smooth. Add hot syrup in a stream, beating on high speed until thickened and cooled. Reduce speed to medium and beat in butter, a little at a time. Beat in Kahlúa and chocolate until combined well. Spread Butter Cream over Chocolate Layer and chill until firm, about 3 hours. Run a knife around edge of pan and carefully remove side of pan. Serves 6–8.

Recipes and Remembrances: Around St. George's Tables (Ohio)

Easy and Delicious Amaretto Cake

1½ cups chopped toasted
  almonds, divided
1 (18¼-ounce) package yellow
  cake mix (without pudding)
1 (4-ounce) package vanilla
  instant pudding mix
4 eggs
½ cup vegetable oil

¾ cup water, divided
¾ cup amaretto, divided
1½ teaspoons almond extract,
  divided
½ cup sugar
2 tablespoons butter or
  margarine

Sprinkle 1 cup almonds in bottom of well-greased and floured 10-inch tube pan. Set aside. In mixing bowl, combine cake mix, pudding mix, eggs, oil, ½ cup water, ½ cup amaretto, and 1 teaspoon almond extract. Beat on low speed of electric mixer until dry ingredients are moistened. Beat on medium speed for 4 minutes. Stir in remaining ½ cup almonds. Pour batter into prepared tube pan. Bake at 325° for 1 hour, or until toothpick inserted in center comes out clean. Cool in pan for 10–15 minutes. Remove from pan and cool completely.

For glaze, combine sugar, remaining ¼ cup water, and butter in small saucepan. Bring to a boil, reduce heat to medium, and gently boil, stirring occasionally, for 4–5 minutes (until sugar dissolves). Remove from heat and cool 15 minutes. Stir in remaining ¼ cup amaretto and remaining ½ teaspoon almond extract. Punch holes in top of cake with wooden pick. Slowly spoon glaze on top of cake, allowing it to soak into cake. Yields 16 servings.

With Great Gusto (Ohio)

Bourbon Pecan Cake

2 teaspoons nutmeg
½ cup bourbon
1½ cups sifted all-purpose
  flour, divided
2 cups pecans
1 cup finely chopped raisins

½ cup butter, softened
1 cup plus 2 tablespoons sugar
3 eggs, separated
1 teaspoon baking powder
Dash of salt
Pecan halves

Preheat oven to 325°. Grease a 10-inch tube pan. Soak nutmeg in bourbon. Mix ½ cup flour with nuts and raisins, coating thoroughly. Reserve.

   Cream butter and sugar until light and fluffy. Add egg yolks, one at a time, beating well after each addition. Beat in remaining flour, baking powder, and salt. Beat in bourbon-nutmeg mixture and continue beating until batter is well mixed. Add nuts and raisins. Beat egg whites until very stiff; fold in. spoon batter into pan. Press down firmly to squeeze out air pockets and allow to stand 10 minutes. Bake at 325° for 1¼ hours or until cake tests done. Cool in pan, right-side-up, 1–2 hours before turning out. Continue cooling.

Note: This cake improves with age. Store in a covered container for several days, wrapped in a bourbon-soaked napkin.

The Conner Prairie Cookbook (Indiana)

Wasp's Nest Cake

1 (3-ounce) box cook and serve
  vanilla pudding
2 cups milk
1 (18¼-ounce) box yellow cake
  mix

1 (12-ounce) package butterscotch
  morsels

On stove top, mix puffing with milk in saucepan, and bring to a boil. Dump in cake mix. Stir and pour into a greased 9x13-inch pan. Sprinkle butterscotch morsels on top. Bake in 350° oven for 30 minutes. Let cool; serve.

Taste & See (Indiana)

Pigout Cake

1 (18¼-ounce) box yellow
   cake mix
2 egg whites, slightly whipped

1 (3-ounce) package instant
   chocolate pudding
2 cups lukewarm water

Mix well and put in greased 9x13-inch pan. Bake 25–35 minutes at 350°. Cool and frost.

FROSTING:
¼ cup softened margarine
1 cup powdered sugar
1 (8-ounce) carton Cool Whip

Heath or Skor candy bars,
   crushed

Mix margarine and powdered sugar. Fold in Cool Whip. Frost cake and sprinkle crushed Heath or Skor candy bars on top. Refrigerate.

Home Cooking with the Cummer Family (Iowa)

"Disorderly Conduct" Cake

1 cup flaked coconut
1 cup chopped pecans
1 (18¼-ounce) package German
   chocolate cake mix

1 stick butter, softened
1 (8-ounce) package cream
   cheese, softened
1 pound confectioners' sugar

Grease and flour a 9x13-inch pan. Spread coconut and pecans in pan. Prepare cake mix according to package directions. Pour batter over pecans and coconut. Mix butter, cream cheese, and sugar. Drop by teaspoons over batter. Bake at 350° for 45 minutes. Cake will be shaky but will set up.

Favorite Recipes from the Delaware Police Department (Ohio)

Red Velvet Cake

4 (½-ounce) bottles red food
  coloring
3 tablespoons cocoa
½ cup vegetable shortening
1½ cups granulated sugar
2 eggs

1 teaspoon vanilla
2¼ cups sifted cake flour
1 teaspoon salt
1 cup buttermilk
1 tablespoon vinegar
1 teaspoon baking soda

Mix food coloring with cocoa; set aside. Beat shortening with sugar. Add eggs, one at a time, beating after each addition. Add food coloring mixture and vanilla. Alternately add flour, salt, and buttermilk. Beat well. Stir in vinegar and baking soda. Bake in 350° for 30 minutes.

FROSTING:

1 stick butter or margarine,
  softened
8 tablespoons vegetable
  shortening

2 cups powdered sugar
3 tablespoons flour
2–3 teaspoons milk
1 teaspoon vanilla

Mix butter until fluffy. Add shortening, one tablespoon at a time, and beat until fluffy. Add sugar, flour, milk, and vanilla; beat well. Do not cook. Ice cooled cake.

Good Cookin' Cookbook (Illinois)

WIKIPEDIA.COM

On November 4, 2008, Barack Obama defeated John McCain in the general election and became the first African/American American to be elected president of the United States. In his victory speech, delivered before a crowd of hundreds of thousands of his supporters in Chicago's Grant Park, Obama proclaimed that "change has come to America." Obama was the junior United States Senator from Illinois from 2005 until he resigned following his election to the presidency. He was inaugurated as the nation's 44th president on January 20, 2009.

Mrs. Lincoln's White Cake

1 cup butter, softened
2 cups sugar
3 cups cake flour
2 teaspoons baking powder
1 cup milk
1 teaspoon vanilla

1 teaspoon almond extract
1 cup chopped blanched
  almonds
6 egg whites
¼ teaspoon salt

Cream butter and sugar until light and fluffy. Sift together flour and baking powder; remove 2 tablespoons; set aside. Add sifted ingredients, alternating with milk, to creamed mixture. Stir in vanilla and almond extract. Combine almonds with reserved flour and add to batter. Beat egg whites until stiff; add salt. Fold into batter.

Pour into 3 greased and floured 8- or 9-inch cake pans. Bake at 350^ until a cake tester comes out clean, 20–25 minutes. Cool 5–10 minutes; remove from pans and cool on racks. Frost.

FROSTING:
2 cups sugar
1 cup water
2 egg whites
½ cup chopped candied
  cherries

½ cup chopped candied
  pineapple
Few drops vanilla or almond
  extract

Combine sugar and water in saucepan, stirring until sugar is dissolved. Bring to a boil; cover and cook about 3 minutes until steam has washed down any sugar crystals that may have formed on side of pan. Uncover and cook until syrup reaches 238°–240°.

Whip egg whites constantly until Frosting is spreading consistency. Add cherries, pineapple, and flavoring.

Honest to Goodness (Illinois)

Bavarian Apple Torte

½ cup butter or margarine,
  softened
⅓ cup sugar

¼ teaspoon vanilla
1 cup all-purpose flour
½ cup chopped pecans

CREAM CHEESE FILLING:
1 (8-ounce) package cream
  cheese
¼ cup sugar

1 egg
½ teaspoon vanilla

APPLE TOPPING:
4 cups peeled, cored, sliced
  apples

½ cup sugar
½ teaspoon ground cinnamon

Cream butter and sugar in a small mixing bowl. Stir in vanilla. Add flour; mix well. Spread in bottom and 2 inches up the sides of a greased 9-inch springform pan. Spread Cream Cheese Filling evenly over pastry. Spoon Apple Topping over Filling. Sprinkle with nuts the last 10 minutes of baking. Bake at 450° for 10 minutes. Reduce temperature to 400° and bake for 25 minutes. Cool before removing from pan.

25th Anniversary Cookbook (Ohio)

Apple Dapple Cake

2 cups sugar
1 cup vegetable oil
3 eggs
3 cups all-purpose flour
1 teaspoon baking soda
1 teaspoon salt

1 teaspoon ground cinnamon
2 teaspoons vanilla
3 cups chopped, peeled apples
2 cups flaked coconut
1 cup chopped dates
1 cup chopped pecans

Mix together sugar and oil. Add eggs and beat well. Blend in flour, baking soda, salt, cinnamon, and vanilla. Stir in apples, coconut, dates, and pecans. Spoon batter into prepared 9- or 10-inch tube pan. Bake 1½ hours at 350°, or until wooden pick inserted in cake comes out clean. Remove immediately.

CARAMEL TOPPING:
1 cup brown sugar, firmly
  packed

½ cup milk
½ cup butter

Combine ingredients in saucepan; heat and stir until blended. Boil 2 minutes. Pour hot topping over hot cake and allow to soak in.

Old-Fashioned Cooking (Illinois)

Apple Baba

4 tart apples, such as Granny
    Smith, peeled, cored,
    quartered, thinly sliced
    crosswise
2¼ cups sugar, divided
1 teaspoon ground cinnamon
4 large eggs
1 cup vegetable oil
½ cup fresh orange juice
2 teaspoons vanilla extract
4 cups unbleached flour
1 teaspoon baking powder
Confectioners' sugar for
    garnish

Preheat oven to 350°. Grease a 10-inch tube pan. Place apples in a large bowl; sprinkle with ¼ cup sugar and cinnamon; set aside. In a large bowl, beat eggs and remaining 2 cups sugar with electric mixer until pale yellow and thick. Gradually beat in oil, orange juice, and vanilla extract.

Sift together flour and baking powder. Gradually add to egg mixture, stirring with a large wooden spoon. You will have a batter the consistency of thick honey. Fold apples into batter, making sure they are well distributed. Pour apple batter into prepared pan, and smooth top with rubber spatula. Bake until top is well browned and splitting, about 1¼ hours. Invert baba onto a rack and cool. Sprinkle with confectioners' sugar before serving. Serves 8–10.

Recipes and Remembrances: Around St. George's Tables (Ohio)

Carrot-Apple Cake

1½ cups sugar
1½ cups vegetable oil
3 eggs
2 teaspoons vanilla
2 cups sifted all-purpose flour
2 teaspoons cinnamon

1 teaspoon each: baking soda,
  baking powder, and salt
2 cups shredded carrots
1 cup coarsely-chopped apples
1 cup raisins
1 cup chopped pecans

Combine first 4 ingredients in a large bowl; blend. Add sifted dry ingredients to first mixture and mix. Stir in remaining ingredients. Bake in 2 greased and paper-lined 9-inch pans or a 9x13-inch pan. Bake at 350° for 35–45 minutes. Cool 10 minutes. Frost with Pecan Cream Cheese Frosting.

PECAN CREAM CHEESE FROSTING:

2 (3-ounce) packages cream
  cheese, softened
1 tablespoon milk
2 teaspoons vanilla

Dash of salt
1 pound powdered sugar
½ cup chopped pecans

Blend first 4 ingredients thoroughly. Beat in sugar until smooth and spreading consistency. Fold in nuts. This makes a lot of frosting and will frost top and sides of layer cake.

Lutheran Church Women Cookbook (Iowa)

Indiana Limestone is a common term for Salem limestone, primarily quarried in south central Indiana. Bloomington, Indiana, has been noted to have the highest quality quarried limestone in the United States. Buildings such as the Empire State Building, the Pentagon, and 35 of the 50 state capitol buildings are made of Indiana limestone.

Orange Carrot Cake

1 cup butter, softened
2 cups sugar
1 teaspoon cinnamon
½ teaspoon nutmeg
1 tablespoon grated orange rind
4 eggs
1½ cups grated carrots
⅔ cup chopped walnuts or
    pecans
3 cups sifted all-purpose flour
3 teaspoons baking powder
½ teaspoon salt
⅓ cup orange juice

In large bowl, cream butter and sugar. Add cinnamon, nutmeg, and orange rind. Beat in eggs, one at a time. Add carrots and nuts. Sift together flour, baking powder, and salt; add alternately with orange juice. Turn into a greased and floured 10-inch tube pan. Bake at 350° for 60–65 minutes, until tester comes out clean. Cool in pan 15 minutes. Turn out and cool completely on wire rack.

ORANGE GLAZE:
1½ cups sifted confectioners'
    sugar
1 tablespoon butter, softened
½ teaspoon grated orange rind
2–3 tablespoons orange juice

In small bowl, mix above ingredients and add enough juice to make a slightly runny Glaze. Pour over cake.

Women's Centennial Cookbook (Ohio)

Old-Fashioned Jelly Roll

¾ cup cake flour
¾ teaspoon baking powder
¼ teaspoon salt
4 eggs
¾ cup sugar
1 teaspoon vanilla
1 cup tart red jelly

Sift flour then measure. Combine baking powder, salt, and eggs in bowl. Beat with egg beater adding sugar gradually until mixture becomes thick and light colored. Gradually fold in flour, then vanilla. Turn into 10x15-inch pan, which has been lined with paper then greased. Bake in hot (400°) oven 13 minutes or until done. Turn cake out on cloth or towel, dusting with powdered sugar. Quickly remove paper and cut off crisp edges of cake. Roll and wrap in cloth. Let cool about 10 minutes, unroll, spread cake with jelly, and roll again. Wrap in cloth; place on cake rack to finish cooling.

Amish Country Cookbook I (Indiana)

Friendship Starter

This recipe trio has a "most often requested" status.

1 cup canned pineapple chunks **2 tablespoons brandy**
1 cup sugar

In large glass jar, combine pineapple chunks, sugar, and brandy, stirring well. Cover and let sit at room temperature for 2 weeks, stirring daily.

AFTER TWO WEEKS:
1 cup maraschino cherries with **1 cup sugar**
  liquid **2 tablespoons brandy**

Combine ingredients and add to first mixture. Let stand at room temperature for 2 weeks more, stirring daily.

AFTER SECOND TWO WEEKS:
1 cup sliced canned peaches
  with syrup

Add to above mixture; let stand at room temperature for 2 weeks more, stirring daily.

Finally, six weeks from starting time, drain fruit, reserving liquid. The liquid is the starter that will be used in the next step of the recipe. The fruit may be served over the top of ice cream if not used in a cake.

Festival Foods and Family Favorites (Indiana)

Because of its popular name, the post office in Santa Claus, Indiana, receives thousands of letters to Santa from all over the world each year. Volunteers known as "Santa's Elves" ensure each child receives a reply from Santa Claus; this tradition has been around since at least 1914. Every year, the post office also creates a special Christmas pictorial postmark for use during the month of December. This practice attracts mail from all over the world wishing to have the official Santa Claus postmark.

Friendship Extender

1½ cups Friendship Starter
   liquid
2–2½ cups sugar

1 (28-ounce) can sliced peaches
   with syrup

Combine in a large glass container and cover loosely; store at room temperature for 10 days, stirring daily.

AFTER 10 DAYS:

1 (16-ounce) can crushed
   pineapple with liquid

2½ cups sugar

Combine ingredients, add to above mixture. Store as before for 10 days, stirring daily.

AFTER 10 MORE DAYS:

2½ cups sugar
1 (16-ounce) can crushed
   pineapple with liquid

1 (10-ounce) jar maraschino
   cherries with syrup

Combine ingredients and add to above mixture. Store as before for 10 days, stirring daily. Note that 30 days have passed since you began this procedure. (This is the procedure your friends will follow when you have passed along some of your Starter liquid.)

ON THE 30TH DAY:

Drain liquid from fruit and divide fruit into 3 equal portions. Divide juice into 1½-cups portions and give to friends along with this 30-day recipe and the one that follows.

Festival Foods and Family Favorites (Indiana)

Friendship Cake

1 (18¼-ounce) box white or
  yellow cake mix, non-pudding
  variety
½–⅔ cup vegetable oil
1 (3.4-ounce) box vanilla or
  pineapple instant pudding

3 or 4 small eggs
About 2 cups drained fruit from
  Starter mixture
1 cup chopped nuts (optional)
1 (3½-ounce) can shredded
  coconut (optional)

Combine all ingredients and bake in a large greased and floured tube or Bundt cake pan for 50–60 minutes at 350°, or until cake tests done. Cake freezes well for up to 1 month and is delicious served with a dollop of whipped cream.

    Many people make up to 3 cakes, reserving one for themselves and sending the others along as part of their gift of Friendship Starter and the recipe.

Festival Foods and Family Favorites (Indiana)

Aunt Judy's Italian Cake

1 (18¼-ounce) box fudge marble
  cake mix
2 pounds ricotta cheese

4 eggs
1 cup sugar
1 teaspoon vanilla

Mix cake mix per instructions on box. Put into greased 9x13-inch pan, but do not bake yet. Mix ricotta cheese, eggs, sugar, and vanilla together. With large spoon, spoon the cheese mixture over top of cake. It should cover the entire surface. Bake at 350° for 1 hour and 5 minutes. Let cool well!

TOPPING:

1 (3-ounce) package instant
  chocolate fudge pudding
1 cup milk

1 (12-ounce) container Cool
  Whip

Mix pudding with milk and add Cool Whip. Spread on cake as frosting. This cake is best when baked the day before needed. Refrigerate.

Cookin' with Friends (Illinois)

Italian Cream Cake

5 eggs
½ cup margarine, softened
½ cup vegetable shortening
2 cups sugar
1 teaspoon baking soda
1 cup buttermilk

2 cups flour, sifted twice
1 (3½-ounce) can coconut
1 cup chopped nuts
1 teaspoon vanilla extract
1 teaspoon coconut flavor
  extract

Separate eggs and beat whites until stiff; set aside. Mix margarine and vegetable shortening until creamy; add sugar. Add egg yolks, one at a time, beating well after each addition. Dissolve baking soda in buttermilk; add alternately with flour; beat well. Add coconut, nuts, and extract flavors. Fold in stiffly-beaten egg whites. Pour into 3 separate greased and floured 9-inch cake pans using approximately 2 cups batter for each pan. Bake in preheated 350° oven for 25 minutes. Spread Cream Cheese icing between layers and on top and sides of cooled cake.

CREAM CHEESE ICING:

1 (8-ounce) package cream
  cheese, softened
½ cup margarine

1 (1-pound) box powdered sugar
1 teaspoon almond extract

Combine ingredients and beat well.

Indiana's Finest Recipes (Indiana)

LIBRARY OF CONGRESS

Carl Sandburg (January 6, 1878–July 22, 1967) spent a lifetime exploring what it meant to be an American. Through his writing, he passionately championed for the everyday working person, those who may neither have had the words nor the power to speak for themselves. Sandburg won Pulitzer prizes in history and poetry. He was always trying new forms of writing. The home where he was born in Galesburg, Illinois, is now a National Historic Site.

Filled Kugelhopf

5 egg yolks
½ cup sweet butter, softened
2 tablespoons sugar
2½ cups all-purpose flour, sifted
1 cake yeast, dissolved in ¼ cup milk
1 teaspoon vanilla
¼ teaspoon salt
Luke-warm sweet cream
Powdered sugar for dusting

Cream egg yolks, butter, and sugar until thick. Add flour, yeast, vanilla, salt, and enough cream to make a very delicate soft dough. Beat with a wooden spoon until dough is smooth, shiny, and no longer sticks to spoon. Cover and allow to rise double in size.

Now place half the dough into a large, well-buttered, deep, round cake or tube pan.

Spread Filling evenly over dough, then cover with the other half of dough. Cake pan should be half full. Allow to rise again for 20 minutes, until pan is filled. Bake in 325°–350° oven for 40–45 minutes or until fully baked. Remove immediately from pan to cool. Dust with powdered sugar and serve.

FILLING:
1 cup ground almonds or walnuts
½ cup finely chopped raisins
3 tablespoons sugar
½ teaspoon cinnamon
½ lemon rind, grated

Combine ingredients well.

Aunt Paula's American Hungarian Cookbook (Ohio)

Corn Cake

1 (16-ounce) can cream-style
  corn
½ cup brown sugar
¾ cup sugar
3 eggs
1 cup oil
1 tablespoon baking powder

2¼ cups all-purpose flour
1 teaspoon baking soda
1 teaspoon salt
1 teaspoon cinnamon
½ cup raisins
½ cup chopped nuts

Mix corn and sugar. Add eggs and oil. Beat well. Mix dry ingredients; add and mix well. Stir in raisins and nuts. Put in sprayed 9x13-inch pan. Bake at 350° for 30–35 minutes. Cool well.

FROSTING:

4 tablespoons margarine
½ cup brown sugar

¼ cup milk
2–3 cups powdered sugar

Bring margarine and sugar to a boil over medium heat. Take from heat; stir in milk. Stir in powdered sugar. Frost cooled cake.

Quasquicentennial / St. Olaf of Bode Cookbook (Iowa)

Cola Cake

2 cups all-purpose flour
2 cups sugar
2 tablespoons cocoa
1 cup margarine
1 cup cola
¼ teaspoon salt

½ cup buttermilk
1 teaspoon baking soda
1½ cups miniature
  marshmallows
2 eggs
1 teaspoon vanilla

Sift together flour, sugar, and cocoa. Heat margarine and cola to boiling. Pour over dry ingredients and mix well. Do not use mixer. Add salt, buttermilk, baking soda, marshmallows, eggs, and vanilla; mix well. Pour batter into greased 9x13-inch pan. Bake in preheated 350° oven 30–35 minutes.

FROSTING:

2 tablespoons cocoa
½ cup margarine
6 tablespoons cola

1 pound confectioners' sugar
1 teaspoon vanilla
1 cup chopped nuts

In small saucepan, combine cocoa, margarine, and cola. Heat to boiling. Pour over confections' sugar; mix well. Add vanilla and nuts; blend well. Spread over hot cake.

Treasured Recipes from Mason, Ohio (Ohio)

Tunnelfudge Muffins

This recipe will have many fans—kids, chocolate lovers, and the chef!

½ cup butter
⅓ cup water
5 squares semisweet chocolate
5 tablespoons cocoa
⅔ cup granulated sugar
2 cups all-purpose flour
1 tablespoon baking powder

¼ teaspoon salt
1 egg
½ cup milk
½ cup sour cream
2 teaspoons vanilla extract
12 Hershey's Kisses candies

Heat oven to 375°. In a small saucepan, melt butter over low heat. Add water and semisweet chocolate squares, and stir until chocolate is melted. Add cocoa and sugar, and cook 5 minutes until sugar is melted. Cool.

In a large bowl, sift together flour, baking powder, and salt. In another bowl, combine egg, milk, sour cream, and vanilla extract, and blend on low speed with an electric mixer. Make a well in the center of dry ingredients, and pour in egg mixture and cooled chocolate mixture. Blend at medium speed.

Fill greased muffin tins. Take one Hershey's Kisses candy and push it down into the center of each cup of batter. Bake 20 minutes or until a tester inserted into a muffin comes out clean. (Insert tester off center to avoid candy.) Cool. Makes 12 muffins.

Muffins—104 Recipes from A to Z (Illinois)

In the early 1900s, more than 198 models of automobiles were manufactured or assembled in 42 Indiana cities. The largest of Indiana's automobile manufacturers was the Studebaker Company. It produced its first car in 1901 and continued making automobiles until they closed in 1963. The Studebaker National Museum in South Bend is one of many classic car museums in Indiana. Others include: the Antique Auto Museum in Elkhart, the Classic Car Museum in Warsaw, the Door Prairie Museum in LaPorte, and the Auburn-Cord Dusenberg Museum in Auburn.

Iowa Dirt Cake

½ cup butter, softened
1 cup sugar
1 (8-ounce) package cream
  cheese, softened
2 packages chocolate or vanilla
  instant pudding

3½ cups milk
1 (12-ounce) container Cool
  Whip
1 (20-ounce) package Oreo
  Cookies, crushed

Blend butter, sugar, and cream cheese. Mix pudding with milk and fold in Cool Whip. Fold in cream cheese mixture. Put ⅔ of crushed Oreos in a 9x13-inch pan. Pat down. Cover with Cool Whip mixture. Sprinkle remaining Oreos on top. Refrigerate to set. You may want to decorate with gummy worms.

Fire Gals' Hot Pans Cookbook (Iowa)

Mt. Mama Mudslide Cake

1 stick margarine, softened
1 cup all-purpose flour
1 cup chopped pecans
1 (8-ounce) package cream
  cheese, softened
1 cup powdered sugar
1 (8-ounce) carton Cool Whip

1 (3.4-ounce) package chocolate
  instant pudding
1 (3.4-ounce) package vanilla
  instant pudding
2 cups cold milk
1 cup chocolate bar, grated

Combine margarine, flour, and nuts. Mix well and press into a 9x13-inch pan. Bake 20 minutes at 350°; let cool. Combine cream cheese and powdered sugar until fluffy. Fold in 1 cup Cool Whip.

Combine pudding mixes with milk. Mix until thick and creamy. Pour over cheese layer. Top with remaining Cool Whip. Grate chocolate bar over top.

Our Favorite Recipes (Indiana)

Special Lemon Cake

1 (18¼-ounce) box yellow
  cake mix
4 eggs
1½ teaspoons lemon extract

¾ cup oil
1 (3-ounce) package lemon
  Jell-O, dissolved in 1 cup
  hot water

Mix well. Bake in moderate 350° oven about 25 minutes. When done, prick with fork.

TOPPING:

1½ cups powdered sugar

2 tablespoons lemon juice

Mix well and put on top of warm cake. It will sink through the pricked holes.

Lehigh Public Library Cookbook (Iowa)

Sour Cream Lemon Pound Cake

1 cup butter, softened
3 cups sugar
6 eggs
¼ cup lemon juice
1 tablespoon grated lemon rind

3 cups all-purpose flour
½ teaspoon baking soda
½ teaspoon salt
1 cup sour cream

Cream butter and sugar. Add eggs, one at a time, beating well after each. Add lemon juice and rind. Mix flour, baking soda, and salt together and add alternately with sour cream to creamed mixture. Pour into greased and floured 10-inch angel food pan (16-cup size). Bake at 325° for 1 hour and 30 minutes, or until it tests done. Cool 15 minutes before turning out on rack to cool. If desired, a Lemon Glaze can be poured over cake.

LEMON GLAZE:

2 cups powdered sugar
¼ cup melted butter

2 tablespoons grated lemon rind
¼ cup lemon juice

Mix all ingredients together and beat until of spreading consistency.

Variations: Orange juice and grated orange rind can be substituted for lemon; 1/4 cup poppy seeds to 1/2 cup finely chopped pecans or walnuts can be added.

German Recipes (Iowa)

Orange Chiffon Cheesecake

CRUST:

1 cup graham cracker crumbs   ¼ cup margarine, melted

Spray a 9-inch springform pan with vegetable spray. Blend crumbs and margarine and press onto bottom of pan. Bake in 350° oven 8–10 minutes. Cool.

ORANGE FILLING:

1 cup orange juice
1 envelope unflavored gelatin
12 ounces low-fat cream cheese
    or cream cheese alternative
1 cup part skim ricotta cheese
12 packets Equal
1 packet sugar-free dessert
    topping

½ cup water
2 medium oranges, peeled,
    seeded, chopped
1 orange, peeled, sectioned, for
    garnish

Pour orange juice into small pan. Sprinkle gelatin over juice and let soften. Heat, stirring until gelatin dissolves. Blend cream cheese and ricotta in a large bowl until smooth. Prepare topping according to package directions, using ½ cup water. Add gelatin to cheese mixture, stirring in Equal. Fold whipped topping into cheese mixture. Stir in chopped oranges. Spoon into prepared Crust. Chill 6 hours or overnight. Garnish with orange sections at serving time. Yields 16 servings.

Tried and True Volume II: Diabetic Cookbook (Ohio)

Ohio has the largest Amish population in the world—more than 35,000. The Darwin D. Bearley Collection of Antique Ohio Amish Quilts contains some 150 quilts ranging from the 1880s through the 1940s. The Ohio Amish Quilts went through three phases. The first was the quilts produced in the late 19th century (1870–1900). These were made mostly in brown and other earth tones and occasionally reds, blues, and greens. In the second phase, which started at the turn of the century, black became a dominant color and was used until 1930. At this point, the third phase began and pastel colors were used exclusively. Colors like lavender, pink, pale green, and yellow are commonly found in the quilts from this period. These colors were also used in the Amish clothing of the same periods.

Mon Ami Oreo Cookie Cheesecake

CRUST:

1¼ cups Oreo cookie crumbs   **¼ cup melted butter**

Mix cookie crumbs with melted butter; press in bottom of 9-inch springform pan and refrigerate ½ hour.

FILLING:

2 pounds cream cheese, softened   **⅓ cup whipping cream**
1½ cups sugar, divided   **2 teaspoons vanilla, divided**
2 tablespoons flour   **1½ cups Oreo cookie crumbs**
4 extra-large eggs   **2 cups sour cream**
2 large egg yolks

In large mixer bowl, beat cream cheese until fluffy. Add 1¼ cups sugar and flour, then blend in eggs and yolks until smooth. Stir in cream and 1 teaspoon vanilla. Pour half this mixture into prepared pan, sprinkle with crumbs, and pour in remaining batter. Bake 15 minutes at 425°; reduce temperature to 225° and bake 50 minutes. Cover loosely with foil if browning too quickly. Increase temperature to 350°; blend sour cream, remaining ¼ cup sugar, and 1 teaspoon vanilla. Spread over cheesecake and bake 7 minutes. Refrigerate overnight. Top with Glaze and garnish.

GLAZE:

1 cup whipping cream, scalded   **1 teaspoon vanilla**
8 ounces semisweet chocolate

Combine scalded whipping cream with chocolate and vanilla, and stir one minute. Refrigerate 15 minutes before pouring over chilled cheesecake.

Recipe by Mon Ami Restaurant and Historic Winery, Port Clinton, Ohio.
Dining in Historic Ohio (Ohio)

Turtle Cheesecake

This cheesecake offers something for everyone—chocolate, caramel, and nuts.

1 cup graham cracker crumbs	1 pound cream cheese, softened
1 cup chocolate wafer crumbs	½ cup sugar
6 tablespoons margarine, melted	1 teaspoon vanilla extract
1 (14-ounce) bag caramels	2 eggs
1 (4-ounce) can evaporated milk	Pecan halves for garnish
1 cup chopped pecans, toasted	

Preheat oven to 350°. In a small bowl, combine crumbs with margarine. Press into bottom of 9-inch springform pan. Bake 10 minutes.

In a 1½-quart saucepan, melt caramels and milk over low heat. Stir until smooth. Reserve ¼–½ sauce for topping. Pour remainder over crust. Sprinkle pecans over caramel layer.

In a medium bowl, combine cream cheese, sugar, and vanilla. Mix at medium speed until well blended. Add eggs, one at a time. Mix well after each addition. Pour over pecans.

Place a 9x13-inch baking pan of water on center rack in oven. Increase oven temperature to 450°. When oven is ready, remove pan of water. Bake cheesecake for 10 minutes at 450°. Then reduce temperature to 250° and continue to bake for 30 minutes. At that time, turn oven off. Leave cheesecake in closed oven an additional 30 minutes. Do not open oven door.

At the end of that 30 minutes, crack oven door open with a hot pad and cool cheesecake another 30 minutes. Pour remaining caramel sauce over top. Garnish with pecan halves. When completely cool, refrigerate. Yields 10–12 servings.

Great Beginnings, Grand Finales (Indiana)

White Chocolate Cheesecake

CRUST:

1 cup crushed chocolate cookie wafers

2 tablespoons margarine, melted

Combine ingredients; mix well. Press in the bottom of springform pan. Set aside.

FILLING:

1 envelope unflavored gelatin
½ cup water
½ cup sugar
1 (8-ounce) package cream cheese, softened

1 cup sour cream
6 ounces white baking chocolate, melted
1 cup whipping cream
½ teaspoon vanilla

TOPPING:

1 cup sliced fresh strawberries

1 kiwi fruit, peeled, sliced

In small saucepan, combine gelatin and water. Let stand 1 minute. Add sugar; stir over medium heat until mixture is dissolved. In large bowl, beat cream cheese and sour cream until creamy. Gradually add melted chocolate, gelatin mixture, whipping cream, and vanilla. Beat until smooth. Pour into Crust. Cover and refrigerate 1½–2½ hours, or until firm.

Shortly before serving, run a knife around edge of pan to loosen cheesecake. Carefully remove sides of pan. Arrange fruit over cheesecake. Store in refrigerator. Makes 16 servings.

Inn-describably Delicious (Illinois)

Cookies and Candies

Snake Alley, a street in Burlington, Iowa, is known as the "Crookedest Alley in the World." It was built by the town's founders in 1894 as an experimental street design (and as a shortcut downhill to the business district). Paved with cobblestones, Snake Alley consists of five half-curves and two quarter-curves over a distance of 275 feet, rising 58.3 feet from Washington Street.

Prized Peanut Butter Crunch Cookie

1 cup butter-flavored Crisco
2 cups firmly packed brown
   sugar
1 cup Jif Extra Crunchy Peanut
   Butter
4 egg whites, slightly beaten
1 teaspoon vanilla
2 cups all-purpose flour

1 teaspoon baking soda
½ teaspoon baking powder
2 cups crisp rice cereal
1½ cups chopped peanuts
1 cup quick oats (not instant or
   old-fashioned)
1 cup flaked coconut

Heat oven to 350°. Combine butter-flavor Crisco, sugar, and peanut butter in large bowl. Beat at medium speed of electric mixer until blended. Beat in egg whites and vanilla.

Combine flour, baking soda, and baking powder. Mix into creamed mixture at low speed until just blended. Stir in, one at a time, rice cereal, nuts, oats, and coconut with spoon.

Drop rounded measuring tablespoonfuls of dough 2 inches apart onto ungreased baking sheet. Bake at 350° for 8–10 minutes or until set. Remove immediately to cooling rack. Makes about 4 dozen cookies.

A Taste of Twin Pines (Indiana)

Crunchy Cookies

2 cups margarine, softened
2 cups sugar
2 teaspoons vanilla
3 cups all-purpose flour
2 teaspoons cream of tartar
2 teaspoons baking soda

2½ cups cornflakes
1 (7-ounce) can coconut
8 ounces white chocolate, cut into
   small chunks (optional)
1½ cups coarsely chopped
   macadamia nuts (optional)

Cream together margarine, sugar, and vanilla. Add flour, cream of tartar, and baking soda to creamed mixture. By hand, add 2½ cups cornflakes (do not crush) and coconut. If desired, fold in white chocolate and nuts. Drop by teaspoonful onto an ungreased cookie sheet. Bake at 350° for 10–12 minutes. Yields 5 dozen.

Holy Cow, Chicago's Cooking! (Illinois)

Pride of Iowa Cookies

1 cup brown sugar
1 cup white sugar
1 cup shortening
2 eggs
1¾ cups all-purpose flour
1 teaspoon baking soda
1 teaspoon baking powder
½ teaspoon salt
1¾ teaspoons oatmeal
½ cup chopped nuts (optional)
1 cup chocolate chips
½ cup flaked coconut (optional)

Cream sugars, shortening, and eggs. Sift flour, baking soda, baking powder, and salt. Add oatmeal, then stir into creamed mixture. Add nuts, chips, and coconut. Bake at 350° for 10–12 minutes.

Country Cupboard Cookbook (Iowa)

White Chocolate Chunk Cookies

½ cup butter, softened
½ cup vegetable shortening
¾ cup granulated sugar
½ cup packed brown sugar
1 egg
1¾ cups all-purpose flour
1 teaspoon baking soda
½ teaspoon salt
2 teaspoons vanilla
10 ounces white chocolate, chopped
½ cup chopped macadamia nuts, toasted

Cream butter and shortening. Gradually add sugars, beating at medium speed until mixed well. Add egg and beat well. In a separate bowl, combine flour, baking soda, and salt. Add dry ingredients to creamed mixture and mix well. Stir in vanilla. Add white chocolate and nuts, and mix. Chill dough 1 hour.

When ready to bake, preheat oven to 350°. Drop dough by 2 tablespoonfuls, 3 inches apart, onto lightly greased baking sheets. Bake at 350° for 10–12 minutes; cookies will be soft. Cool slightly on baking sheet. Remove to wire rack to cool completely.

Crowd Pleasers (Ohio)

Marie Wallace's
World's Best Cookies!

Once in a while a really good and different recipe comes along, and this recipe falls into that category. There are interesting additions that you certainly wouldn't expect (cornflakes?!), but the cookie is buttery and very tender—not crisp. They literally melt in your mouth!

1 cup butter, softened
1 cup sugar
1 cup light brown sugar, firmly
   packed
1 egg, slightly beaten
1 cup oil
1 cup quick rolled oats
1 cup crushed cornflakes
   (measure after crushing)

3½ cup all-purpose flour
1 teaspoon baking soda
1 teaspoon salt
1 teaspoon vanilla
½ cup coconut
1 cup finely chopped pecans
Red or green glazed cherries for
   decoration (optional)

Cream butter with sugars. Add egg and oil; mix well. Add oats, cornflakes, flour, baking soda, salt, and vanilla; mix well. Stir in coconut and nuts. Roll into 1-inch balls of dough and place on a lightly greased cookie sheet. Flatten balls with a fork in a crisscross pattern. Dip fork in water between cookies. If desired, place glazed cherry half in the center of each cookie. Bake at 350° for about 10 minutes, or until light brown. Do not overbake. Makes 8–10 dozen cookies.

Christmas Thyme at Oak Hill Farm (Indiana)

Hawthorn Hill Coconut Macaroons

These cookies were always served to the elementary school children who were carollers at Hawthorn Hill (Wright Brothers' home) at Christmastime twenty years or more ago. My father requested the recipe from the National Cash Register Company for me to use in a 4-H foods demonstration at the County Fair. It was a winner then, and it is still a winner today.

½ cup egg whites (about 4
  large egg whites), room
  temperature
1 cup sugar

2½ cups granulated coconut,
  or flaked coconut granulated
  in food processor or blender
1 teaspoon vanilla

Beat egg whites until stiff peaks form when beaters are raised. Add sugar very slowly with beater at medium speed. By hand, fold in coconut carefully. Fold in vanilla carefully. Drop by tablespoonfuls onto a Teflon cookie sheet or a regular cookie sheet covered with parchment or brown wrapping paper. Bake in a preheated 325° oven for about 18 minutes or until light golden in color. Cool slightly before removing from paper with a stiff spatula. Yields about 2½ dozen cookies.

Discover Dayton (Ohio)

Swedish Jam Shortbread

1 (18¼-ounce) box butter cake
  mix
½ cup finely-chopped nuts
¼ cup butter, softened
1 egg

1 (10-ounce) jar raspberry
  preserves or jam
½ cup powdered sugar
2½ teaspoons water
½ teaspoon almond extract

Heat oven to 350°. Grease and flour a 9x13-inch pan. In a large bowl, combine cake mix, nuts, butter, and egg at low speed until crumbly. Press mixture into prepared pan. Spread with preserves. Bake 20–25 minutes, or until edges are light brown.

Make glaze with remaining ingredients, mixing until smooth. If needed, add additional water, a drop at a time, for desired consistency. Drizzle over warm shortbread. Cool completely. Cut into bars. Makes 36 bars.

A Taste of Fishers (Indiana)

Double-Chocolate Sugar Cookies

1 (12-ounce) package semisweet
   chocolate chips, divided
1 cup butter or margarine,
   softened
1½ cups sugar, divided
1 large egg

2 tablespoons milk
1 teaspoon vanilla extract
3 cups all-purpose flour
1 teaspoon baking powder
½ teaspoon baking soda

Melt 1 cup chocolate chips in a heavy saucepan over low heat. Reserve remaining chocolate chips; set aside. Beat butter at medium speed with electric mixer until fluffy. Gradually add 1 cup sugar, beating well. Add egg, milk, and vanilla, mixing well. Add melted chocolate, mixing until blended. Combine dry ingredients, except ½ cup sugar, and add to butter mixture, mixing well. Add remaining chocolate chips. Roll dough into balls, 1 tablespoon at a time. Roll balls in ½ cup sugar. Place on cookie sheet. Bake at 400° for 8–10 minutes. (Cookies will be soft and will firm up as they cool.) Yields 4½ dozen cookies.

The L.o.V.E. Chocolate Cookbook (Iowa)

Dutch Handkerchiefs

1 cup butter
2 cups all-purpose flour
¼ cup water

1 egg white
1 cup sugar
1 teaspoon almond flavoring

Cut butter into flour. Add water gradually as if making a pie crust. Roll very thin and cut into 4-inch squares. Beat egg white until stiff. Fold in sugar and flavoring. Place about 2 teaspoons of egg white mixture into the center of each square and fold corners toward center of square. Place on a greased cookie sheet and bake at 350° until lightly browned.

Dandy Dutch Recipes (Iowa)

Lemonade Cookies

1 cup butter, softened
1 cup sugar
2 eggs, beaten
3 cups sifted all-purpose flour
1 teaspoon baking soda
1 (6-ounce) can frozen lemonade, thawed

Cream butter and sugar. Add eggs and blend. Combine flour and baking soda. Add to mixture and mix well. Add 4½ ounces (¾ can) lemonade; mix well. Drop by teaspoonful on ungreased cookie sheet. Bake at 350° for 10–12 minutes.

The "Friends" Cookbook (Ohio)

Caramel-Filled Chocolate Cookies

2½ cups all-purpose flour
¾ cup unsweetened cocoa powder
1 teaspoon baking soda
1 cup plus 1 tablespoon granulated sugar, divided
1 cup packed brown sugar
1 cup margarine or butter, softened
2 teaspoons vanilla
2 eggs
1 cup chopped pecans, divided
48 Rolo Chewy Caramels in Milk Chocolate (9-ounce package)
4 ounces vanilla candy coating, melted

Preheat oven to 375°. In a small bowl, combine flour, cocoa, and baking soda. Blend well. In a large bowl, beat 1 cup granulated sugar, brown sugar, and margarine until light and fluffy. Add vanilla and eggs and beat well. Mix in dry ingredients. Stir in ½ cup pecans. For each cookie, using floured hands, shape about 1 tablespoon of dough around 1 caramel candy, covering completely.

In a small bowl, combine remaining ½ cup pecans and remaining 1 tablespoon sugar. Press one side of each dough ball into pecan mixture. Place, nut-side up, 2 inches apart on ungreased baking sheets. Bake at 375° for 7–10 minutes or until set and slightly cracked. Cool 2 minutes. Remove from baking sheet and cool completely on wire racks. Drizzle melted vanilla coating over cookies.

Crowd Pleasers (Ohio)

Indiana Mud Cookies

16 graham crackers
1 (14-ounce) can sweetened
  condensed milk

1 (6-ounce) package chocolate
  chips

On a piece of waxed paper, roll graham crackers (a few at a time) into crumbs with a rolling pin. Put crumbs in a bowl. Add condensed milk and chocolate chips. Drop by spoonfuls onto greased cookie sheet. Bake at 350° for about 12 minutes. When they are done, let cool before you remove them from pan. Serve with ice cold milk and lots of paper napkins!

The Indiana Kid's Cookbook! (Indiana)

Church Windows

For an easy, quick cookie, this is especially pretty for the holidays. Something special means making Church Windows.

1 (12-ounce) package semisweet
  chocolate chips
1 stick margarine
1 cup chopped walnuts or pecans

1 (10½-ounce) miniature colored
  marshmallows
Powdered sugar or coconut

Melt chocolate chips and margarine; cool. Add chopped nuts and marshmallows. Divide mixture in half and form 2 large logs. Roll each log in powdered sugar or coconut. Wrap in aluminum foil and chill for 24 hours. Slice into ⅓-inch cookies. Makes approximately 3 dozen.

Sharing Our Best (Indiana)

The Basilica of St. Francis Xavier is the Catholic parish for the residents of Dyersville, Iowa. It is one of only 52 basilicas in the United States, and the only one outside a large metropolitan area. The Gothic-style building was finished in 1888. It has 64 stained glass windows. One notable window features Saint Francis Xavier ministering to the Indians. The maker of the window had mistakenly used images of Native Americans instead of images of people from India. But the window was never changed.

Chocolate-Covered Cherry Cookies

1½ cups all-purpose flour
½ cup cocoa
¼ teaspoon salt
¼ teaspoon baking powder
¼ teaspoon baking soda
½ cup margarine, softened
1 cup sugar

1 egg
1½ teaspoons vanilla
10 ounces maraschino cherries, drained, reserve juice
1 (6-ounce) package semisweet chocolate chips
½ cup condensed milk

Sift together flour, cocoa, salt, baking powder, and baking soda. Beat together margarine and sugar until fluffy. Add egg and vanilla; beat well. Add dry ingredients and beat until well blended. Shape dough into 1-inch balls. Place on ungreased cookie sheet. Press down center of dough with thumb. Place a cherry in center of each cookie.

In a small saucepan combine chocolate chips pieces and condensed milk. On very low heat, heat until chocolate is melted. Stir in 4 teaspoons cherry juice. Spoon about 1 teaspoon frosting over each cherry, spreading to cover cherry (frosting may be thinned with more juice, if needed).

Bake in 350° oven about 10 minutes or until done. Remove to wire rack to cool. Makes about 4 dozen.

Treasures and Pleasures (Ohio)

Cherry Chip Cookies

¾ cup margarine, softened
1 cup brown sugar
1 egg
1 teaspoon vanilla
2¼ cups all-purpose flour
1 teaspoon baking powder

½ teaspoon salt
½ cup small cut maraschino cherries
1 cup miniature chocolate chips
½ cup flaked coconut

Using mixer, cream together margarine and brown sugar. Add egg and vanilla; mix well. Mix flour, baking powder, and salt; add gradually to creamed mixture. Mixture will be stiff. Using spoon, stir in cherries, chocolate chips, and coconut. Chill in refrigerator about 2 hours. Roll chilled dough between hands into ½-inch small balls. Place on greased cookie sheets. Bake at 350° for 8 minutes or until light brown. Makes 85 small cookies.

College Avenue Presbyterian Church Cookbook (Illinois)

Chocolate Chip Pudding Cookies

3½ cups all-purpose flour
1½ teaspoons baking soda
1½ cups butter or margarine,
   softened
1 cup firmly packed brown
   sugar
½ cup sugar

1 (6-ounce) package vanilla
   instant pudding
1½ teaspoons vanilla
3 eggs
3 cups chocolate chips
½ cup chopped nuts

Mix flour with baking soda. Combine butter, both sugars, pudding mix, and vanilla in a large bowl; beat until creamy and smooth. Beat in eggs. Gradually add flour mixture; then stir in chips and nuts. Drop by rounded teaspoonfuls onto ungreased baking sheet. Bake at 375° for 8–10 minutes. Makes about 10 dozen.

Thompson Family Cookbook (Iowa)

World's Best Cookie Bars

LAYER 1:

1 cup all-purpose flour
½ cup butter, softened

¼ cup sugar

Mix with pastry blender and press into a 9x13-inch pan. Bake at 375° for 10 minutes.

LAYER 2:

1 cup graham cracker crumbs
1 teaspoon baking powder
1 (14-ounce) can condensed
   milk

½ cup chocolate chips
½ cup chopped nuts (optional)

Mix together and pour over Crust. Bake at 325° for 25 minutes. Cool.

LAYER 3:

½ cup butter, softened
1½ cups powdered sugar

1 teaspoon vanilla

Whip, and frost.

New Beginnings (Iowa)

Whoopie Pies

FILLING:

1 cup milk
4 tablespoons flour or
  2 tablespoons cornstarch
½ cup margarine, softened

1 cup Crisco
1 cup sugar
1 teaspoon vanilla
¼ teaspoon salt

Cook milk and flour together. This will be very thick. Cool completely. Cream together the margarine, Crisco, and sugar. Add vanilla and salt. When cooled, beat mixture with an electric mixer on high speed for at least 5 minutes. Will be very creamy. Spread Filling between 2 Cookies.

COOKIE:

½ cup oil
1 cup sugar
½ cup cocoa
1 cup milk
1 egg

2 cups all-purpose flour
1½ teaspoons baking soda
½ teaspoon salt
1 teaspoon vanilla

Mix ingredients in order given and beat until well mixed. Drop on ungreased cookie sheet from a tablespoon. Bake 7–10 minutes in a 375° oven, or until done. Yields 40 cookies.

By Our Cookstove (Ohio)

AUTHENTICHISTORY.COM

Swing to the Big Band sounds of Glenn Miller in Clarinda, Iowa. The house where the popular American band leader, composer, and arranger of the swing era was born has been restored with period furnishings to reflect the time around 1904 when Miller was born. Each year on the second weekend in June, visitors and entertainers from around the world converge in Clarinda to celebrate the music and memory of Alton Glenn Miller.

Turtle Shells

1 package Azteca salad shells
  (in dairy case at grocery)
1 (12-ounce) package caramels
½ cup canned sweetened
  condensed milk

1 cup pecan pieces
1 cup milk chocolate chips

Preheat oven to 350°. Cut shell in 8 pie-shaped wedges. Bake on ungreased baking sheets for 7–9 minutes or until light golden brown. Remove shells and place on wax paper.

Place caramels and milk in microwave-safe bowl. Microwave on MEDIUM for 3 minutes, stirring often. Spread caramels onto cooled shells; top with pecans. Microwave chocolate on MEDIUM for 3 minutes; stir and repeat 2 minutes, stirring often. Drizzle chocolate over caramel and pecans. Makes 32 candies. Delicious.

Country Cooking (Indiana)

Indiana Fortune Cookies

¾ cup butter or margarine,
  softened
2 cups sugar
1 teaspoon vanilla

3 eggs
1 cup all-purpose flour, sifted
60 intriguing fortunes written on
  small strips of paper

In a mixing bowl combine butter and sugar until fluffy. Add vanilla. Then add eggs to mixture, one at a time. Beat well after adding each egg. Then add flour and beat thoroughly. Heat oven to 375°. Grease cookie sheets, then dust lightly with flour. Drop rounded teaspoons of dough at least 2 inches apart on each sheet. Bake 20 minutes and remove. With a wide spatula, loosen each cookie from sheet. Place a folded fortune on each cookie. Gently fold cookies in half with fortune inside. Pinch edges together, then twist in the centers. Makes 60 fortune cookies.

Note: While putting a fortune inside each cookie, keep the cookie sheet warm. This will make the cookies easier to work with.

The Indiana Kid's Cookbook! (Indiana)

Butter Brickle Bars

1 (18¼-ounce) box yellow cake
  mix

⅓ cup margarine, softened
1 egg, slightly beaten

Mix like pie crust and pat into a 10x15-inch jellyroll pan.

1 (6-ounce) package butter
  brickle chips (Heath bars)
1½ cups chopped pecans

1 (14-ounce) can sweetened
  condensed milk

Mix and dot over top of crust. Bake at 350° for 20 minutes.

The Berns Family Cookbook (Iowa)

Chocolate Toffee Crunch Bars

⅓ cup butter, melted
¾ cup packed brown sugar,
  divided
2 cups finely crushed vanilla
  wafers

½ cup firm butter
1 (6-ounce) package mini
  chocolate chips
½ cup finely chopped nuts

Preheat oven to 350°. In bowl, combine ¼ cup brown sugar and crumbs. Stir in butter. Press in 9x13-inch pan. Bake 8 minutes.

Heat ½ cup butter and remaining ½ cup brown sugar in a pan over medium heat until boiling. Boil 1 minute. Pour immediately over cookie base and spread to edges. Bake at 350° for 10 minutes. Let stand 2 minutes. Sprinkle with chocolate chips (mini-chips work best). Let stand 2–3 minutes, then spread chips. Sprinkle with nuts.

25th Anniversary Cookbook (Ohio)

Fabulous Pecan Bars

Wherever and whenever you want to serve (or give) about the best cookie ever, do consider this recipe.

CRUST:

½ cup cold butter   ¼ cup ice water
1½ cups all-purpose flour

Use a pastry blender to cut butter into flour. Mixture should resemble cornmeal. Add water and toss with a fork. Gather dough into a ball. Wrap in plastic wrap and refrigerate for 1 or 2 hours. Butter and flour a 9x13-inch pan. Roll dough out to about an 11x15-inch rectangle. Fit dough into prepared pan and let it come up about 1 inch on all sides. Pierce dough with a fork. Chill while making Filling.

FILLING:

1½ cups light brown sugar,   ⅓ cup sugar
  packed   1 pound pecans, chopped
1 cup butter   (but not too fine)
½ cup honey   ¼ cup whipping cream

Preheat oven to 400°. Combine brown sugar, butter, honey, and sugar in a heavy saucepan, and bring to a boil over medium heat, stirring constantly. Boil until thick and dark, 3–4 minutes. You must stir constantly. Remove from heat. Stir in pecans and whipping cream. Pour over dough in pan. Bake 25 minutes. Check after about 15 minutes. If Filling is browning too much, reduce oven heat to 375° and continue baking. Cool cookies in pan. Cut into strips. Makes 5 or 6 dozen strips, depending on how large you cut them. Almost better than pecan pie.

Christmas Thyme at Oak Hill Farm (Indiana)

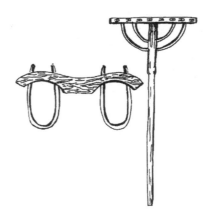

Crème de Menthe Bars

1¼ cups butter, divided
½ cup cocoa
3½ cups sifted powdered sugar,
    divided
1 beaten egg
1 teaspoon vanilla
2 cups graham cracker crumbs
⅓ cup green crème de menthe
1½ cups semisweet chocolate
    chips

BOTTOM LAYER:

In saucepan combine ½ cup butter and cocoa. Heat and stir until well blended. Add ½ cup powdered sugar, egg, and vanilla. Stir in cracker crumbs; mix well. Press into ungreased 9x13-inch pan.

MIDDLE LAYER:

Melt ½ cup butter. Mix in crème de menthe at low speed of mixer. Beat in remaining 3 cups powdered sugar until smooth. Spread over chocolate layer. Chill 1 hour.

TOP LAYER:

Combine remaining ¼ cup butter and chocolate chips. Cook and stir over low heat until melted. Spread over mint layer. Chill 1–2 hours. Store in refrigerator. Freezes well.

A Collection of Recipes from St. Matthew Lutheran Church
(Illinois)

Chocolate Cherry Bars

This tastes like the Black Forest Cake.

1 (18¼-ounce) box chocolate
    cake mix
1 (21-ounce) can cherry pie
    filling
1 teaspoon almond extract
2 eggs, beaten

Grease and flour jellyroll pan. In large bowl, combine all ingredients. Stir by hand until well mixed. Pour into prepared pan. Bake at 350° for 25–30 minutes, or until cake tester comes out clean.

Frost with chocolate frosting, if desired. Or put mixture into greased and floured 9x13-inch pan; bake for about 35 minutes. Frost with sweetened whipped cream and chocolate curls.

Our Best Home Cooking (Illinois)

Caramel Layer Choco-Squares

1 (16-ounce) package light
  caramels
$\frac{2}{3}$ cup evaporated milk, divided
1 (18$\frac{1}{4}$-ounce) box German
  chocolate cake mix

$\frac{2}{3}$ cup butter, softened
$\frac{1}{2}$ cup chopped nuts
1 (12-ounce) package chocolate
  chips

In a heavy saucepan, melt caramels in $\frac{1}{3}$ cup milk over low heat; set aside. In a large bowl, combine remaining ingredients, except chocolate chips. Mix until dough is crumbly but holds together. Press half the dough into a greased and floured 9x13-inch pan. Bake at 350° for 6 minutes. Remove from oven. Sprinkle chocolate chips over dough. Pour caramel mixture over chips. Top with remaining dough. Bake 15–20 minutes. Chill. Cut into squares. Makes 2 dozen.

Nutbread and Nostalgia (Indiana)

Pecan-Caramel Cream Squares

16 caramels, unwrapped
24 large marshmallows
$\frac{1}{2}$ cup milk
1 cup chopped pecans, toasted

1 cup whipping cream
1 cup graham cracker crumbs
4 tablespoons butter, melted

Put caramels, marshmallows, and milk in top of double boiler. Place over boiling water. Cook, stirring occasionally, until mixture is melted and smooth, about 25 minutes. Remove from heat and cool. Stir in pecans. Whip cream and fold into caramel mixture. Combine crumbs and butter; reserve $\frac{1}{4}$ cup. Press remainder into bottom of a 6x10-inch dish. Top with caramel mixture. Sprinkle with reserved crumbs. Chill several hours or overnight. Cut into squares. Serves 6.

Note: May be doubled and put into a 9x13-inch dish.

Favorite Recipes from Poland Women's Club (Ohio)

S'Morsels

1 cup all-purpose flour
¾ cup graham cracker
  crumbs
⅔ cup butter or margarine,
  softened
¼ cup sugar

¼ cup packed brown sugar
¼ teaspoon salt
1 cup marshmallow crème
1½ cups semisweet chocolate
  morsels.

Preheat oven to 325°. In mixer bowl blend flour, cracker crumbs, butter, sugar, brown sugar, and salt until crumbly. Press into greased 9x13-inch pan. Bake for 15 minutes. Spread marshmallow crème over base; sprinkle with chocolate morsels. Bake for 5 minutes longer. Cool. Cut into squares.

Our Favorite Recipes (Illinois)

Pumpkin Pie Squares

1 cup sifted all-purpose flour
½ cup quick Quaker Oats
1 cup brown sugar, divided
½ cup plus 2 tablespoons
  butter, softened, divided
1 (16-ounce) can pumpkin
1 (12-ounce) can evaporated
  milk

2 eggs
¾ cup sugar
1 teaspoon salt
1 teaspoon cinnamon
½ teaspoon ground ginger
¼ teaspoon ground cloves
½ cup chopped pecans

Combine flour, oats, ½ cup brown sugar, and ½ cup butter in mixing bowl. Mix until crumbly, using an electric mixer on low speed. Press into ungreased 9x13-inch pan. Bake at 350° for 15 minutes.

Combine pumpkin, evaporated milk, eggs, ¾ cup sugar, salt, and spices in mixing bowl; beat well. Pour into crust. Bake at 350° for 20 minutes.

Combine pecans, remaining ½ cup brown sugar, and 2 tablespoons butter; sprinkle over pumpkin filling. Return to oven and bake 15–20 minutes, or until filling is set. Cool in pan, and cut in 2-inch squares.

Our Best Recipes to You, Again (Indiana)

Sour Cream Apple Squares

Perfect for brunch or dessert!

2 cups all-purpose flour
2 cups firmly-packed brown
   sugar
½ cup butter softened
1 cup chopped walnuts
1–2 teaspoons cinnamon
1 teaspoon baking soda

½ teaspoon salt
1 cup sour cream
1 teaspoon vanilla
1 egg
2 cups peeled, finely chopped
   apples (2 medium)

Preheat oven to 350°. In large bowl, combine flour, brown sugar, and butter until crumbly. Stir in nuts. Press 2¾ cups of crumb mixture into ungreased 9x13-inch pan.

To remaining mixture, add cinnamon, baking soda, salt, sour cream, vanilla, and egg. Blend well. Stir in apples. Spoon evenly over base. Bake at 350° for 25–35 minutes until toothpick comes out clean. Cut into squares. Yields 12–15 servings.

Cookin' to Beat the Band (Indiana)

Moon Bars

1 cup water
1 stick margarine
1 cup all-purpose flour
4 eggs
2 packages vanilla instant
   pudding

1 (8-ounce) package cream cheese,
   softened
1 (8-ounce) carton Cool Whip
Chocolate syrup
Nuts (optional)

Boil water and margarine. Add flour; stir well. Add eggs, one at a time; stir well. Bake at 400° for 30 minutes in jellyroll pan. Cool. Mix pudding according to directions. Add softened cream cheese. Mix and put on baked crust. Cool. Add Cool Whip. Drizzle with chocolate syrup. Top with nuts, if desired.

Trinity Lutheran Church Centennial Cookbook (Iowa)

Marshmallow Brownies

¾ cup shortening or
  margarine
1⅓ cups sugar
3 eggs
1⅓ cups all-purpose flour
½ teaspoon baking powder

2 tablespoons cocoa
⅓ teaspoon salt
1½ teaspoons vanilla
¾ cup chopped nuts
1 small bag miniature
  marshmallows

Mix all but marshmallows in order given. Bake at 325° for 20 minutes. Take out of oven and cover with marshmallows. Put back in oven for 3 minutes. Pour Icing over top.

ICING:
¾ cup brown sugar
⅓ cup water
3 tablespoons cocoa

4 tablespoons butter
1½ teaspoons vanilla
2 cups powdered sugar

In saucepan, boil first 5 ingredients for 3 minutes; let cool. Add powdered sugar.

Amish Country Cookbook I (Indiana)

Bravo Brownies

½ cup vegetable oil
6 tablespoons cocoa
1 egg, beaten
1 cup sugar
1¼ cups all-purpose flour

½ teaspoon baking soda
½ teaspoon salt
1 teaspoon vanilla
¾ cup orange juice
1 cup chocolate chips

Combine all ingredients except chocolate chips, and beat until smooth. Stir in chocolate chips. Bake at 350° in greased 9x9-inch pan for 30 minutes. Done when toothpick inserted in center comes out clean. Cut after cool. Serves 9–12.

Heavenly Food II (Ohio)

Dump Brownies

2 cups sugar
1¾ cup all-purpose flour
1 cup oil
5 eggs
1 teaspoon vanilla

½ cup cocoa
½ teaspoon salt
1 (6-ounce) package chocolate
   chips

Dump all ingredients, except chips, in a mixing bowl. Mix well until blended. Pour into a greased 9x13-inch pan. Top with chocolate chips. Bake in a 350° oven 20–25 minutes.

Note: If you are low on chocolate chips, frost with Never Fail Chocolate Frosting.

NEVER FAIL CHOCOLATE FROSTING:

1½ cups sugar
6 tablespoons milk
6 tablespoons butter

½ cup chocolate chips
1 teaspoon vanilla

In saucepan, bring sugar, milk and butter to a boil. Boil 1 minute. Add chocolate chips and vanilla. Beat until right consistency for frosting. Will frost a 9x13-inch cake.

Fontanelle Good Samaritan Center Commemorative Cookbook
(Iowa)

Cedar Rapids, Iowa, is one of only a few cities in the world that has its government buildings on an island in the center of the city. The City Hall and Linn County Courthouse are located on Mays Island, an island on the Cedar River.

Peanut Butter Logs

Make your own candy bars with this recipe. The kids will like these for after-school snacks and you'll like them while watching television at night!

1 cup peanut butter
¼ cup margarine, softened
1½ cups sifted powdered sugar
3 cups Rice Krispies
1 cup chopped dry roasted
   peanuts

1 cup semisweet chocolate
   morsels
2 tablespoons margarine

Cream together peanut butter and ¼ cup margarine. Stir in sifted powdered sugar and then Rice Krispies. Portion dough by tablespoons and shape into little logs. Roll in roasted peanuts; set aside.

Melt chocolate morsels with 2 tablespoons margarine in small saucepan over low heat, stirring constantly. (Or heat on HIGH in microwave in glass measure 1 minute or until soft and melted. Stir to smoothness.) Drizzle over top of logs. Chill.

Sharing Our Best (Indiana)

Buckeyes

Ohio is known as the Buckeye State, and these candies are made to resemble the buckeye seed. (The real buckeye is reputedly poisonous.)

1 stick butter or margarine,
   softened
1 (1-pound) box confectioners'
   sugar
1½ cups peanut butter

1 teaspoon vanilla extract
1 (12-ounce) package real
   chocolate chips
¼ stick paraffin

Cream butter, confectioners' sugar, peanut butter, and vanilla. Form into small (buckeye-size) balls and refrigerate overnight.

Melt chocolate chips and paraffin in top of double boiler. Stick a toothpick in the candy ball and dip it into chocolate mixture. Leave part of the ball uncovered so that it resembles a buckeye; smooth over the toothpick hole. Place on wax paper to cool and harden. These candies can be frozen. Yields 3–4 dozen.

Cincinnati Recipe Treasury (Ohio)

Creamed Pecan Nuts

Most delicious!

½ cup brown sugar, packed
¼ cup white sugar
¼ cup sour cream

1½ teaspoons vanilla
1½ cups pecan halves

Combine sugars and sour cream in saucepan. Cook over low heat, stirring constantly, until sugars are dissolved. Cook until soft ball form in cold water. Remove from heat. Add vanilla and pecans. Stir until light sugar coating begins to form on nuts. Turn out on wax paper. Separate nuts by hand; let cool.

Seasoned with Love (Illinois)

Nut Cups

FILLING:

2 cups chopped pecans
2 eggs, beaten
1½ cups brown sugar

Pinch of salt
1 teaspoon vanilla
2 tablespoons melted butter

Combine all ingredients thoroughly. Set aside.

PASTRY:

2 (3-ounce) packages cream
  cheese, softened
2 sticks butter or margarine,
  softened

2 cups all-purpose flour
Powdered sugar (optional)

Combine cream cheese and butter; gradually add flour, mixing with hands. Divide dough into 4 equal parts. Each quarter of the dough will be enough for 12 mini-muffin cups. Divide each quarter into 12 balls and place one ball in each mini-muffin cup. Press with thumb or finger into bottom and around sides to form cup. Fill each with 1 teaspoon nut Filling. Bake at 350° for 15–20 minutes. When cool, you may sprinkle with powdered sugar, if desired. Makes 48 cookies that melt in your mouth. They keep well.

Cookies & Tea (Ohio)

Elephant Ears

1½ cups milk
2 tablespoons sugar
1 teaspoon salt
6 tablespoons shortening
2 packages dry yeast

4 cups all-purpose flour
Oil for frying
Sugar/cinnamon mixture
 (½ cup sugar and 1 teaspoon
 cinnamon)

In a saucepan combine milk, sugar, salt, and shortening; heat until shortening is melted. Do not let mixture boil. Cool mixture to lukewarm. Add yeast and stir until dissolved; stir in flour 2 cups at a time. Beat after each addition until smooth. Put in a greased bowl, cover with a damp cloth and let rise until double, about 20 minutes. Dust hands with flour, pinch off pieces of dough about the size of a golf ball. Stretch each piece into a thin 6- to 8-inch circle. Fry, one at a time in oil (350°) until dough rises to the surface. Turn and fry on other side until light brown. Drain on absorbent paper and sprinkle with sugar/cinnamon mixture.

Amish Country Cookbook II (Indiana)

Homemade Mint Patties

1 (1-pound) bag powdered sugar
1 (14-ounce) can condensed
 milk
Peppermint oil or flavoring to
 taste

1 (12-ounce) bag semisweet
 chocolate chips
1 (1-inch) square paraffin

Put powdered sugar in a bowl and add condensed milk; milk well. Add flavoring and form into a ball like pie dough. Leave in bowl and chill overnight.

Next day form into little balls and chill several hours. Melt chips and wax. Dip balls into chocolate and let set till firm.

Our Favorite Recipes II (Indiana)

Des Moines Fudge

1 cup butter or margarine
3 cups sugar
1 envelope unflavored gelatin
1 cup milk
½ cup white corn syrup
3 squares unsweetened
  chocolate
2 teaspoons vanilla
1 cup chopped nuts

Use some of the butter to grease sides of heavy saucepan. Mix sugar and gelatin in pan. Add milk, corn syrup, chocolate, and butter. Cook over medium heat, stirring frequently until it reaches 238° on a candy thermometer. Pour into a large mixer bowl and cool for 15 minutes. Add vanilla and beat until thick. Add nuts and pour into buttered 9x9-inch pan. Cool well before cutting. This fudge keeps for 4–6 weeks in refrigerator.

The L.o.V.E. Chocolate Cookbook (Iowa)

Pumpkin Fudge

2 cups sugar
2 tablespoons pumpkin
¼ teaspoon pumpkin pie
  spice
¼ teaspoon cornstarch
½ cup evaporated milk
½ teaspoon vanilla

Cook together sugar, pumpkin, spice, cornstarch, and milk until soft-ball stage (between 234°–240° on candy thermometer). Add vanilla and cool. Beat until creamy. Pour onto buttered plate. Cut in squares when cool.

St. Gerard's 75th Jubilee Cookbook (Ohio)

Peanut Brittle

Easy and delicious!

1 cup sugar
1 cup white syrup

1 cup raw peanuts
1 teaspoon baking soda

Heat sugar and syrup until clear. Add raw peanuts and boil until it is amber in color (about like a penny). Remove from heat and add baking soda. Stir well (will be frothy). Pour into a well-buttered cookie sheet. Cool and break into pieces. Can add large flaked coconut, if desired.

Country Cupboard Cookbook (Iowa)

Creamy Caramels

1½ cups half-and-half
1½ cups whipping cream
2 cups sugar
¼ teaspoon salt

1⅓ cups light corn syrup
2 teaspoons vanilla
1 cup toasted walnuts

Butter a 9-inch square pan. Combine half-and-half and whipping cream in 4-cup measure. Mix sugar, salt, corn syrup, and 1 cup of cream mixture in heavy 3- to 4-quart saucepan. Cook over medium heat, stirring constantly until syrup reaches 234° (soft ball). Add one more cup of cream and stir until mixture again reaches 234°. Add remaining cream and stir until mixture reaches 250° (hard ball). Remove from heat, add vanilla and nuts. Pour into pan, cool and wrap.

Affolter-Heritage Reunion Cookbook & More (Ohio)

Irene's Divinity

2 egg whites, room
   temperature
2 cups sugar
½ cup white corn syrup

½ cup water
Salt
Vanilla
1 cup chopped pecans

Beat egg whites until stiff; set aside. In saucepan, boil together sugar, corn syrup, and water to soft-ball stage (between 234°–240° on a candy thermometer). Pour ½ of syrup over beaten egg whites, beating it in. Boil remaining syrup to hard-ball stage (between 250°–265°); add slowly to mixture. Beat until right consistency for candy. Add a pinch of salt and flavor with vanilla. Stir in nuts. Drop by teaspoon on greased sheet. Store in covered tin.

Favorite Recipes of Collinsville Junior Service Club (Illinois)

Pies and Other Desserts

WWW.WIKIPEDIA.COM

The gilded Golden dome and statue of Mary atop the Main Building is the centerpiece of the University of Notre Dame. Founded in 1842 as an independent Catholic university in South Bend, Indiana, today is is recognized for its academic excellence and its athletic prowess . . . The Fighting Irish.

Frost-on-the-Pumpkin Pie

1½ cups confectioners' sugar, divided
½ teaspoon vanilla extract
½ teaspoon cinnamon
1 cup heavy cream, whipped
1 tablespoon unflavored gelatin
¼ cup cold water
3 eggs, separated

⅓ cup granulated sugar
1¼ cups pumpkin
½ cup milk
½ teaspoon cinnamon
½ teaspoon allspice
¼ teaspoon ginger
¼ teaspoon nutmeg
1 (9-inch) baked pie shell

Fold 1¼ cups confectioners' sugar, vanilla extract, and cinnamon into whipped cream; chill.

Soften gelatin in cold water. Mix well beaten egg yolks with granulated sugar, pumpkin, milk, and spices. Cook in a heavy pan, stirring constantly, until thick (about 5 minutes). Add gelatin and stir until dissolved. Chill thoroughly.

Beat remaining ¼ cup confectioners' sugar into 3 egg whites; beat until stiff; fold into pumpkin mixture. Turn half of pumpkin mixture into pie shell; cover with half of whipped cream mixture. Repeat layers. Chill for several hours or overnight. Serves 8.

First There Must Be Food (Illinois)

Paradise Pumpkin Pie

1 (8-ounce) package cream cheese, softened
¾ cup sugar, divided
½ teaspoon vanilla
3 eggs, beaten, divided

1 (9-inch) pie shell, unbaked
1¼ cups pumpkin
¼ teaspoon nutmeg
1 teaspoon cinnamon
1 cup evaporated milk

Combine cream cheese, ¼ cup sugar, vanilla, and 1 beaten egg. Pour into pie shell. Combine remaining ingredients and carefully spoon on top of creamed mixture. Bake at 350° for 65–70 minutes.

Favorite Recipes from Poland Women's Club (Ohio)

Easiest Apple Pie

This is one of the flakiest pie crusts I've ever eaten. I like it better than the traditional pie crust.

6 Granny Smith apples, peeled, thinly sliced
1 cup plus 1 tablespoon Splenda, divided
2 tablespoons cornstarch
¾ teaspoon ground cinnamon
⅛ teaspoon ground cloves
1 (16-ounce) box filo dough sheets
1 egg white, beaten

Preheat oven to 425°. Place apples in a microwave-safe bowl. Toss apples gently with 1 cup Splenda, cornstarch, cinnamon, and cloves. Cover and microwave 5–7 minutes, stirring every couple of minutes until apples are tender and fully heated.

While apples are cooking, cut filo dough in half to form a rectangle. Wrap one stack and save to use another time. Spray each sheet of dough with nonfat cooking spray before stacking 10 sheets of filo on top of each other to form bottom of pie crust. Place sheets across pie plate like tire spindles crossing in the center. Allow extra length to hang over edge of pie plate. Put cooked sweetened apples into pie plate.

With remaining 10 sheets of dough, make top crust by doing the exact same thing as for bottom crust. Do not press dough into bottom of plate. With scissors, cut dough hanging off the edge of pie plate. If needed, spray in between layers of filo dough sheets with nonfat cooking spray and tightly squeeze sheets together to help seal top and bottom layers of crust together. Brush top with beaten egg white. Cover edge with aluminum foil. Bake at 425° for 10 minutes. Remove foil; bake another 5–7 minutes or until top is light golden brown. Once removed from oven, sprinkle remaining 1 tablespoon Splenda on top.

Busy People's Low-Carb Cookbook (Ohio)

Topsy Turvy Pecan Apple Pie

½ stick butter, softened
Pecan halves
⅔ cup brown sugar, packed
2-crust pastry

6 cups apples, sliced, mixed with
  ½ cup sugar, and sprinkles of
  apple pie seasonings (flour,
  cinnamon, nutmeg)

Smooth butter around sides and bottom of pie pan. Stick pecans in butter, then press brown sugar evenly over pecans. Put on 1 layer of crust extending about an inch beyond edge of pan. Add apple mixture next, and then top crust. Lap extended crust over top crust and flute edges.

Prick top with fork. Bake 10 minutes at 450° then reduce heat to 350° and continue baking 30–45 minutes, or until done. Flip upside down to serve.

Home Cookin' Is a Family Affair (Illinois)

Country Apple Pie with Lemon Glaze

Pastry for 2-crust pie
5–7 apples
¾ cup sugar
1 teaspoon cinnamon

2 tablespoons flour
1 tablespoon butter or
  margarine

Line a 9-inch pie plate with bottom of crust. Pare, core, and slice apples. Combine with mixture of sugar, cinnamon, and flour. Place in pastry-lined plate. Dot with butter. Place top crust over filling. Trim and seal. Prick or cut slots to allow steam to escape. Bake at 400° for 30–40 minutes or until apples are cooked and crust is lightly browned. If crust gets too brown before pie is done, place a sheet of foil over pie and continue baking.

LEMON GLAZE:

1 tablespoon butter, melted
1 tablespoon lemon juice

Powdered sugar (enough to
  thicken)

Mix above ingredients in small bowl. Wait about 10 minutes after pie is out of oven. Spread over pie.

A Matter of Taste (Ohio)

Lemon Cake Pie

1 lemon, juice and grated rind
1¼ cups milk
1 cup sugar
2 heaping tablespoons flour

2 eggs, separated
1 tablespoon butter, melted
1 (9-inch) pie crust, unbaked

Beat all ingredients (except 2 egg whites that have been beaten stiff) together; fold in beaten egg whites. Pour into curst, bake in slow (325°) oven for 1 hour or until done.

Oma's (Grandma's) Family Secrets (Iowa)

Peaches and Cream Pie

A cake-like crust adds an interesting texture to this popular dessert.

CRUST:
¾ cup flour
1 teaspoon baking powder
½ teaspoon salt
1 (3-ounce) package vanilla
   pudding mix (not instant)

3 tablespoons margarine,
   softened
1 egg
½ cup milk

Combine all ingredients and beat with mixer 2 minutes. Pour into greased 9-inch pie plate. Set aside.

FILLING:
1 (29-ounce) can peaches, sliced,
   drained, reserve juice
1 (8-ounce) package cream
   cheese, softened

½ cup sugar
3 tablespoons peach juice

Place peaches over Crust. Combine remaining Filling ingredients and spoon over top of fruit to within one inch of edge of dish.

TOPPING:
1 tablespoon sugar

½ teaspoon cinnamon

Mix Topping ingredients together and sprinkle over pie. Bake in pre-heated 350° oven 35–40 minutes. Refrigerate and serve cold. Must be prepared several hours ahead. Yields 8 servings.

Simply Sensational (Ohio)

Raspberry Cream Cheese Pie

Good combination of flavors.

30 vanilla wafers, crushed
½ cup butter, melted
1 (8-ounce) package cream
  cheese, softened
1 cup powdered sugar

1 teaspoon vanilla extract
1 cup non-dairy whipped topping
1 (10-ounce) box frozen
  raspberries, drained
3–4 chocolate toffee candy bars

Preheat oven to 325°. Combine wafers and butter; pat into 9-inch pie plate. Bake 15 minutes. Turn off oven and leave crust in oven for 10 minutes; remove and cool.

Mix cream cheese, powdered sugar, vanilla, and whipped topping. Pour in raspberries. Mix and pour into crust. Crush candy bars in blender; sprinkle on top of pie. Chill 1 hour before serving. Yields 6–8 servings.

Great Beginnings, Grand Finales (Indiana)

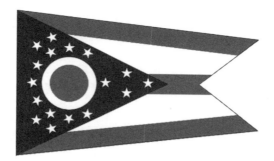

Ohio has the only state flag with a pennant shape. Adopted in 1902, its large blue triangle represents Ohio's hills and valleys, and the stripes represent roads and waterways. The white circle with its red center not only represents the first letter of the state name, but also its nickname, "the Buckeye State." The seventeen stars grouped about the circle symbolize that Ohio was the seventeenth state admitted to the Union.

Di's Ohio Sour Cherry Pie

This is the recipe that won Diane Cordial of Powell the Grand Prize at Crisco's American Pie Celebration National Championship. A distinguished panel of food experts from across the country saluted Di and declared her Ohio pie the best pie in America, beating entries from the 49 other states. Crisco, of course, is a product of Ohio-based Procter & Gamble. Way to go, Bucks!

FILLING:

1 (20-ounce) bag frozen, unsweetened, pitted tart cherries, thawed (4 cups)
1¼ cups sugar
¼ cup cornstarch

2 tablespoons butter or margarine
½ teaspoon almond extract
½ teaspoon vanilla extract
1–2 drops red food color

In medium saucepan, combine sugar and cornstarch; add cherries. Cook and stir on medium heat until mixture comes to a boil. Remove from heat; stir in butter, extracts, and food color. Let stand for 1 hour at room temperature.

PASTRY:

3 cups all-purpose flour
2 tablespoons sugar
1 teaspoon salt
1 cup Crisco solid vegetable shortening

½ cup water
1 eggs, slightly beaten
1 tablespoon vinegar
1 tablespoon milk
1 tablespoon sugar

Preheat oven to 375°. In medium bowl, combine flour, sugar, and salt; cut in shortening until crumbly. Add egg and vinegar; stir until dough forms a ball. Divide into thirds. On floured surface, roll each third out to ⅛-inch thickness. Line pie plate; trim edges even with plate. Turn cherry filling into pastry-lined plate.

On second pastry circle, cut out the word "Ohio" and a shape of the state. Moisten edges of pastry in plate. Lift second pastry circle onto filling. Trim ½ inch beyond edge of pie plate; fold top edge under bottom crust, flute edges. Brush top of pie with milk; sprinkle with sugar. Bake 35–40 minutes, or until golden brown.

With third pastry circle, cut out 3-inch shapes of the state of Ohio; cut small hole in center of each. Bake 5–8 minutes or until golden brown; cool. To serve pie, place maraschino cherry piece in each hole. Place cutout on toothpick; insert in each piece of pie. Makes 1 (9-inch) pie.

Bountiful Ohio (Ohio)

Rhubarb Cream Pie

Mmmmm good!

1 pound rhubarb, cut into 1-inch pieces
1¼ cups plus 2 tablespoons sugar, divided
2½ tablespoons tapioca
1 (9-inch) pie crust, unbaked

1 (8-ounce) package cream cheese, softened
2 eggs, beaten
1 cup sour cream
1 teaspoon vanilla

Cook rhubarb, ¾ cup sugar, and tapioca until thickened. (Red food coloring may be added, if desired.) Pour into an unbaked 9-inch pie crust. Mix well the cream cheese, ½ cup sugar, and eggs. Pour over rhubarb, and bake in a 350° oven for 35 minutes, until brown and puffy. When cool, mix sour cream, remaining 2 tablespoons sugar, and vanilla together; spread over top. Cool in refrigerator until ready to serve. Serves 6–8.

Specialties of Indianapolis II (Indiana)

Rhubarb Custard Pie

CRUST:

1 cup all-purpose flour
½ cup margarine, softened

1 tablespoon sugar

Mix until crumbly and push into 9-inch pie plate. Bake at 350° until light brown.

CUSTARD:

3 cups finely chopped rhubarb
3 egg yolks
2 tablespoons flour

1½ cups sugar
1½ tablespoons margarine
2 egg whites

Mix ingredients and cook until thick like custard. Pour into baked pie shell.

MERINGUE:

2 egg whites
6 tablespoons sugar

¼ teaspoon cream of tartar

Combine ingredients and whip until stiff. Top Custard with Meringue. Bake another 5 minutes to slightly brown tips of Meringue.

St. Paul's Woman's League 50th Anniversary Cook Book (Iowa)

Indiana Sugar Cream Pie

1 cup whipping cream
1 cup coffee cream
¾ teaspoon vanilla
½ cup all-purpose flour
1 cup sugar

¼ teaspoon salt
Pastry lined 9-inch pie pan
1 tablespoon butter
½ teaspoon nutmeg

Combine heavy cream, coffee cream, and vanilla. In another bowl, combine flour, sugar, and salt. Slowly, using an electric mixer or wire whisk, add cream mixture to flour mixture until smooth. Let stand while rolling out pastry crust.

Dot bottom of crust with small pieces of butter. Sprinkle nutmeg evenly over bottom of pie shell. Briefly beat cream mixture again before pouring into prepared pie shell. Bake at 450° for 10 minutes; stir filling and lower heat to 325°. Bake 20–25 minutes longer. Shake pie pan every 8–10 minutes while baking. Serves 8.

Indiana's Finest Recipes (Indiana)

15-Minute Custard Pie

4 slightly beaten eggs
½ cup sugar
¼ teaspoon salt
1 teaspoon vanilla

2½ cups scalded milk
1 (9-inch) pie shell, unbaked
Nutmeg

Preheat oven to 475°. Thoroughly mix eggs, sugar, salt, and vanilla; beat slightly. Slowly stir in hot milk. At once, pour into unbaked pastry shell. To avoid spills, fill at oven. Dash top with nutmeg. Bake in very hot over 5 minutes. Reduce heat to 425°. Bake 10 minutes longer, or until knife inserted halfway between center and edge comes out clean. Cool on rack. Serve cool or chilled. Keep unused portion refrigerated. This custard does not get watery and is very tasty.

175th Anniversary Quilt Cookbook (Ohio)

Coconut Macaroon Pie

¼ cup chopped pecans
1 (8-inch) unbaked pie shell
½ cup water
¼ cup all-purpose flour
1 (3½-ounce) can flaked
   coconut

2 eggs, slightly beaten
1½ cups sugar
¼ teaspoon salt
½ cup butter, melted

Sprinkle pecans over bottom of pie shell. Combine remaining ingredients; pour into pie shell. Bake in slow oven (325°) until golden brown and almost set, about 45 minutes. Cool and serve.

Home Cooking (Indiana)

Iowa Pride Chess Pie

Delicious warm or chilled.

1 cup granulated sugar
½ cup light brown sugar,
   firmly packed
1 tablespoon flour
1 tablespoon yellow cornmeal
⅛ teaspoon salt
3 large eggs

½ cup butter, melted
3 tablespoons milk or light
   cream
1½ teaspoons white vinegar
1 teaspoon vanilla
1 (9-inch) pie shell, unbaked

Toss sugars, flour, cornmeal, and salt together with a fork. Add eggs, butter, milk or cream, vinegar, and vanilla. Beat mixture with electric beater until smooth. Pour into unbaked pie shell. Cover edges of crust with narrow strips of foil for first 25 minutes of baking to prevent over browning. Bake at 350° for 35–40 minutes or until a clean knife inserted in center comes out clean. Can be frozen. Serves 6.

Recipes from Iowa with Love (Iowa)

Heavenly Cream Cheese Pie

CHOCOLATE NUT CRUST:

1 (6-ounce) package semisweet
   chocolate chips

1 tablespoon shortening
1½ cups chopped nuts

Line a 9-inch pie pan with foil. Over hot (not boiling) water in a double boiler, melt chocolate chips and shortening. Stir in nuts. Spread in pie pan over bottom and sides. Chill in refrigerator until firm, about 1 hour. Lift out of pan and peel off foil. Replace crust in pan; chill until ready to fill.

FILLING:

1 (6-ounce) package semisweet
   chocolate chips

1 (8-ounce) package cream
   cheese, softened

¾ cup sugar, divided

⅛ teaspoon salt
2 eggs, separated
1 cup whipping cream
3 tablespoons brandy, or 2
   tablespoons Grand Marnier

Melt chocolate chips over hot (not boiling) water in a double boiler. Cool 10 minutes. In a large bowl, combine cream cheese, ½ cup sugar, and salt; beat until creamy. Beat in egg yolks one at a time. Stir into cooled chocolate; set aside.

In a small bowl, beat egg whites until foamy. Gradually beat in remaining ¼ cup sugar, and beat until stiff, glossy peaks form. Set aside.

In another small bowl, beat 1 cup whipping cream and brandy until soft peaks form. Fold flavored whipped cream and beaten egg whites into chocolate mixture. Pour into crust. Chill in refrigerator 3 hours or until firm.

TOPPING:

1 tablespoon brandy or Grand
   Marnier

1 cup whipping cream

Beat brandy and whipping cream until soft peaks form. Garnish on top of pie before serving.

Country Collections Cookbook II (Ohio)

Walnut Pie

½ cup brown sugar, packed
2 tablespoons flour
1¼ cups light corn syrup
3 tablespoons butter
¼ teaspoon salt

3 eggs
1½ teaspoons vanilla
1 cup large pieces English
  walnuts
1 (9-inch) pie shell, unbaked

Mix brown sugar and flour in saucepan. Add corn syrup, butter, and salt; warm over low heat just until butter is melted. Beat eggs with vanilla. Stir in sugar mixture. Turn into pie shell and sprinkle with walnuts. Bake below oven center at 375° for 40–45 minutes, or until filling is set in center. Cool before cutting.

Our Heritage (Iowa)

Buckeye Pie

4 large egg yolks
2½ cups milk
¼ cup cornstarch
1 cup light brown sugar

2 teaspoons vanilla
½ cup creamy peanut butter
1 (9-inch) pie shell, baked,
  cooled

Whisk egg yolks and milk in a bowl. In saucepan, combine milk mixture, cornstarch, and brown sugar. Cook over medium heat, stirring constantly, until mixture thickens and boils. Remove from heat and add vanilla. Stir in peanut butter. Cover pudding with plastic wrap to prevent skin from forming. Cool to room temperature. Spread in pie shell and cover with Topping.

TOPPING:

2 tablespoons unsalted butter
2 tablespoons corn syrup
1 tablespoon water

2 ounces semisweet chocolate
1 ounce milk chocolate
Whipped cream

Combine butter, corn syrup, and water in saucepan. Bring to a boil and remove from heat. Add both chocolates. Wait 5 minutes for chocolate to melt, then whisk until smooth. Cool 15 minutes and spread over filling. Refrigerate. Remove from refrigerator about 20 minutes before serving. Serve with whipped cream.

Entertaining Made Easy (Ohio)

Chocolate Mousse Pie

CRUST:

3 cups chocolate wafer crumbs (Oreos)

1 stick unsalted butter, melted

Combine crumbs and butter. Press on bottom and completely up sides of 10-inch springform pan. Refrigerate 30 minutes (or chill in freezer).

FILLING:

1 pound semisweet chocolate
2 eggs
4 egg yolks

2 cups whipping cream
6 tablespoons powdered sugar
4 egg whites, room temperature

Soften chocolate in top of double boiler over simmering water. Let cool to lukewarm (95°). Add whole eggs; mix well. Add yolks and mix until thoroughly blended.

Whip cream with powdered sugar until soft peaks form. Beat egg whites until stiff, but not dry. Stir a little of the cream and whites into chocolate mixture to lighten. Fold in remaining cream and whites until completely incorporated. Turn into Crust and chill at least 6 hours, or preferably overnight.

TOPPING:

2 cups whipping cream

Sugar

Whip cream with sugar to taste until quite stiff. Loosen Crust on all sides using sharp knife; remove springform. Spread all but about ½ cup cream over top of mousse. Pipe remaining cream into rosettes in center of pie. Makes 10–12 servings.

I Love You (Iowa)

Chocolate Cream Pie

A chocolate pie like no other.

½ cup granulated sugar
3 heaping tablespoons Nestlé Quik (no substitute)
3 heaping tablespoons cornstarch
¼ teaspoon salt

3 egg yolks
2 cups whole milk
1 teaspoon vanilla
2 tablespoons butter or margarine
1 (9-inch) pie shell, baked

Mix dry ingredients together. Slightly beat egg yolks, and add milk. Add to dry mixture and cook over medium heat until thick. Add vanilla and butter. Cool. Pour into baked pie shell.

Touches of the Hands & Heart (Ohio)

Blackberry Crisp

BLACKBERRY FILLING:

¾ cup sugar
2 tablespoons flour

5 cups fresh or frozen blackberries

Preheat oven to 375°. Mix sugar and flour; then toss gently with blackberries to coat evenly. Transfer to a 9x9-inch baking dish that is well buttered.

CRUST TOPPING:

1 cup all-purpose flour
1 cup sugar
1 teaspoon baking powder

1 egg, beaten
1 stick butter, melted

Combine flour, sugar, and baking powder; blend. Make a well in center of dry ingredients and blend in beaten egg, mixing until topping is crumbly. Sprinkle over berry mixture. Drizzle melted butter evenly over crumbly topping. Place baking dish on a baking sheet or foil to prevent spillovers. Bake 45 minutes, or until crisp.

Gardener's Delight (Ohio)

Rhubarb Surprise

8 cups chopped rhubarb
½ cup butter
3 cups sugar, divided
1½ cups all-purpose flour
½ teaspoon salt
1½ teaspoons baking powder
½ cup milk
2 tablespoons cornstarch
1 cup boiling water

Spread chopped rhubarb evenly in 9x13-inch greased pan. Cream butter, 1½ cups sugar, flour, salt, and baking powder alternately with milk. Spread mixture over rhubarb. Combine remaining 1½ cups sugar and cornstarch. Sprinkle evenly over batter. Pour boiling water evenly over all. Bake 1 hour at 375°.

Heavenly Dishes (Ohio)

Million Dollar Dessert

1 box Jiffy Yellow Cake Mix
1 (8-ounce) package cream
   cheese, softened
2 cups milk, divided
1 (4-ounce) package vanilla
   instant pudding
1 (21-ounce) can pie filling (any
   flavor)
1 (8-ounce) container Cool Whip

Mix cake mix as directed. Put into 9x13-inch pan. Bake 12–15 minutes at 350°. Let cool. Combine cream cheese with ½ cup milk. Mix pudding with remaining 1½ cups milk, then mix together with cream cheese mixture. Spread on cake and let set. Cover with pie filling. Serve topped with Cool Whip. Makes 12–15 servings.

Inn-describably Delicious (Illinois)

The Grand Finale Grand Trifle

4 cups pound or yellow cake
  chunks
1 cup fresh or frozen, thawed
  strawberries in syrup
4 ounces port wine
4 ounces cream sherry
8 large scoops rich vanilla ice
  cream or custard

1 cup fresh or frozen, thawed
  raspberries in syrup
1½–2 cups heavy cream,
  whipped
¼ cup toasted slivered almonds
8 maraschino or chocolate
  covered cherries for garnish

In 8 large brandy sniffers or a 2-quart clear glass bowl, layer ingredients in order given, and garnish with cherries. Chill about an hour to blend flavors. Serves 8.

Dining in Historic Ohio (Ohio)

Punch Bowl Cake

1 angel food cake mix (or 1
  "boughten" cake)
2 (3-ounce) boxes vanilla regular
  pudding
1½ quarts fresh strawberries,
  sliced
1 (16-ounce) box frozen
  strawberries, thawed

1 (15-ounce) jar strawberry
  glaze
1 (15-ounce) can crushed
  pineapple, drained
1 (16-ounce) carton whipped
  topping

Make cake as directed and bake. While cake is baking, make up pudding so cake and pudding can cool. After cake is baked and cooled, crumble half into bottom of a punch bowl. Mix berries and glaze together. Add half the pudding, pineapple, berries and glaze, and whipped topping to cake in bowl. Repeat layers. Cover and refrigerate at least overnight.

First Christian Church Centennial Cookbook (Iowa)

Peanut Buster Dessert

CRUST:

1 cup all-purpose flour
1 stick butter or margarine,
    softened

⅔ cup chopped peanuts, dry
    roasted, unsalted

Mix flour and butter like pie crust. Add peanuts and spread in a 9x13-inch greased pan. Bake at 350° for 15–20 minutes until golden brown. Set aside until cool.

FIRST TOPPING:

⅓ cup creamy peanut butter
1 (8-ounce) package cream
    cheese

1 cup powdered sugar
2 cups Cool Whip

Cream first 3 ingredients, then blend in Cool Whip. Spread on top of cooled baked dough.

SECOND TOPPING:

1 (3-ounce) package French
    vanilla instant pudding
3 cups cold milk

1 (3-ounce) box chocolate
    instant pudding

Mix all together with mixer until thick. Spread on top of cream cheese topping.

THIRD TOPPING:

1 (8-ounce) container Cool Whip
Chopped peanuts

1 large Hershey's Chocolate Bar,
    crushed

Spread Cool Whip on top of pudding mixture. Sprinkle with chopped peanuts and crushed chocolate bar. Refrigerate.

Note: You can use one small box vanilla and one box chocolate pudding; use 1½ cups cold milk for each box. Spread one on top of the other.

Cooking GRACEfully (Ohio)

Pioneer Bread Pudding

2 cups stale but not dry bread
  cubes
2 cups milk
3 tablespoons butter

¼ cup sugar
2 eggs
Dash of salt
¼ teaspoon vanilla

Place bread cubes in a 1-quart buttered baking dish. Scald milk with butter and sugar. Beat eggs slightly, add salt, then stir in warm milk and vanilla. Pour over bread cubes. Set baking dish in a pan containing warm water up to the level of the pudding and bake about 1 hour at 350°, or until a knife comes out clean when inserted in center of pudding. Makes 4–6 servings. Serve warm with plain cream, currant jelly, or Lemon Pudding Sauce.

LEMON PUDDING SAUCE:

½ cup sugar
1 tablespoon cornstarch
1 cup boiling water
2 tablespoons butter

1 tablespoon grated lemon rind
3 tablespoons lemon juice
⅛ teaspoon salt

Combine sugar and cornstarch; add boiling water slowly and stir until dissolved. Cook slowly, stirring constantly, until thickened and clear. Remove from heat and add remaining ingredients. Serve warm.

Neighboring on the Air (Iowa)

The Eternal Indian, better known as the Black Hawk Statue, is a sculpture in Lowden State Park near the city of Oregon, Illinois. The 48-foot-tall concrete monument towers over the Rock River on a 77-foot bluff. Sculptor Lorado Taft said the statue was inspired by the Indian leader Black Hawk. Black Hawk was born in the village of Saukenuk on the Rock River, in present-day Rock Island, Illinois, in 1767. Black Hawk's legacy is legendary. Of all the wars fought in United States history, the Black Hawk War is the only one named for a person. In 1833, Black Hawk's life story became the first Native American autobiography published in the United States.

Annie's Apple Pudding

This fabulous pudding is similar to the date pudding that makes that wonderful sauce as it bakes.

1–1⅓ cups sugar (depends on
   tartness of apples)
⅔ cup shortening
2 eggs, beaten
6 cups peeled, chopped apples

1 cup chopped pecans or walnuts
2 teaspoons baking soda
2 teaspoons ground cinnamon
1 teaspoon ground nutmeg
2 cups all-purpose flour

Cream sugar and shortening. Add eggs, one at a time, and beat well after each addition. Fold in chopped apples and nuts. Sift together baking soda, spices, and flour, and add to apple mixture. Spread mixture into greased 9x13-inch pan and pour following Sauce over the top.

SAUCE:
1½ cups brown sugar, packed
2 tablespoons flour
1 cup water

¼ cup butter
1 teaspoon vanilla

Stir together sugar and flour, then add remainder of ingredients in a heavy saucepan. Bring to a boil and boil gently for 3 minutes, stirring often. Pour this hot Sauce over the batter. Do not stir. Bake at 325° for 1 hour. Serves 10–12.

Christmas Thyme at Oak Hill Farm (Indiana)

Apfelstrudel-Vanillesauce

2 cups all-purpose flour
2 eggs
¼ cup lukewarm water
Pinch of salt
½ teaspoon vinegar
4–5 pounds tart apples
⅓ cup sugar

3 tablespoons cinnamon
6 tablespoons butter, melted
4 tablespoons bread crumbs
1 cup chopped almonds, or other
   nuts
1½ cups raisins

Heap flour on bread board and make a depression in center large enough to hold the beaten eggs, water, salt, and vinegar. Knead this into a firm dough which, when cut, will reveal air pockets. Set dough, covered, in a warm place.

Peel and grate apples and sprinkle with sugar and cinnamon. Dust a cloth with flour and on it, roll out dough, the thinner the better. Melt butter. Mix in bread crumbs and coat dough. Sprinkle with apples, nuts, and raisins. Roll dough over in cloth several times to form a loaf (strudel) of several alternating layers of dough and filling. Brush finished loaf with more melted butter, put on greased baking sheet, and bake in hot (400°) oven until crust is crisp and well browned. This may be served with Vanilla Sauce.

VANILLA SAUCE:

1 cup milk
1 teaspoon vanilla
1 tablespoon sugar

2 egg yolks
½ teaspoon cornstarch

Heat milk and vanilla, then let cool. Blend sugar, egg yolks, and cornstarch until smooth and stir into milk. Beat in double boiler over moderate heat until mixture thickens. Remove from heat and stir until cool.

Guten Appetit (Indiana)

Creamy Caramel Apples

1 bag caramels
1 (14-ounce) can condensed
  milk

1 (8-ounce) carton Cool Whip
Sliced apples
Chopped nuts

In fondue pot, melt peeled caramels and condensed milk. Then add Cool Whip and stir mixture. Slice apples in bowl, pour some caramel mixture over them and sprinkle nuts on top.

Good Cookin' Cookbook (Illinois)

Cinnamon Candied Apples

These are incredibly beautiful in a footed glass or crystal compote. (Cool apples and syrup before placing into a crystal bowl or compote.)

1 cup sugar
2 cups water
1 cup cinnamon red hot candies

Small, firm apples, such as
  Jonathan

Combine sugar, water, and red hots in a fairly large, deep saucepot. Bring to a boil and simmer until red hots are dissolved and thoroughly melted. Peel small, firm apples. Drop addles into boiling syrup—keep syrup boiling, so just add 3 or 4 apples at a time. Cook until apples (or small, firm, peeled pears) are just tender, but not mushy. This is enough syrup to cook 6–8 apples.

Christmas Thyme at Oak Hill Farm (Indiana)

Bailey's Irish Cream Turtle Torte

A wonderful frozen ice cream pie.

1½ cups shortbread cookie
   crumbs (like Keebler's Pecan
   Sandies)
¼ cup light brown sugar,
   packed
¼ teaspoon ground nutmeg
¼ cup butter, melted
1 quart butter pecan ice cream
¾ cup Bailey's Irish Cream
   Liqueur, divided

1 (12-ounce) jar caramel ice
   cream topping
1 cup coarsely chopped pecans,
   toasted, divided
1 quart chocolate ice cream
1 (12-ounce) jar fudge ice cream
   topping

Lightly butter sides of a 10-inch springform pan. Line sides with strips of wax paper, then butter the bottom and paper-lined sides. In a bowl, combine cookie crumbs, sugar, and nutmeg. Stir in melted butter. Pat evenly on bottom of pan and refrigerate. Spoon slightly softened butter pecan ice cream into a bowl and swirl in ½ cup of Irish Cream. (Do not overmix.) Pack this into chilled crust. Pour caramel topping into a small bowl and stir in 2 tablespoons of Irish Cream. Drizzle over butter pecan layer, then sprinkle with ¾ cup pecans. Freeze 1 hour.

Spread slightly softened chocolate ice cream on top of frozen first layer. Pour fudge topping into another small bowl and stir in remaining 2 tablespoons Irish Cream. Spoon this over chocolate ice cream. Cover with foil and freeze until firm, 6 hours or overnight.

To serve, remove sides of pan. Carefully peel off wax paper. Place bottom of springform pan on serving plate. Garnish top with remaining ¼ cup pecans. Let torte stand 10 minutes before slicing. If desired, serve with a dollop of whipped cream atop each serving. Serves 14–16.

It's About Thyme (Indiana)

Chocolate Pâte

PÂTE:

15 ounces semisweet chocolate
1 cup heavy cream
4 tablespoons unsalted butter
4 egg yolks

¾ cup powdered sugar
6 tablespoons dark rum
Sweetened whipped cream for
  garnish

Grease a 4-cup loaf pan. Place wax paper in pan, leaving a small overhang. Grease sides and bottom of paper lining. Set aside.

Melt chocolate with cream and butter in the top of a double boiler over simmering water. Beat with a wire whisk until mixture is smooth and glossy. Remove from heat and add yolks, one at a time, beating well after each addition. Whisk in powdered sugar until smooth. Mix in rum. Pour mixture into prepared pan and cover with plastic wrap. Freeze overnight.

When ready to serve, remove Pâte by gently loosening wax paper from pan. If it sticks, set pan in hot water for a few seconds. Invert Pâte onto a serving plate and remove wax paper. Using a hot knife, cut Pâte into ⅓- to ½-inch slices.

RASPBERRY SAUCE:

2 (10-ounce) packages frozen
  raspberries in syrup, thawed
¼ cup sugar

2–3 tablespoons Grand Marnier
  liqueur

Drain 1 package raspberries, discarding juice. Reserve juice when draining second package of berries. Purée all berries, reserved juice, sugar, and liqueur in a food processor or blender. Strain purée to remove seeds. Chill until ready to use.

To serve, place a slice of Pâte in a pool of Raspberry Sauce on each plate. Top with a generous dollop of whipped cream. Yields 8–10 servings.

Causing A Stir (Ohio)

Crunchy Ice Cream Dessert

Prepare dessert the day before serving.

DESSERT:

½ gallon vanilla ice cream
¼ cup butter
½ cup firmly packed brown
  sugar
2 cups crisp rice cereal squares
⅔ cup chopped pecans
⅔ cup flaked coconut

Place ice cream in large bowl and soften at room temperature for 2 hours. Melt butter with brown sugar in skillet over medium heat, stirring constantly. Remove from heat. Add cereal, pecans, and coconut to skillet, mixing well. Press ½ of cereal mixture into a 9x13x2-inch baking pan. Spread ice cream on cereal layer and top with remaining cereal mixture. Freeze overnight.

HOT FUDGE SAUCE:

1 (6-ounce) package semisweet
  chocolate chips
1 (14-ounce) can sweetened
  condensed milk
1 (7-ounce) jar marshmallow
  crème

Melt chocolate chips in top of double boiler over simmering water. Stir in condensed milk and marshmallow crème, heating and stirring until well blended. To serve, cut ice cream into squares and top with Hot Fudge Sauce. Serves 15.

I'll Cook When Pigs Fly (Ohio)

List of Contributors

Located in Utica, Illinois, Starved Rock State Park contains 18 sandstone canyons carved over the last 12,000 years by surface water runoff and groundwater outflow. Starved Rock itself is a large eroded butte overlooking the Illinois River. The park is one of the busiest state parks in Illinois with yearly attendance averaging over one million visitors.

Listed below are the cookbooks that have contributed recipes to this book, along with copyright, author, publisher, city and state. The information in parentheses indicates the BEST OF THE BEST cookbook in which the recipe originally appeared.

Affolter-Heritage Reunion Cookbook & More, Mary Calendine, Hiddenite, NC

America Celebrates Columbus ©1999 The Junior League of Columbus, OH

The American Gothic Cookbook ©1996 Penfield Press, Iowa City, IA

Amish Country Cookbook I ©1979 Bethel Publishing, Evangel Publishing House, Nappanee, IN

Amish Country Cookbook II ©1986 Bethel Publishing, Evangel Publishing House, Nappanee, IN

Amish Country Cookbook III ©1993 Bethel Publishing, Evangel Publishing House, Nappanee, IN

The Amish Way Cookbook ©1994 Adrienne Lund, Jupiter Press, Chagrin Falls, OH

An Apple for the Teacher ©1993 Illinois Retired Teachers Association, Springfield, IL

Angels and Friends Cookbook I ©1981 Angels of Easter Seal, Youngstown, OH

Angels and Friends Cookbook II ©1991 Angels of Easter Seal, Youngstown, OH

Angiporto, Inc. ©1991 Angiporto, Inc. Barbara McCormack and Deedee Borland, Lake Forest, IL

Applause Applause, Roberta Coleman, Coggon, IA

Aren't You Going to Taste It, Honey? ©1995 The Toledo Blade Company, The Blade Marketing Department, Toledo, OH

Aspic and Old Lace ©1987 The Northern Indiana Historical Society, Sound Bend, IN

Asthma Walk Cook Book, American Lunch Association of Ohio, Kaiser Wells Asthma Walk Team, Norwalk, OH

Aunt Paula's American Hungarian Cookbook ©1998 Albert E. Misek, by Mathilde Misek, Solon, OH

Back Home Again ©1993 The Junior League of Indianapolis, IN

Beginnings ©2000 The Junior League of Akron, OH

Berns Family Cookbook, Berns Family, Waukon ,IA

Best Recipes of Illinois Inns and Restaurants ©1988 Amherst Press, Margaret Guthrie, Amherst, WI

Best Recipes of Ohio Inns and Restaurants ©1988 Palmer Publications, Margaret E. Guthrie, Amherst Press, Amherst, WI

Blue Willow's "Sweet Treasures," C.J. Gustafson, Harcourt, IA

Bountiful Ohio ©1993 James Hope and Susan Failor, Gabriel's Horn Publishing Co., Bowling Green, OH

Brunch Basket ©1984 Junior League of Rockford, IL

Busy People's Fun, Fast, Festive Christmas Cookbook ©2005 Dawn Hall, Rutledge Hill Press, Nashville, TN

Busy People's Low-Fat Cookbook ©2003 Dawn Hall, Rutledge Hill Press, Nashville, TN

Busy People's Low-Carb Cookbook ©2005 Dawn Hall, Rutledge Hill Press, Nashville, TN

By Our Cookstove ©1983 Shekinah Christian School, Shekinah Christian Ladies Auxiliary, Plain City, OH

C-U in the Kitchen ©1983 Champaign-Urbana Hadassah, Champaign, IL

Carol's Kitchen ©1993 Carol J. Moore, Galesburg, IL

Carroll County Humane Society Members & Friends Cookbook Volume II, Carroll County Humane Society, Malvern, OH

A Cause for Applause, Elgin Symphony League, Elgin, IL

Causing A Stir ©2000 Junior League of Dayton, OH

Celebrating Iowa, First United Methodist Church UMW, Iowa City, IA

Champions: Favorite Foods of Indy Car Racing ©1993 by C.A.R.A., Championship Auto Racing Auxiliary, Indianapolis, IN

Christmas Thyme at Oak Hill Farm ©1994 Thyme Cookbooks, Marge Clark, West Lebanon, IN

Cincinnati Recipe Treasury ©1983 Mary Anna DuSablon, Ohio University Press, Athens, OH

A Collection of Recipes from St. Matthew Lutheran Church, Rebecca Quilters, Galena, IL

College Avenue Presbyterian Church Cookbook, Presbyterian Women of College Avenue Church, Aledo, IL

Columbus Colony Creations, Columbus Colony Elderly Care, Westerville, OH 43081

Community Centennial Cookbook, Harcourt Community, Harcourt, IA

The Conner Prairie Cookbook ©1990 Conner Prairie Press, Edited by Margaret A. Hoffman, Noblesville, IN

Cook Book: Favorite Recipes of Our Best Cooks, Central Illinois Tourism Council, Springfield, IL

Cook of the Week Cookbook, Humboldt Independent Newspaper, Humboldt, IA

Cook, Line & Sinker, Rocky River Junior Women's Club, Rocky River, OH

A Cook's Tour of Iowa ©1988 University of Iowa Press, Chicago, IL

The Cookery Collection ©1990 Conner Prairie Press, Dorothy Nelis Nicholson, Anderson, IN

Cookies & Tea, College Women's Club of Dayton, OH

Cookin' with Friends, Friends of the Graves-Hume Library, Mendota, IL

Cookin' to Beat the Band, Tri Kappa, Elkhart, IN

Cooking with Daisy's Descendants, Elaine Gilbert Davis, Fairmount, IL

Cooking Along the Lincoln Highway in Ohio, Bucyrus Tourism and Visitors Bureau, Bucyrus, OH

Cooking with Marilyn ©1988 Marilyn Harris, Pelican Publishing Co., Gretna, LA

Cooking with Hope Ridge Families, Hope Ridge United Methodist Women, Mentor, OH

Cooking on the Wild Side ©1995 Zoological Society of Cincinnati, Cincinnati Zoo and Botanical Garden, Cincinnati, OH

Cooking with Class, Garden Club of Apple Valley in Ohio, Howard, OH

Cooking Up a Care, Always Friends (Light the Night Team), West Milton, OH

Cooking GRACEfully, Grace Presbyterian Church, Martins Ferry, OH

Country Cooking, Upper Deer Creek United Church of Christ, Galveston, IN

Country Cupboard Cookbook, Panora Church of the Brethren Women, Panora, IA

Country Collections Cookbook II, Fry's Valley Moravian Church, New Philadelphia, OH

Country Lady Nibbling and Scribbling ©1994 Alice Howard, Country Lady Productions, Elgin, IA

Crowd Pleasers ©2002 The Junior League of Canton, OH

The Cubs 'R Cookin' ©1994 Cubs' Wives for Family Rescue, The Chicago Cubs, Chicago, IL

Dandy Dutch Recipes ©1991 Penfield Press, Iowa City, IA

Dawdy Family Cookbook, Kae Dawdy Coates, Roodhouse, IL

Dawn to Dusk ©1998 Jonna Sigrist Cranebaugh, Olde World Bed & Breakfast, Dover, OH

The Des Moines Register Cookbook ©1995 The University of Iowa Press, Chicago, IL

The Diabetic's Healthy Exchanges Cookbook ©1996 Healthy Exchanges, Inc., JoAnna M. Lund, DeWitt, IA

Dining in Historic Ohio ©1987 Marty Godbey, McClanahan Publishing, Kuttawa, KY

Discover Dayton ©1979, 1986 The Junior League of Dayton, OH

Don't Forget the INNgredients!, Jan Westfall Rogers, Spitzer House Bed & Breakfast, Medina, OH

Down Home Cookin' without the Down Home Fat ©1996 Dawn Hall, Cozy Homestead Publishing, Inc., Swanton, OH

Down Home Cooking from Hocking County, Logan Hocking Chamber of Commerce, Logan, OH

Easy Cooking with Herbs & Spices ©1993 Triset De Fonseka, Cincinnati, OH

Elsah Landing Heartland Cooking ©1984 The Elsah Landing Restaurant, Inc., Helen Crafton and Dorothy Lindgren, Grafton, IL

The Elsah Landing Restaurant Cookbook ©1981 The Elsah Landing Restaurant, Inc., Helen Crafton and Dorothy Lindgren, Grafton, IL

Enjoy, Martha Harrison, Toledo, IA

Entertaining Made Easy ©2004 Barbara J. Smith, London, OH

Family Celebrations Cookbook, Saline County Homemakers Extension Association, Harrisburg, IL

Favorite Recipes of Collinsville Junior Service Club, Collinsville Junior Service Club, Collinsville, IL

Favorite Recipes from the Delaware Police Department ©2006 Delaware Police Department, Delaware, OH

Favorite Recipes-First Church of God, Gallipolis, OH

Favorite Recipes, St. Nicholas Orthodox Church, Barton, OH

Favorite Recipes from the Heart of Amish Country, Rachel Miller, Sugarcreek, OH

Favorite Herbal Recipes Vol. III, Herbs for Health and Fun Club, Centralia, IL

Favorite Recipes from Poland Women's Club, Poland, OH

Feeding the Flock-Trinity United Methodist Women ©2003 Trinity UM Women, Chillicothe, OH

Festival Foods and Family Favorites ©1995 Sara Anne Corrigan, Evansviille, IN

A Festival of Recipes, Annunciation Greek Orthodox Church, Dayton, OH

The Fifth Generation Cookbook, Carol L. Wise, Findlay, OH

50 Years and Still Cookin'!, Christ Child Society of Akron, OH

Fire Gals' Hot Pans Cookbook, Garrison Emergency Service Auxiliary, Garrison, IA

Firebelles Cookbook, New Philadelphia Fire Department Ladies Auxiliary, New Philadelphia, OH

First There Must Be Food ©1987 Volunteer Services Department, Chicago, IL

CONTRIBUTING COOKBOOKS

First Christian Church Centennial Cookbook, Christian Women's Fellowship, First Christian Church of Mason City, IA

500 Recipes Using Zucchini, Southington Garden Club, Southington, OH

The Fishlady's Cookbook ©1991 Patricia Kendall, Templegate Publishers, Springfield, IL

Five Star Sensations ©1991 Auxiliary of University Hospitals of Cleveland, OH

Five Loaves and Two Fishes II, First United Methodist Church Women, Springfield, IL

Fontanelle Good Samaritan Center Commemorative Cookbook, Fontanelle Good Samaritan Center, Fontanelle, IA

Food for Thought ©2005 Alzheimer's Association NW Ohio Chapter, Toledo, OH

For Crying Out Loud . . . Let's Eat! ©1988 The Service League of Hammond, IN

Franklin County 4-H Favorites, Franklin County 4-H Teen Council, Grove City, OH

Franklin County Homemakers Extension Cookbook, Franklin County Homemakers Extension, Benton, IL

The French-Icarian Persimmon Tree Cookbook ©1992 Louise Lum, Pollard Press, Icarian Living History Museum, Nauvoo, IL

The "Friends" Cookbook, Friends of Darke County Parks, Pitsburg, OH

Gardener's Delight, The Ohio Association of Garden Clubs, Inc., Green Springs, OH

Generations of Good Cooking, St. Mary's Parish, Oxford, IA

Generations ©1994 Junior League of Rockford, IL

German Recipes ©1994 Penfield Press, Iowa City, IA

Good Cookin' Cookbook, New Life Class, Benton, IL

Grand Detour Holiday Sampler, Karen Stransky, Dixon, IL

Great Beginnings, Grand Finales ©1991 The Junior League of South Bend, IN

The Great Iowa Home Cooking Expedition, New Life Fellowship, Lisbon, IA

Guten Appetit, German-American Klub, Indianapolis, IN

The Heart of Cooking II ©1994 The Heart Center of Fort Wayne, IN

Heartland ©1991 Marcia Adams, Random House, Westminster, MD

Heartline Cookbook ©1992 Pat DiGiacomo, Wooster, OH

Heavenly Food II, United Methodist Women, Sunbury United Methodist Church, Sunbury, OH

Heavenly Dishes, United Methodist Women of Union Pisgah Church, Attica, OH

Heirloom Recipes and By Gone Days ©1993 Heirloom Enterprises, , Sherry Maurer, Zoar, OH

Herrin's Favorite Italian Recipes Cookbook, Herrin's Hospital Auxiliary, Herrin, IL

Holy Cow, Chicago's Cooking! ©1993 The Church of the Holy Comforter, Kenilworth, IL

Home Cookin' Is a Family Affair, Aldersgate United Methodist Women, Marion, IL

Home Cooking with the Cummer Family, Dubuque, IA

Home Cooking, 49'ers Club of Dana, Hillsdale, IN

Home Cooking II, 49'ers Club of Dana, Hillsdale, IN

Honest to Goodness ©1990 The Junior League of Springfield, IL

Hoosier Heritage Cookbook, Mental Health Assn. in Hancock County, Greenfield, IN

Hopewell's Hoosier Harvest II, Hopewell Presbyterian Church, Franklin, IN

I Love You, Sondra Smith, Iowa City, IA

I'll Cook When Pigs Fly ©1998 The Junior League of Cincinnati, OH

The Indiana Kid's Cookbook! ©1995 Gollapade Publishing Group, Peachtree City, GA

Indiana's Finest Recipes, Beech Grove Central Elementary PTA, Beech Grove, IN

Inn-describably Delicious ©1992 Tracy M. Winters and Phyllis Y. Winters, Winters Publishing, Greensburg, IN

Iowa Granges: Celebrating 125 Years of Cooking, Iowa State Grange, Cedar Rapids, IA

It's About Thyme ©1988 Marge Clark-Thyme Cookbooks, West Lebanon, IN

The James Whitcomb Riley Cookbook ©1990 Dorothy June Williams and Diana Williams Hansen, Guild Press of Indiana, Carmel, IN

Jubilee, Emmanuel Memorial Episcopal Church, Champaign, IL

The Kettle Cookbook, The Soup Sisters of the Salvation Army, Cleveland, OH

kinderFun Kuisine ©1988 Healthy Young Children Ent, Inc., Linda Leszynski, Avon Lake, OH

Lehigh Public Library Cookbook, Lehigh Public Library , Lehigh, IA

Light Kitchen Choreography ©1994 Cleveland Ballet Council, Cleveland, OH

The L.o.V.E. Chocolate Cookbook, Jean Van Elsen Haney, Waterloo, IA

The Lucy Miele 6-5-4 Cookbook ©1988 Lucy Meile, Hill House Publishers, Stockton, IL

The Lucy Miele Too Good to Be Low-Fat Cookbook ©1988 Lucy Miele, Hill House Publishers, Stockton, IL

Lutheran Church Women Cookbook, Lutheran Church Women of Missouri Valley, IA

Madison County Cookbook ©1994 St. Joseph's Catholic Church, Winterset, IA

Marcus, Iowa, Quasquicentennial Cookbook, QQC Cookbook Committee, Marcus, IA

A Matter of Taste, Paulding County Republican Women, Paulding, OH

MDA Favorite Recipes, Maple Dale Elementary School, Cincinnati, OH

More Nutritious Still Delicious ©2006 Nutrition Council of Greater Cincinnati, OH

More Hoosier Cooking ©1982 Indiana University Press, Edited by Elaine Lumbra, Bloomington, IN

More to Love . . . from The Mansion of Golconda ©1993 Marilyn Kunz, Golconda, IL

Muffins–104 Recipes from A to Z ©1993 Dorothy Jean Publishing, Dot Vartyan, Evanston, IL

Neighboring on the Air ©1991 University of Iowa Press, Chicago, IL

New Beginnings, First Congregational United Church of Christ, DeWitt, IA

New Tastes of Iowa ©1993 Kathryn Designs, Peg Hein and Kathryn Lewis, Austin, Texas

Noteworthy ©1986 Noteworthy Publications, Women's Board of the Ravinia Festival, Highland Park, IL

Nutbread and Nostalgia ©1979 The Junior League of Sound Bend, IN

Oeder Family & Friends Cookbook, Diana Browning, Lebanon, OH

Ohio State Grange Cookbook, Ohio State Grange, Fredericktown, OH

Ohio Cook Book ©2002 Golden West Publishers, Donna Goodrich, Phoenix, AZ

Old-Fashioned Cooking, Raleigh Historical Society, Raleigh, IL

Oma's (Grandma's) Family Secrets, Linda F. Selzer, Homestead, IA

125 Years–Walking in Faith, Women's Fellowship, First Congregational Church, Spencer, IA

175th Anniversary Quilt Cookbook, Oak Grove Mennonite Church, Smithville, OH

One Magnificent Cookbook, The Junior League of Chicago, IL

Opaa! Greek Cooking Chicago Style
©1991 Bonus Books, Inc., George J.
Gekas, Chicago, IL

Our Favorite Recipes, Union County
Hospital Auxiliary, Anna, IL

Our Best Home Cooking, Pearl Luttman,
Red Bud, IL

Our Best Recipes to You, Again, High
Street United Methodist Church,
Muncie, IN

Our Collection of Heavenly Recipes,
Victory Christian School PTF,
Kinsman, OH

Our Favorite Recipes II, English
Wesleyan Women's Missionary
Society, English, IN

Our Heritage, Gayla Voss, Fonda, IA

Pioneer Pantry, Telephone Pioneers of
America, Lucent Technologies
Chapter #135, Lisle, IL

Plain & Fancy Favorites, Montgomery
Woman's Club, Cincinnati, OH

The PTA Pantry ©1994 The Fairlawn
Elementary School PTA, Akron, OH

*Quasquicentennial / St. Olaf of Bode
Cookbook,* St. Olaf Lutheran Church,
Bode, IA

Recipes from Iowa with Love ©1981 New
Boundary Concepts, Inc., Peg Hein
and Kathryn Cramer, Strawberry
Point, Prior Lake, MN

*Recipes and Remembrances: Around St.
George's Tables,* St. George's
Episcopal Church, Dayton, OH

*Recipes from "The Little Switzerland of
Ohio,"* First United Church of Christ,
Sugarcreek, OH

Recipes from Jan's Cake & Candy Crafts,
Janet Travis, Anderson, IN

Recipes of the Durbin, Mary Durbin,
Homer, IN

Recipes & Remembrances, Dotson
Family, Lima, OH

Return Engagement ©1989 The Junior
Board of the Quad City Symphony
Orchestra Association, Davenport, IA

Rose Hill Recipes, Bay Village Historical
Society, Bay Village, OH

Seasoned with Love, St. Joseph's Ladies
Auxiliary, North Royalton, OH

Seasoned with Love, Debra Rose,
Sprintgerton, IL

*SEP Junior Women's Club 25th
Anniversary Cookbook,* Debb DeBoef,
Mitchellville, IA

The Shaker Cookbook ©1984 The Shaker
Historical Society, Caroline Piercy
and Arthur Tolve, Gabriel's Horn
Publishing Co., Bowling Green, OH

Share with Love, Georgetown United
Methodist Women, Georgetown, OH

Sharing the Best from Our Kitchen
©2004 Patricia Irvin, Colonel Taylor
Inn, Cambridge, OH

Sharing Our Best, Eileen Hardway,
Martinsville, IN

Sharing Our Best, The Elizabeth House
for Assisted Living, Maumee, OH

Sharing Our Best, The Old Homestead,
Waukon, IA

Sharing Our Best, Ashland Church of
God Ladies Ministries, Ashland, OH

*Sharing Traditions from People You
Know* ©1996 American Cancer
Society/Iowa Division, Des Moines,
IA

Simply Sensational ©1986 The
Children's Medical Center TWIGS,
Dayton, OH

Singing in the Kitchen, Mavis Punt,
Sioux Center, IA

SoupÇon I ©1974 The Junior League of
Chicago, IL

SoupÇon II ©1982 The Junior League of
Chicago, IL

Spanning the Bridge of Time ©1996 Diana L. Neff, Princeton, IA

Specialties of Indianapolis II ©1993 Home Economists' Guild of Indianapolis, Indianapolis, IN

Spitfire Anniversary Cookbook, Quimby Spitfire Ladies Auxiliary, Quimby, IA

A Sprinkling of Favorite Recipes, Ronald McDonald House, Youngstown, OH

St. Joseph's Parish Cookbook, St. Joseph's Altar and Rosary, Greeley, IA

St. Gerard's 75th Jubilee Cookbook, St. Gerard Church, Lima, OH

St. Paul's Woman's League 50th Anniversary Cook Book, St. Paul's Lutheran Women's Missionary League, Marion, IA

Still Gathering ©1992 Auxiliary to the American Osteopathic Association, Chicago, IL

Stirring Up Memories, Platte Center Presbyterian Church, Creston, IA

T.W. and Anna Elliott Family Recipes, T.W. and Anna Elliott Family, La Porte City, IA

Taste & See, Women Ministries of Sardinia Baptist Church, Westport, IN

A Taste of Columbus Vol. III, Beth and David Chilcoat, Corban Productions, Worthington, OH

A Taste of Fishers ©1993 Fishers Tri Kappa, Fishers, IN

A Taste of Grace, Grace Lutheran Women, DeWitt, IA

A Taste of the Murphin Ridge Inn ©2004 Sherry McKenney, Murphin Ridge Inn, West Union, OH

A Taste of the World, Central College Auxiliary, Pella, IA

A Taste of Twin Pines, Twin Pines Alumni, W. Lafayette, IN

Thank Heaven for Home Made Cooks, C.H.O.S.E.N. Youth Group, South Side Church, Litchfield, IL

Thompson Family Cookbook, Janice Winter, Lakota, IA

Touches of the Hands & Heart, Karen Maag, Columbus Grove, OH

Treasured Recipes, Trinity United Methodist Church, Delphos, OH

Treasured Recipes from Mason, Ohio, Mason Historical Society, Mason, OH

Treasures and Pleasures ©1995 Shawnee United Methodist Church, Lima, OH

A Treasury of Recipes for Mind, Body & Soul ©2000 Laurie Hostetler, Grand Rapids, OH

Tried and True by Mother of 2's, Westshore Mothers of Twins Club, Westlake, OH

Tried and True Volume II: Diabetic Cookbook, East Central Chapter-American Diabetes Association, Newark, OH

Trinity Lutheran Church Centennial Cookbook, Trinity LWML, Mallard, IA

25th Anniversary Cookbook, Lancaster Montessori School, Lancaster, OH

Up a Country Lane Cookbook ©1993 University of Iowa Press, Chicago, IL

Visitation Parish Cookbook, St. Rita's Circle of Visitation Parish, Stacyville, IA

Viva Italia ©1994 Maria Volpe Paganini, Concord, OH

Wildlife Harvest Game Cookbook ©1988 Wildlife Harvest Publications, Inc., Goose Lake, IA

Winners ©1985 The Junior League of Indianapolis, IN

With Great Gusto ©1987 The Junior League of Youngtown, OH

Women's Centennial Cookbook, Oak Chapel United Methodist Women, Wooster, OH

Woodbine Public Library Community Cookbook, Woodbine Public Library, Woodbine, IA

Index

The National Underground Railroad Freedom Center in Cincinnati, Ohio, stands as a monument to freedom, bringing to life the importance of struggles for freedom throughout history. The center is located on the banks of the Ohio River—the historic dividing line between North and South, slave and Free states.

INDEX

INDEX

INDEX

INDEX

INDEX

The recipes included in the REGIONAL COOKBOOK SERIES have been collected from the

BEST OF THE BEST STATE COOKBOOK SERIES

   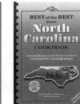  

VOLUME FIVE

Best of the Best from the
Midwest
Cookbook

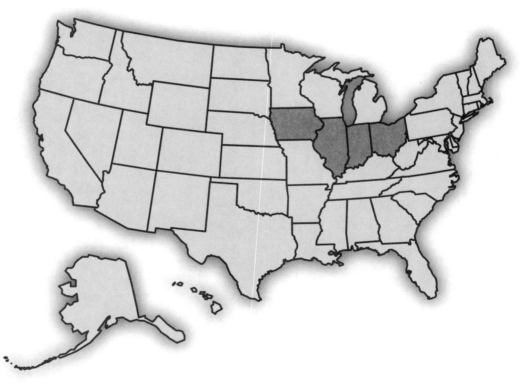

Selected Recipes from the
Favorite Cookbooks of
Iowa, Illinois, Indiana, and Ohio